DATE DUE

11-24-07			
9- -08			

Demco

Imagining the Nation

ASIAN AMERICA

A series edited by Gordon H. Chang

The increasing size and diversity of the Asian American population, its growing significance in American society and culture, and the expanded appreciation, both popular and scholarly, of the importance of Asian Americans in the country's present and past—all these developments have converged to stimulate wide interest in scholarly work on topics related to the Asian American experience. The general recognition of the pivotal role that race and ethnicity have played in American life, and in relations between the United States and other countries, has also fostered this heightened attention.

Although Asian Americans were a subject of serious inquiry in the late nineteenth and early twentieth centuries, they were subsequently ignored by the mainstream scholarly community for several decades. In recent years, however, this neglect has ended, with an increasing number of writers examining a good many aspects of Asian American life and culture. Moreover, many students of American society are recognizing that the study of issues related to Asian America speak to, and may be essential for, many current discussions on the part of the informed public and various scholarly communities.

The Stanford series on Asian America seeks to address these interests. The series will include work from the humanities and social sciences, including history, anthropology, political science, American studies, law, literary criticism, sociology, and interdisciplinary and policy studies.

David Leiwei Li

IMAGINING THE NATION

Asian American Literature and Cultural Consent

STANFORD UNIVERSITY PRESS

Stanford, California

1998

Stanford University Press
Stanford, California
© 1998 by the Board of Trustees of the
Leland Stanford Junior University

Printed in the United States of America

CIP data appear at the end of the book

For X.Y. and A.L.L.

Acknowledgments

This book originated with my dissertation at the University of Texas, Austin. For their able guidance, I want to thank Tony Hilfer, Wayne Lesser, Evan Carton, Jeanette Faurot, and the off-campus member of my dissertation committee, Elaine Kim of the University of California, Berkeley, whose expertise was much sought after. During its evolution, the manuscript benefited from reading by colleagues both at my home institution and at large. Appreciation is due Alice Gambrell, Tania Modleski, and Vincent Cheng of the University of Southern California, Sau-ling Wong of Berkeley, and Amy Ling of the University of Wisconsin, Madison. Brook Thomas of the University of California, Irvine, Lisa Lowe of the University of California, San Diego, and Tony Hilfer of the University of Texas, Austin, were particularly helpful in suggesting "radical trimming"; the book owes its "weight loss" to them. I also wish to thank Ron Gottesman for his friendship and for initiating my family into the cultures of Los Angeles. Appreciation is also due Muriel Bell and Jan Spauschus Johnson of Stanford University Press and Gordon Chang for their enthusiasm for the book, and Janet Mowery for her fine-tuning of the manuscript.

The completion of the book would have been impossible without the generous junior faculty leave provided by the College of Letters, Arts, and Sciences at the University of Southern California, and the Zumberg Fellowship from the same institution.

Finally, I am grateful to my parents' help in caring for Art while this book underwent major revisions, for the enduring love of Cherry Wen-ying, and for the delight of Art Ling, our child. The book is dedicated to my American family.

D.L.L.

Contents

Imagining the Nation

Introduction

Alienation, Abjection, and Asian American Citizenship

Since Maxine Hong Kingston won the National Book Critics Circle award for *The Woman Warrior* (1976), we have witnessed a steady output of Asian American texts and their gradual ascendance as deserved objects of academic study. At the same time, the theory and practice of Asian American studies have experienced radical transformations. "Region" seems to have overridden "race," and the "global" seems to have overtaken the "local" in the ongoing disciplinary redefinition of "Asian America(n)." What are the forces behind the unprecedented Asian American literary emergence? What has occasioned its paradigmatic shift from an insistence on the geopolitical centrality of the United States to an eager embrace of the Pacific Rim? What does the changing significance of "Asian America(n)" say about the nature of the nation and the status of American democracy?

This study of contemporary Asian American literary production approaches these questions in the context of citizenship. It conceives the reading and writing of Asian American literature as a significant performance not only of the political delineation of the ethnic community but also of the cultural narration of the nation. By analyzing how literary "Asian America" is represented, I intend to reveal the historical contradiction of a United States caught between the utopian impulse of democratic consent and the residual practice of national inheritance. Close readings of how Asian American texts both embody and negotiate this contradiction at once affirm the imaginative power of cultural critique and express the possibility of realizing a radical American democracy.

I

An understanding of contemporary Asian American literature as the product and productive textual mediation of political, social, and economic relations entails a genealogy of the formations of U.S. citizenship. We shall historicize the "Asian" in the different periods of "American" construction to see how the "Asian" both troubles and is troubled by the definitions of "America(n)." To do so, we must first turn to the mid-nineteenth century, when the idea of the nation and the ingredients of its citizenry were being reshaped. Powered by the engine of monopoly capital, young America was advancing restlessly in the dual movements of national consolidation and imperial venture. Westward expansion, in other words, was at once a territorial colonization, the European immigrant settling of "vacant" Indian land, and a step toward an American empire on and beyond the Pacific. But empire-building is inevitably a two-way street: American entry into the fabled Asia-Pacific marketplace also brought Asian immigrants to America. The presence of Asian immigrants in the United States, however, seemed to both affirm the law of surplus labor and dispute the narrative of Western civilization's unstoppable stride (see Cheng and Bonacich 1984; Horsman 1981). Not only did the "strangers from a different shore" (Takaki 1989) counter the inevitable fulfillment of Manifest Destiny; they also threatened to adulterate the national fantasy of Anglo-Saxon purity, thus inviting the institutional "exercise [of] the tyranny of a free people . . . on those who are not to receive full citizenship within it" (Pocock 1975: 542–45).

Although American citizenship is believed to have evolved from quasi-medieval assumptions of natural, perpetual, and hierarchical forms of allegiance ("ascriptive" citizenship) to the contractual and volitional principles of democratic political membership ("consensual" citizenship) (see Kettner 1978), the consideration of race, national origin, and culture in the actual admission practices tells a different story.[1] As Peter Schuck and Rogers Smith argue, American citizenship has never been exclusively "consensual." There has always been an interpretive imbalance between John Locke's "individualistic liberalism," which has been the attributed conceptual cornerstone of the American Revolution, and the less-acknowledged influence of "Atlantic republicanism" that underlies that of an American empire.[2] Although which of the two tends to dominate the earliest of American national consciousness should not expressly concern us, it is helpful to note their tension after the American gaze beyond the Appalachians. If a republic's unity supposedly hinges on its homogeneity, as Schuck and Smith believe, its survival depends on expansion, and expansion will have to entail unwelcome elements of difference that are likely to undermine the foundation of republican self-identity (28–29). In the imperial process of absorbing diverse lands and labor, the United States had to cope with the looming heterogeneity of its peoplehood and contain the "impurity" of its citizenry.

Opposed to the alleged Lockean tradition of civic membership at American independence, the "Atlantic Republicanism" of an expanding nation insists that "consent to membership must be mutual, granted by the representatives of the existing citizenry." True to the Machiavellian spirit of imperial governance, which ordains that "republics must rule conquered rivals as subject peoples, not as fellow citizens. . . . The [American national] community's power to refuse consent to the membership of those who would [arguably] disrupt their necessary homogeneity," as Schuck and Smith conclude, "was never seriously questioned" (1985: 30–31; 27–29). Such an Atlantic republican practice of citizenship not only unduly favors the established community over the rights of the prospective citizen, thus openly contradicting Locke's "individualistic liberalism" of volitional allegiance; it also legitimates racial and cultural homogeneity by turning the ascriptive characteristics of one's birth into requisites of national competence. The Supreme Court decisions on such cases as *Cherokee Nation v. Georgia* (1831) and *Scott v. Sandford* (*Dred Scott*, 1856) and the whole chapter of legislated Asian exclusion that began with *People v. Hall* (1854) are typical of the republic's consensual cleansing of its common nationality, and they reflect the contradictions of American citizenship.[3]

My intention is not to reiterate the history of Asian exclusion; it is to illuminate the inextricable but often repressed relation between the acts of Asian exclusion and American national formation. Since the "nationalism-nation relation" typically "opposes a 'reality,' the nation, to an 'ideology,' nationalism," since "no nation, that is, no nation state, has an ethnic base," "except precisely in the sense of the product of a *fictive* ethnicity," as Etienne Balibar persuasively posits, an "imaginary unity" has to be "instituted in real [historical] time *against* other possible unities" (Balibar and Wallerstein 1991: 46, 49; original emphasis). In this context, the acts of Asian exclusion—from debates on the Fourteenth Amendment (Schuck and Smith 1985: 76–77, 152; Hutchinson 1981: 57–58; Saxton 1971: 36–37; Hing 1993: 201–2), through the 1882 Chinese Exclusion Act, the "Gentlemen's Agreement" of 1908 barring Japanese immigration, the Immigration Act of 1917 creating the "Asiatic barred zone" that extended racial exclusion to exclusion by region, the Immigration Act of 1924 denying admission for permanent residence to persons racially ineligible for citizenship, the Tydings-McDuffie Act of 1934 stripping Filipinos of their noncitizen American national status, to the Japanese Internment during World War II—were direct expressions of massive American anxiety about the nature of the nation and the contour of the citizenry.[4]

As state-sanctioned forms of discipline, these successive legal citations of the unamalgamatable "Oriental" helped complete "the cycle" of what Balibar calls the "historical reciprocity of nationalism and racism" (Balibar and Wallerstein 1991: 53). As alternatives to enslavement and expropriation, both of which had exhausted their value by the last quarter of the nineteenth century, the acts of exclusion at once secured the national space of the United States by repelling its putative Asian invaders and signaled the de jure transfiguration of its former undesirables. The juridical and legislative processes through which the "Oriental" became exclusively racialized as "foreign," one must note, are also the processes through which blacks and Indians were formally segregated and the "Irish" became inclusively "white" (Ignatiev).[5] The historical construction of the "Oriental" as the perpetual figure of *xenos*, as both antithetical and antagonistic to the United States, therefore reveals not only the spectral centrality of the Asian in the determination of a formative European American *ethnos*, but also the ways in which the historical consanguinity between racial essence and national legitimacy has been cemented.

The history of Asian exclusion is a history of the nation-state's "monopoly of legitimate symbolic violence" in making explicit identity and difference, citizens and aliens (Bourdieu 1985: 732). It is a history that consolidates the contradiction of democratic consent in what Benjamin Ringer terms the "duality" of America's "Plural Terrain" and "People's Domain." It is also a history of "orientalism," to adopt Edward Said, in an "exceptional" American form (1978).[6] If this history of orientalist intranational regulation is intricately tied to earlier international movements as imperialist ventures and massive immigrations, the changes in global political economy since then will inevitably alter the construction of the United States and the definition of American citizenship. The accompanying table provides a clearer picture of this history and its subsequent transformation. As the Asian American genealogy in the table indicates, American orientalism is expressed in two historically distinct but related periods, with their corresponding modes of production, forms of political culture, and figures of representation.[7]

The legal prohibition of Asian American citizenship coincides roughly with what I label period I, "Oriental alienation" (1854–1943/1965). The American passage from market to monopoly capital in this period is a "passage to India," which not only demands the blockage of an Asian-Pacific passage but also requires "the metaphysics of Indian-hating."[8] American orientalism of this period is a Janus-faced racial Anglo-Saxonism: it manifests itself both in the expansion of the empire similar to and concurrent

An Asian American Genealogy of American Orientalism

	I. Oriental alienation (1854–1943/1965)	II. Asian abjection (1943/1965–present)
Modes of production	Monopoly capitalism	Late/transnational capitalism
Forms of political culture	Old orientalism ┌──────┴──────┐ Nationalism Imperialism	Neo-orientalism ┌──────┴──────┐ Neoconservatism Neocolonialism
Figures of representation	Oriental *xenos* as an object of prohibition	Asian *xenos* as an abject/unviable subject

with European colonial missions and in the domestic purification of American citizenry against such a national expansion. The term "alienation" refers to the ways with which the figure of the "Oriental" is made "foreign" to the "nation" (the United States). It characterizes the historical process through which the Asians in America are politically excluded and legally disenfranchised, and it describes their simultaneous psychological and affective estrangement in the United States.

Since the end of World War II and the replacement of Asian exclusion legislation with the landmark Immigration Reform Act, we have witnessed the increasing availability of late/transnational capitalist structures, such as multinational business, global division of labor and production, and international banking. The fundamental shift in the mode of capital is directly responsible at once for the changes of citizenship and civil rights laws in the United States and for the onset of neo-orientalism in what I label period II, "Asian abjection" (1943/1965–present). The Janus manifestations of neo-orientalism, domestic neoconservatism (value determinism) and neo-colonialism abroad (coprosperity), have together transformed the dominant representation of the Asian and given rise for the first time in history to significant Asian American contestations of their given identity.

The difference between the periods is most evident in subject positions and citizenship status of Asian Americans. In period I, the "Oriental" was legally constructed as the most visible, most menacing kind of difference, as the Other to the (European) American self, and as the object of national prohibition. Barred from immigration and naturalization, the Oriental personified the historical tension between America's universalist promise of democratic consent and its race-, gender-, and culture-specific practice of citizenship. In period II, however, "Orientals" in the United States became "Asian Americans" when they began to be recognized as either citizens or legal aliens. Since that racial, civilizational, and geopolitical Other no longer stands opposed to the national subject, at least in terms of the law, the Asian American is, by all official accounts, identical to "authentic" citizens (in particular the "free white" descendants of the Mayflower) and is given equal protection under the law.[9] However, such an identification of the Asian American as possibly representative of the United States' national imaginary has not yet occurred. As the most recently incorporated legal subject of the nation, the Asian American instead inhabits a rearticulated tension between the nation's commitment to formal equality and the dominant cultural revival of national inheritance. In period II, the Asian American has been turned into an "abject," into that which is neither radical enough for institutional enjoinment of the kind in period I nor competent enough to enjoy the subject status of citizens in a registered and recognized participation of American democracy. Although period II pronounced the death of the explicit legal exclusion of the Asian in period I, it did not yet herald a birth of full Asian American inclusion. This is because in period II the regulatory function of the law in defining citizens and aliens is increasingly subsumed by mass media and public education. As apparatuses of social and cultural reproduction, mass media and systems of education continue to secure the common sense of Asian Americans as aliens, thus both precluding their sense of national entitlement and inhibiting their American actualization.

II

My conceptualization of "Asian abjection" in the contemporary United States formation is informed by Julia Kristeva's psychoanalytical interpretation of the genesis of individual subjectivity. In *The Powers of Horror*, Kristeva contends that the emergence of the "self" depends on the constitution of the "not-self." In addition to excluding that which is ostensibly "the object" or the Other, the "subject" also needs to separate itself from what she terms "the abject." To illustrate, she cites the example of "refuse" or waste. "Dung" "signifies" for Kristeva "the other side of the border, the place where I am not and which permits me to be." In this, the abject is understood as the part of ourselves that we willfully discard. "I expel myself . . . I abject myself," she concludes, "within the same motion through which 'I' claim to establish myself" (1982: 3).

Kristeva's description of the abject has received considerable attention in feminist legal scholarship and gay and lesbian studies. Addressing the question of "embodiment" and "identification" within the "heterosexual hegemony," Judith Butler argues that the abject not only "designates" the "unlivable" and the "uninhabitable" but also "constitute[s] the defining limit of the subject's domain" (1993: 3). Similarly, Iris Young describes abjection as a unique form of contemporary oppression that is executed not as brutal state tyranny but as an underground, unconscious, yet structural "immobilization" and "reduction" of a group (1990: 41–42). While the transformation of the Asian from the object of legal exclusion to inclusion reflects the nation-state's legal guarantee of individual rights regardless of race, gender, and sexual orientation, the abjection of the Asian rearticulates in contemporary form the ancient contradiction in U.S. citizenship.

In the 1960s, legislative assurances of the fundamental civil rights of all citizens shook the racialist formation of the nation and produced an unprecedented clash between what Louis Althusser calls the "Repressive State Apparatus" and the "Ideological State Apparatus."[10] The law, in other words, began to undermine the dominant cultural argument for inherent national inheritance, which until then had secured the legal foundation of American citizenship. What this meant for the re-membered Asian American, at least in theory, was the freedom to inhabit the nation as an abstract geopolitical entity. However, a nation is composed of both the institutional and the imaginary, the political that regulates the juridical and territorial boundaries, and the cultural that defines origins and continuities, affiliations and belongings. Rather than pronouncing the demise of culture as citizenship's constitutive element, the state's insistence on fundamental formal equality has enhanced the role of culture as the pivotal site of national contestation. A euphemism for race, culture has become an objective political force to either sustain or subvert the state's social rearrangement, and Asian Americans are compelled again to justify their newly acquired citizenship on cultural grounds. This is because culture disseminates the sense of the nation as an "imagined community" (Anderson 1983), and the "cultural wars" (Graff 1992) over the origin and destiny of the nation also begin to bear directly on the legal definitions of merits and entitlements.

The period of "Asian abjection" is marked by its own paradox. No longer the explicit Other to be disciplined, the Asian in the United States must be strictly contained in permitted quarters yet readily conflated with his or her ancestral nation.[11] This paradox of "Asian-American" representation itself expresses the contradiction within transnational capitalism as it reorganizes international relations, influences decolonization, and alters intranational social relations.[12] The categorical birth of "Asian(-)America(n)" is the result of at least two transnational developments that are not necessarily compatible. First is the Western rearrangement of the world through late or transnational capital. Globally, the need to maintain American hegemony in the "free world," to exploit low-skilled labor in and import professional labor from the Asia-Pacific region to compensate for the drastic cut in domestic social spending (especially in education), began to change the geopolitical relationship of Asian countries with the United States. Locally, the 1965 immigration reforms were less an indicator of the state's commitment to formal equality for all the races than a response to both the ascendance of transnational capital and the Cold War political economy (Ong, Bonacich, and Cheng 1994: 3–31). As the result of these global and local changes, the postwar removal of structural barriers (restrictive laws in citizenship, employment, and education, for example) opened social access for the U.S.-born Asians and facilitated the arrival and acceptance into U.S. society of professional and entrepreneurial immigrants from Asia, making possible the rise of an Asian American middle class.[13] However, it was the second transnational chain of events, the convergence of global decolonization and the domestic civil rights movement, of third world nationalism and U.S. ethnic nationalism, that acted as a catalyst to turn the newly acquired dominant cultural capital within the Asian American constituency into demands for self-definition.

The inauguration of "Asian America(n)" as a viable social, cultural, and political entity is thus caught between contradictory transnational forces. The entry of Asian Americans into the nation via the civil rights movement and third world national independence must be regarded as a form of oppositional politics intended to revise the exclusionist U.S. history and reconstitute the national space. At the same time, Asian American inclusion may also have been a strategy of the dominant culture to maintain its continuing "positional superiority" (Said 1978: 7) by reforming alliances and managing ethnic consent. In its affinity with movements of resistance, Asian America embraced the interests of underclasses and subordinate races within and without the nation, while in its incorporation by the dominant culture, it was assumed to share the interests of both the inter- and the intranational elites. The result is a basic conflict between the emergent Asian American discourse of self-delineation and the neo-orientalist discourse that attempts to "derealize" the self through abjection. In my formulation, the dominant discursive "Asian abjection" functions at two levels at once. On the one hand, it works as a form of sanctioned articulation—Asian Americans are to speak in the official voice of the nation. On the other hand, it works as a form of substituted articulation—Asian Americans are to be spoken for by a delegated dominant authority. In both instances, however, abjection is a form of denied Asian American articulation that serves to immobilize the race- and culture-specific national embodiment of the Asian American.[14]

III

If the massive movement of people and expansion of land occasioned national instability in the nineteenth century and prompted the Anglo-Saxon repressive violence of Asian exclusion, the dominant culture's abjection of Asian Americans was a strategic response to the rupture of national contour and character in our time. The struggle over the nature of American democracy continued to pivot on the role of the Asian within, just as the abjective formation of the "Asian model minority" heralded the neo-orientalist redefinition of citizenship rights.[15]

A 1966 article in *U.S. News and World Report* made the point:

> At a time when Americans are awash in worry over the plight of racial minorities, one such minority, the nation's 300,000 Chinese-Americans, is winning wealth and respect by dint of its own hard work. . . . At a time when it is being proposed that hundreds of billions be spent to uplift Negroes and other minorities, the nation's 300,000 Chinese-Americans are moving ahead on their own—with no help from anyone else. (Quoted in Tachiki et al. 1971: 6)

While the boot-strap narrative of American social mobility is not particularly new, the inclusion of the Asian in the company of European Horatio Algers against the marked absence of the Booker T. Washingtons laid the foundation for a full-blown neoconservative comeback in national politics and policy reversals.[16] In the model minority discourse, the Asian American is incorporated into the narrative of European assimilation to serve two primary functions: first, to reaffirm the validity of the American democratic promise that other minorities of color have collectively failed to take advantage of; and second, to erase the repetitive historical differentiations of citizenship between white ethnicities and people of color.[17] The revision of history thus paves the way for such neoconservative arguments of meritocracy that Asian Americans have come to exemplify.[18]

A consummate master of this newspeak, Ronald Reagan would years later praise Asians for their preservation of the "bedrock values" of America: "the sacred worth of human life, religious faith, community spirit . . . fiscal responsibility, cooperation, and love." Regardless of his expressed admiration of Asians, the message that emerged is that we Americans need "your values, your hard work" in "our political system."[19] In this rhetorical juxtaposition of you and me, of "your values" and "our system," a fundamental structural continuity between the past "Yellow Peril" and the present "model minority" is made patently evident. While the discourse of "alienation" typically constructs Asiatics as unamalgamatable, and the discourse of abjection casts them as essentially assimilable, one cannot fail to note that Asians remain principally external to America and American institutions in both formations. Asian Americans are next to the subject, perhaps too close for comfort not to have a partition erected between them. The structural exteriority of the Asian in Reagan's speech reveals a complementarity between "alienation" and "abjection"; it anticipates as well the potential modal switch of discourses with serious consequences for the Asian American constituency. Not at all an oxymoron, the object and the abject Asian are two sides of the same alien. With model minority discourse firmly entrenched, the abject of today could be readily become the object of tomorrow, potentially leading to the repetition of such state measures as disenfranchisement or internment.[20]

Here, we must again appreciate Kristeva's formulation of the abject both as a bodily scheme and as a border-setting mechanism. The assimilable Asian cannot belong but must be measured by his *proximity* to the center/same, which welcomes copies, imitations, and mimicries for the security of its own value while insisting on their inauthenticity and their illegitimacy. The abject Asian, similarly, is not radical enough to be clearly differentiated and objectified, yet her difference is clear enough for a defensive posture to be established against her: the abject, in other words, must be kept at a respectable *distance*. Not an object, the assimilable and abject Asian is eventually assigned to what Judith Butler calls the "domain of unviable (un)subjects . . . who are neither named nor prohibited within the economy of the law" (1991: 20).

The formation of the Asian within as a "model minority" is a classificatory wonder of the dominant social strategy: it detaches Asians from their association with other racial "minorities" by hailing them as a white-appointed "model," while it distinguishes them from the unmarked "true" nationals by calling Asians their "minor." The model minority discourse thus redraws the contract of Asian American citizenship by aggressively managing (and here I borrow from Gramsci's brilliant analysis of hegemony) "to win active *consent* of those over whom it rules" (1971: 244). Consent to the model minority discursive abjection has become a legitimate form of Asian American allegiance. Strangled between the authentic white subject and the oppositional black subject, the Asian American is at once defined and "derealized"; his claim to a distinctive self and national embodiment will have to be fought out not only between the East and the West, Asia and America, but also between black and white, labor and capital.[21]

IV

The abjective discourse of the Asian American model minority reveals the contemporary contradiction of American citizenship as a particular form of the Enlightenment "utopian paradox" that Pierre Bourdieu puzzles over in the context of French democracy (1984: 397). For Bourdieu, the failure of democracy is the failure of universal education to prepare citizens for universal suffrage. Such a failure typically occurs when formal education begins, when the differentiation in the modes of cultural acquisition, preference for "total, early, imperceptible learning within the family from the earliest days of life" ("familiarization") over the "belated, methodical [school] learning" ("assimilation"), for example, comes to determine not only a class's cultural competence but its particular relation to culture (65). Since national culture is the culture of the bourgeois, who are conferred a sense of legitimacy in it the way the working class is not, the latter's technical competence in the culture cannot ensure its sense of entitlement. Because "technical competence is to social competence what the capacity to speak is to the right to speak," and because "social competence" is itself a status that legitimate owners of the dominant culture pass down to their heirs, "competence in the sense of specific culture is to competence in the sense of status property as existence is to essence." Bourdieu concludes: "only those who ought to have it can really acquire it and only those who are authorized to have it felt called upon to acquire it" (409–10).

Bourdieu's insights on how class privilege is reinscribed in French democracy to subvert the practice of universal suffrage sheds new light on how abjection works in the American context to reproduce the dominant sense of national distinction. As a mechanism of subjective regulation that apparently exceeds the realm of the law, abjection ensures the "social competence" of democratic exercise by only "recogniz[ing] as legitimate the relation to culture (or language) which at least bears the visible markers of its genesis" (Bourdieu 1984: 68). Since social competence is believed to reside in the subject's originary relation to the nation, "genealogy" is sneaked in to symbolically equate with "the legitimacy of filiation" (Balibar and Wallerstein 1991: 55–56). The United States again reverted to the privileged domain of white subjects as the reproduction of social competence reenforces the correspondence of race and rights that the law explicitly repudiates.

The granting of citizenship can be no guarantee of Asian American representation, for legal inclusion only recognizes national competence in the formal or "technical" sense. Although the law necessarily ensures the contractual terms of citizenship in abstraction, it can hardly change the cultural condition of Asian American abjection. This is because the law cannot—even if it is willing to try—possibly adjudicate the psychocultural aspects of subject constitution; neither can it undo the historically saturated epistemological structures and structures of feeling, which continue to undermine the claims of Asian American subjectivity.[22] Visibly different from the normative look of the nation and suspiciously alien to its cultural origin, Asian Americans can hardly have the requisite "social" competence that is not theirs to inherit in the first place.

This in/out position of the Asian American abject, as formal nationals and cultural aliens, has at least two significances. First, the Asian American illuminates the unique contradiction of legal and cultural competences in contemporary American citizenship. Second, by inhabiting the nation as a space of contradiction, the Asian American also constitutes a critique of the national community and proposes an alternative reconstruction. The body of this study treats contemporary Asian American literary articulations as both compulsory cultural struggles for national legitimacy and productive textual negotiations of the national contradiction. It focuses in particular on the varied literary strategies of overcoming alienation and abjection that at once constitute the contradiction of American citizenship and the specificity of Asian American experience.

To accomplish this main objective, Part I, "Emergence," traces Asian American definitional endeavors in the 1970s. It investigates two divergent approaches, one idiosyncratically "ethnic nationalist," insisting on a U.S.-based imaginary that refutes both white cultural domination and the ancestral symbolic, the other decidedly "diasporic" and "feminist," turning toward cultural Asia and mainstream America in order to secure its voice in public culture. Following these paradigmatic tensions of the emergence, Parts II and III sample texts that engage the dominant orientalist geocultural divide and explore how Asian American culture is contested and constructed. "Claiming America" looks into Asian American revisions of national meaning and acts of national self-legitimation. "Whither Asia" looks at Asian American appropriations of the ascendant transnationalist discourses, their interrogation of tradition and (be)longing. While these two parts closely read Asian American narrations of the nation, Part IV returns to the politics of representation, first by reexamining Asian American identity in the nexus of essence and performance, and second by reconceiving it as an incumbent intra-ethnic contract both facilitating and delimiting agency. "Representation Reconsidered" thus prepares for a theoretical overview of contemporary Asian American literary history to which the concluding chapter turns. There, the strategies of Asian American articulation are studied both in phases of their critical development and in terms of difference and diaspora.

Despite their success in calling Asian America into being, these strategies can neither transcend the contradiction of American citizenship nor conceal the structures of Asian American alienation and abjection. The strategy of "claiming America," for example, is liable to concede to the European American cultural exclusivity of the nation and succumb to its nativist capabilities. Asking "whither Asia," on the other hand, runs the risk of being co-opted into orientalism and displacing Asian Americans once more onto their "immutable" ancestral origins. "Transvestic and transpirational" masquerades, furthermore, may lead the Asian to sacrifice the particularity of Asian American body and affectivity for the access of universal rights and claims. These limitations on Asian American imaginings of the nation have finally come to demonstrate that "the American creed" encoded in the Declaration of Independence, the Constitution, and the Bill of Rights actually entails "the American dilemma," if American democracy's translation of Enlightenment universals continues to embody a particular European culture while canceling out other practices and collectivities constituting the same nation.[23]

In "Universalism, Particularism, and the Question of Identity," Ernesto Laclau traces the utopian paradox of the Enlightenment to the ways in which the European body has been postulated as the universal in and by itself, at once embodying a particular culture and expressing a universal human essence. Such a formulation, in Laclau's view, has enabled both a particular substantiation of universality and the elimination of bodies that do not represent "universal human interests" (1992: 86). To break out of this imperializing formation of the subject, he asks us to "differentiate the *form* of universality as such from the actual *contents* with which it is associated" (85), and proposes a new conceptualization of the universal "as an incomplete horizon suturing a dislocated particular identity" (89).

Approaching the universal and the particular in "Citizenship and Political Identity," Chantal Mouffe has also argued for a citizenship beyond the communitarian and the liberal conceptualizations. Since the communitarians "want to revive the civic republican conception of citizenship as the key identity that overrides all others, their approach runs the risk of sacrificing the rights of the individual." Since politics for the liberals is "only the terrain where different groups compete for the promotion of their specific interests," they are likely to "sacrifice the citizen to the individual" (Mouffe 1992: 29). To avoid the pitfalls of both, Mouffe demands that "the political community be conceived as a discursive surface and not as an empirical referent" (30). In a move reminiscent of Laclau when he argues that "the universal is the symbol of missing fullness, and the particular exists only in the contradictory movement of asserting a differential identity and simultaneously canceling it through its subsumption into a nondifferentiating medium" (89), Mouffe reasons, nation, "as a surface of inscription of a multiplicity of demands where a 'we' is constituted, requires the correlative idea of the common good, but a common good conceived as a vanishing point, something to which we must constantly refer but that can never be reached" (30).

The "missing fullness" of Laclau is for Mouffe this new idea of "common good," a "'grammar of conduct' that coincides with the allegiance to the constitutive ethico-political principles of modern democracy: liberty and equality for all" (ibid.). Similar to Laclau, who resuscitates democratic possibility by emptying the universal of "any necessary body, any necessary content" so that "different groups compete to give their particular aims a temporary function of universal representation" (90), Mouffe envisages citizenship as a form of "common political identity of persons [in] different communities" and with "different conceptions of the good," all submitting to the "res publica" of democratic conduct to treat each other as free and equal (30–31).

Laclau's and Mouffe's theoretical ruminations on citizenship propose a way out of the reproductive cycle of American legitimacy that Asian American articulations of the nation have exposed and that both Kristeva's psychoanalysis and Bourdieu's social critique have helped us apprehend. Through a collective identification with the radical democratic interpretation of the principles of liberty and equality, the "we" that Mouffe has conceived "through the principle of democratic *equivalence* . . . does not erase plurality and differences" and "respects diverse forms of individuality" (1992: 30–31). This radical democratic conception of citizenship works against such *gemeinschaft* community cemented by a substantive idea of the common good as in Atlantic republicanism. It also works against the ambiguous cultural particularism turned universal that denies other constitutive features of the nation and suppresses their diverse collectivities. With it, the distinction between the private and the public is maintained, as it is between the individual and the citizen, yet the pairs do not constitute discrete and exclusive realms: "every situation is an encounter between the private and public because every enterprise is private while never immune from public conditions prescribed by the principles of citizenship" (31).

Situating this conception of citizenship in Laclau's adamant disassociation of the form and content of universality, we can finally envision a radical American democratic vista that commits to the separate but equal station of its citizens by both upholding the principles of life, liberty, and the pursuit of happiness and dissolving the bands of race and rights, cultural practice and legal competence. The conceptualization of American citizenship as a formal commitment to such democratic abstractions as liberty and equality for all will expand the horizon of human freedom while breaking the historical integrity of institutional strengths and individual endowments. It will enable the emergence of a national identity that can be embodied in difference while affiliating with one another, "e pluribus unum." And it will anticipate an American peoplehood, consisting of concrete social agents, regardless of the conditions and circumstances of their birth, all striving for the fulfillment of democratic equivalence. If anything, Asian

American literary imagination is an indispensable contribution to the finding and forging of this liberating language of radical democracy, this volitional cultural consent to liberty and equality for all.

V

Centrally concerned with the construction of an imaginative (writerly),
imagined (textual and social), and not at all imaginary (tangible and palpa-
ble) Asian American community, this book engages the heated academic
debate about the canon and its spillover discussion in the mass media about
national culture and character. Persistently occupied with the macroscopic
mapping of an Asian American determination through "alienation" and
"abjection," this book anchors the "postscriptive" Asian American literary
emergence within its "prescriptive" sites.[24] The attention to the contradictory material manifestation of "race" and "nation" that the category, "Asian
American" comes to problematize reflects my attempt to delineate a provisional paradigm in and against which the specific structures of Asian American feeling can be meaningfully articulated and analyzed.

On this note, readers familiar with the framing argument of Lisa Lowe's
Immigrant Acts (1996), a book of rare intellectual breadth that brings theories of race, postcoloniality, and Marxism to bear on Asian American cultural politics, will find that we both focus on "nation." However, I share
neither her conclusion that Asian American culture is an autonomous alternative of resistance to the dominant formation of the nation (5–6), nor
her postulation of an Asian American subject who is able to supersede the
narrative of the nation and the "discourse of citizenship" (33). As should be
clear by now, in my view the Asian American formation is not necessarily a
solution to but a problem in and of the contradictions of American citizenship, which can only be resolved through a radical divorce of racial inheritance and national competence.

A few qualifications on the scope of the book and its spheres of interest
are now in order. First, despite its emphasis on the narrative of the nation,
the book is not a study of national culture per se but rather a very limited
analysis of its expression in book, entertainment, and academic cultures: the
production and reception of Asian American "literature" in its cross-
institutional sites—composing, publishing, popular consumption and classroom use, scholarly dissemination and preservation. Second, while I recognize the inevitable political nature of all forms of representation, I do not
believe that the symbolic struggle over image and identity in the aesthetic
realm can necessarily substitute for the real struggle over social resource
and justice.[25] Literary studies is not electoral politics, grassroots organizing,

or social movements. It is, rather, the cultural practice of testing boundaries, critiquing existing social arrangements, and imagining more emancipatory relations. As such, literary criticism is indispensable yet limited, a textual exercise of border crossing whose effectiveness outside the classroom and the academy should not be exaggerated. Third, although this book implies a pan–Asian American literary formation, its textual analysis does not encompass the full range of Asian American ethnicities. Given the book's evolution, this is something that I cannot satisfactorily resolve and very much regret. But this apparent shortcoming also makes evident that the book cannot expect to transcend the materiality of Asian American representation it analyzes. To say that there is a definitive Asian American culture would be premature at this point. If there were, there would also have been a complete resolution of the American democratic contradiction, and accordingly, the expiration of "Asian America(n)"'s categorical and historical functions. The book will have served its purpose if it is able to both provoke debate and prompt effort toward the fulfillment of these goals.

A study of how an Asian American identity is embodied and disseminated in the world of letters, *Imagining the Nation* is fundamentally engaged in the question of how the sense of the nation and its social relationships are constructed and deconstructed through reading and writing in competing institutional sites. With texts by Asian American writers as the object of investigation, I ask repeatedly who reads them for whom under what circumstances and with what purposes in mind. I raise a similar set of questions about writing: for whom does the Asian American author write, and in what social and institutional contexts? Instead of assuming a fixed correspondence of reading and writing positions with their projected effects, I follow Asian American literary production and reproduction from the ethnic nationalist / cultural separatist phase of the late 1960s and early 1970s, through the feminist/academic phase of the late 1970s and early 1980s, to the current heteroglossiast phase, in which voices of difference and diaspora, identity and collectivity coexist within an indisputable professional dominance of what was once a cultural ghetto. This linear critical narrative is juxtaposed with the traversing of geocultural boundaries of the orientalist divide, to open the possibilities of an Asian American identity, not as object or abject but as a subject of difference in the democratic (re)public. As the book's trajectory indicates, the uneven institutionalization of Asian American literary studies is a story twice told. It is a tale about the rise of an ethnic "professional-managerial class," whose coming of age and the arrival of an "Asian American renaissance" are not just coincidental. And it is the chronicle of a class formation that at once complicates racial and national identities and crystallizes the intra-ethnic and intercultural contestations over Asian American subjectivity.[26]

During the writing of this book, the focus of Asian American studies shifted from an emphasis on the local, U.S.-centered formation of a counter-racial identity to a focus on the global links to the Pacific Rim. Such a disciplinary shift coincides not only with the diversification of the American canon but also with the current "post-Americanist narratives" that both valorize the poststructuralist suspicion of social solidarity and announce the theoretical demise of the nation-state. Benefiting from and building upon inquiries in American studies, ethnic / Asian American studies, and transnational studies, I seek to treat "national" and "transnational," "identity" and "difference," not as binary oppositions but as mutually constitutive concepts. The book's interdisciplinary approach may fall under the broad rubric of cultural studies, which is to me less an academic discipline than a critical methodology. By conceiving literature as the cultural product and productive aesthetic negotiations of the political, social, and economic conditions, I have correlated literary studies with the more encompassing forms of cultural practice, heightened the ideological and institutional dimensions of definitional struggle, and brought into play the multiple effects of race, class, gender, and generation on the formation of the nation and the reformation of citizenship.

As a work of materialist cultural criticism, this work affirms the inventive and interventional power of "Asian America(n)," not as a thing in itself but as an insistent dialogue among dominant, ethnic, and diasporic communities. To write Asian America is to share equal national time and space (see Fabian 1983) and to "talk stories" (Kingston), incessant and incomplete, of our imbricated and intersubjective past, present, and future. In some respects, the book is also the critical meditation of an informal Asian American, an immigrant/resident alien in the language of the law, a trespasser in the eyes of many, and an academic "outside in the teaching machine" (Spivak 1993), who, in thinking through his own lost links and transplanted roots, has partaken of the collective imagination of more equitable societies and more emancipatory human relationships.

Emergence

Having charted the dominant cultural narration of the United States, we are ready to examine its critical Asian American challenge during the era of the civil rights movement. Central to this examination is how the prescriptive acts of oriental prohibition are turned into enabling ethnic self-inscriptions, and what the differences in writing strategies reveal about the emergent paradigms of Asian American representation.

The *Aiiieeeee!* group's rejection of immutable ancestral cultural affiliation and its repudiation of white cultural suppression animate the discussion of Chapter 1, which investigates both this writing collective's ethnic nationalist affirmation of a time- and place-bound "sensibility" and its tonal alliance with the black aesthetic movement. The relative inability of *Aiiieeeee!*'s vocal discourse of opposition to open up channels of dissemination in the dominant culture, and the almost simultaneous national recognition of an individual ethnic talent provide the critical context of Chapter 2, which highlights the multiple contingencies that occasion the popular and canonical ascent of *The Woman Warrior* by Maxine Hong Kingston and its contested aesthetic and ideological value among different reading communities.

While the *Aiiieeeee!* group's insistence on locating Asian American experience in the geography and historiography of the United States establishes an empowering home base, theirs seems an imagination in search of a distinctive aesthetic form. Kingston's magical use of Chinese folklore, on the other hand, suggests a fresh Asian American form that, however, seems still in need of a nation. The inadmissibility of the ethnic polemic into the national cultural arena, and the enshrinement of an ethnic art only to be displaced onto another place and another time, highlight the predicament of Asian American articulation as it confronts the nation's arbitrary integration of its geopolitical and sociocultural boundaries.

Aiiieeeee! and the Predicament of Asian American Articulation

T he civil rights movement of the 1960s in general and the third world strikes in 1968 at San Francisco State University in particular made urgent the overwhelming question of what is an "Asian American" amid the clamor for national redefinition.[1] The question is far from the exclusive concern of writers and critics: the anthropological study of Francis L. K. Hsu, *The Challenge of the American Dream* (1971), the sociological study of Victor G. and Brett de Bary Nee, *Longtime Californ'* (1972), and the historical study of Him Mark Lai and Philip P. Choy, *Outlines: History of the Chinese in America* (1973) exemplify the variety of responses and foreshadow the conflict between the largely psychocultural and the primarily sociohistorical explanations of Asian American identity. If the formation of "Asian America" as a geocultural space and "Asian American" as a subject position is from its inception a debate, such a debate reveals how the different endeavors define "race" and "culture."

I

One of the earliest debates over emergent Asian American identity centered on Stanley and Derald Sue's essay "Chinese-American Personality and Mental Health" (1971).[2] To challenge the universal Western subject and to appropriate white psychological discourse for the ethnic community, the Sues came up with a view of Chinese Americans as products of interplaying forces, among them traditional Chinese values, Western influences, and racism. While inevitably caught in the conflicting matrix of forces, the Chinese American, according to the Sues, tends to be of three basic types, the "traditionalist," the "marginal man," and the "Asian American" (Sue 1971: 36–38). The traditionalist is one who conforms to parental expectations; the marginal man is one who abandons ancestral culture to embrace Western ways; and the Asian American is one who rebels against both in search of a new self. To the Sues, the problem with the traditionalist is that "Chinese patterns of deference and reserve" prevent the subject both from expressing his or her "personal feelings" to their elders and from "aggressively respond[ing] to racism" (38–39). The problem with the marginal man is that the subject "finds his self worth defined in terms of acceptance by Caucasians" and consequently "develop[s] a form of 'racial self hatred'" (40). The difficulty with the Asian American lies in the subject's "obsessive concern with racism" (43). Their proposal, after analyzing all three personality types, calls for the individual to develop his or her "*own* conception of pride" (45).

Although the Sues' sample was highly selective (U.S.-born Chinese American college students from middle-class backgrounds) and its presumed universal application was also a problem, the primary charge against the Sues' typology of personality was that internal factors override social forces. In "The Ghetto of the Mind," Ben Tong declared that the Sues' paradigm "fits squarely into the existing WASP-oriented psychotherapeutic frame of reference. . . . By insisting that Chinese-Americans take pride in living with these personality options," he argued, "our ethnic psychotherapists contribute to the maintenance of those very same stereotypes which they fear 'studies' and 'tests' are perpetuating" (1971: 1, 3). Tong's dissatisfaction is not as much with the Sues' description of Asian American identity crisis as it is with their proposal of adjustment, which in his view omits race as the structuring device of American society and psyche. Instead of conceding to the instrumentality of psychoanalysis as a form of dominant social control, Tong sees the pathology of Asian American personality as the malady of a historically perpetuated institutional racism whose cure requires "something of a radical political nature" (24). The disagreement between the Sues and Ben Tong is as much a disagreement between the methods of coping and confrontation as it is between the ethnic reformist whose model is Jewish assimilation and the ethnic revolutionary· who is inspired by African American rebellion.[3] From its beginning, Asian American identity talk has clearly been caught between the available black and white ethnic alternatives. The decision about whom to affiliate with is apparently settled on the basis of culture.

The Sues express the element of culture in identity in the form of a puzzle: "If Chinese as a group exhibit maladaptive characteristics," they wonder aloud, "what will this mean in terms of their struggle to attain self identity and pride through Chinese culture?" (47). The Sues appear to have been caught up in the paradox of their own paradigm: while implicitly affirming a Chinese culture of reserve and resolve (Sue and Sue 1971: 47), they seem unable to convince themselves of the culture's positive value. Since their ideal identity is a combination of "the marginal man" and "the Asian American," and since both types are predicated on the demise of Asian culture, one cannot help but wonder about the Sues' faith in the ancestral culture itself (45).[4] This raises the questions whether culture is a hand-me-down set of static values, and where pride is to be found if a culture is proven deficient, questions that are the premise of Ben Tong's criticism.

Tong makes two integral historical observations, one about the prevailing perception of Asian docility and the other about its presumed cultural origin. First, he claims that "Chinese American heritage" is not "synonymous with Great Traditions of Cathay" (Tong 1971: 4). Although apparently responding to the Sues' culturalist explanation, Tong is in fact addressing the more global abjective effect of the model minority discourse. He seems particularly concerned with attempts to contain an emergent Asian American constituency by celebrating its inherent Asian cultural strengths. The denial of Chinese American heritage's grand civilizational claims unhinges the model minority discourse's conflation of the Confucian culture of China with the Cantonese immigrant culture of America. Tong's claim that Chinese Americans are immigrant descendants of Cantonese peasantry, a peripheral people within high Chinese culture who did not have access to the privilege of the Chinese elite, namely, the ruling scholar-official class (7), shatters the myth of a glorious and continuous tradition that imbues model minority discourse with much of its explanatory charm.[5]

The image of "the meek and mild Chinaman," Tong argues, is "originally a façade, a consciously manufactured appearance—a *survival mechanism* to be activated or shelved at will, in conjunction with the requirements of the historical moment" (ibid.: 8). However, while masking did begin as a deliberate tactic, the "total repression by a white racist society," from the legislative terror of exclusion to the denial of Chinese testimony in court, fundamentally distorted the tactic and drove the "Chinaman façade into the very nerve and sinew of individual personality" (9, 11–12). To dignify their imposed silence, the Chinese rationalized their withdrawal by appealing to the "ascetic strains in Confucianism," and this "unreacting expressionlessness" was quickly legitimized by the whites as the Chinese virtue of "know[ing] their place." The result is stunning: what was invented as an adaptive mask by early immigrants became for succeeding generations of U.S.-born Chinese Americans a cultural trait (14).

Tong's analysis leads us to the important aspects of essence and performance in identity.[6] The difference between acting "meek and mild" as a façade and as a reality rests largely on the level of consciousness of the actor. Awareness of the act gives the mask its subversive meaning. However, repetitions of the act not only tend to erode the intentionality of the mask but also contribute to its automaticity and its appearance as reality. "The self-fulfilling prophecy" of "the meek and mild" identity that Tong deplores is thus the work of the racist institution that at once conditions the necessary repetition of the role and deprives it of its original meaning (ibid.: 20). Since historically Asian Americans were denied access to the political and cultural production of the nation, and heavily restricted in finding alternative means of propagating ethnic consciousness, they were forced into a sorry state of dependency on the dominant definition of themselves.

By emphasizing that Chinese American passivity is not the material manifestation of inherited Chinese traits but the product of American racism, Tong is able, on the one hand, to redirect the issue of personality from the secluded realm of pure culture and psychology to the messy terrain of history and politics; on the other hand, he is able to pave the way for an evocation of Asian American legacy that is "*yet to be* discovered and affirmed . . . in agricultural fields, mines and railroad projects of nineteenth century America" (4; emphasis mine). But the future tense in the recuperation of a past symbolic speaks of the dominant discursive blackout and a simultaneous ethnic self-dismissal of a once vital tradition. The Sues' failure to note it and Tong's inability to deliver it intact can be attributed to their shared historical limitation, for what the present inherits is a loss, a discontinuity that both contributes to the pathological state of the Asian American psyche and determines, as we will repeatedly witness, much of its varied resistance. For Tong and his like-minded radical intellectuals, this loss will not justify the diagnosis of innate cultural inhibition. Rather, it excites the possibility of quest, the prospect of filling out, and the necessity of confrontation.

II

The concerns of the Sues and Tong with identity are resonant in Frank Chin and Jeffery Paul Chan's essay "Racist Love," published at the time of the debate between the former. "In terms of the utter lack of cultural distinction, the destruction of an organic sense of identity, the complete psychological and cultural subjugation of a race of people," Chin and Chan write, "the people of Chinese and Japanese ancestry stand out as white racism's only success" (1972: 66). "If the system works," they reason, "the stereotypes assigned to the various races are accepted by the races themselves as reality, as fact and racist love reigns" (65). Similar to Ben Tong, who notes how the dominant culture manufactures and then manages Asian American passivity, Chin and Chan characterize racist love as "a low maintenance engine of white supremacy" that conditions not only "the mass society's perceptions" but also "the subject minority" itself into "becoming the stereotype, live it, talk it, embrace it, measure group and individual worth in its terms, and believe it" (66–67). Without apparent benefit from Antonio Gramsci, whose work was appearing in English, Chin and Chan seem to have come to a similar understanding of "hegemony" and its solicitation of consent from the subaltern subject: the stereotype and the subject in the Asian American case became one.

The problem of Asian American identity, Chin and Chan believe, lies in its schizophrenic model of "dual personality," which has its structural roots in what Edward Said would characterize six years later as orientalism:

> The so-called "blending of East and West" divides the Chinese-American into two incompatible segments: (1) the *foreigner* whose status is dependent on his ability to be accepted by the white natives; and (2) the *handicapped native* who is taught that identification with his foreignness is the only way to "justify" his difference in skin color. . . . The privileged foreigner is the assimilable alien . . . posed as an exemplary minority against the bad example of the blacks . . . and trained to respond to the black [and] not the white majority as the single most potent threat to his status. The handicapped native is neither black nor white in a black and white world. . . . His pride is derived from the degree of his acceptance by the race of his choice at being consciously one thing and not the other. (Chin and Chan 1972: 72)

The authors of "Racist Love" have traced the problem of Asian American identity to the discursive alienation and abjection that freeze the Asian as the perpetual alien and deny its status of citizenship. Notably, however, Chin and Chan's focus is not on the blatantly prohibitive phase of legislative discipline that gave us Chinese exclusion and Japanese internment, but on the apparently benign phase of post–World War II orientalism that began to incorporate Asians into U.S. democracy. It is this phase of apparent tolerance and assimilation that transformed the enemy alien of old into the amiable alien of today. Racist love, which by the peak of the civil rights movement had taken the form of model minority discourse, effectively consolidated its positioning of the Asian as a manipulable auxiliary to white interests and an unviable subject of the nation.

The investigations of identity by Tong and by Chin and Chan were characteristic of the emerging Asian American discourse, which was steeped in what one might call "ethnic nationalism." In their dismissal of culturalist explanations and orientalist divisions of the citizen and the alien, they reclaimed the United States as the unambiguous geocultural site of Asian American self-definition. In their genealogy of American racism, they not only assumed a conscious American national identity that takes into account the historicity and commonality of Asian experience in the United States, but also rejected lingering intra-Asian animosity from the lands of origin and nostalgic political allegiances to ancestral countries. In addition, the recognition of racism became the point around which different Asian groups could forge alliances with other ethnic minorities in an effort to emerge from the margins of second-class citizenship to a full enjoyment of American democracy. The naming of "Asian America," or the "emergence of yellow power in America" (from Uyematsu 1971, an essay of kindred spirit to the authors we have been discussing), was signaled by a steadfast dis-identification with the dominant whites and a clear identification with the victimized people of color. The delineation of Asian American identity is an ethnic nationalistic act of redrawing boundaries, an act that at once displaces the model minority discourse from the metropolitan center, helps create a counterhegemonic "minority discourse" of civil disobedience and civil rights, and makes anti-assimilation a stance typical of the insurgent Asian American consciousness (Uyematsu 1971: 9–10).[7]

The ethnic nationalistic discourse of antiracism and anti-assimilation seeks not an autonomous Asian nation in the United States but a profound transformation of the terms of American democracy that will bring full citizenship to Asian Americans as well as other people of color. The social impact of this political and cultural initiative cannot be underestimated. The development of an Asian American identity, as described in Tong and in Chin and Chan, is typically a compulsory conversion process that begins with a rejection of internalized whiteness and concludes with a self-reeducation in revolutionary blackness. Although the specificity of Asian American experience is repeatedly evoked, an impatience among the intellectual vanguard to share the spirit of the black power movement has more or less determined their militant articulations of Asian American identity.[8] Ben Tong's recall of the "rural Cantonese peasant-laborer lineage" is informed by "the form of *black* personages who represent a broader spectrum of possibilities than the meek-and-mild stereotype" (Tong 1971: 18, 21). In a similar vein, Chin and Chan's acceptance of Asian Americans as an "Uncle Tom minority" and their eagerness to prove otherwise through "a recognized style of manhood" betray not only an indebtedness to black struggle but also a valorization of macho aggression. These Asian American writers are apparently willing to concede to a leader and follower partnership that transfers the historical Asian subordination within the white nation to a new bloc of black nationalism (Chin and Chan 1972: 74, 76).[9] The result, however, is an ideal of Asian American identity that appears irredeemably inauthentic between the dichotomous space of black and white America.

Chin and Chan's sharp observation about the discriminating function of "racist love" and "racist hate" is undercut when they begin to presume such differences to be transhistorically permanent. In their eagerness for panethnic coalition and in their appeal to an antagonistic identity image, the writers attempt to replace the "subject-abject" relation of their own historical moment with the "subject-object" relation of an earlier era of state exclusion, thus significantly blurring the period distinctions of Asian American "alienation" and "abjection" and considerably simplifying the articulation of Asian American identity.

What Chin and Chan refuse to acknowledge in their argument against "racist love" is that the post–World War II period of abjection represents for Asian Americans no small measure of progress from the period of racist legislative hate. Both want to forget that their acute awareness of historical injustice is gained not only through the civil rights movement but also through unprecedented access to the institutions of learning from which their parents and grandparents had been barred. Although American public schools socialized the postexclusion generations into the universal ideal of white Americanness, promising Asian Americans social mobility on the condition of their ethnic self-erasure, they also helped inculcate abstract democratic values capable of being appropriated for the subversion of racist hierarchies. But the widening access of Asian Americans, especially to education, also paradoxically diminished the solidarity and power of the historically segregated ethnic group, whether it was the ghetto community or the family, to shape the visions and aspirations of their young.

Under these circumstances, Chin and Chan's refusal to recognize the era of "racist love" as the beginning of formal equality appears to be not just an effective rejection of the model minority discourse and an empathetic response to black nationalism. It is also symptomatic of the desire to recover the lost ethnic cultural continuity and to negotiate the generational differences that compound Asian American identity. Harking back to the time of exclusion, when a presumed integral and defiant Asian American identity existed, thus serves many purposes all at once. First, the restoration of exclusion-era social relations situates the contemporary Asian American in an ideological position that is identical to that of the African American against white hegemony. Second, it smooths over the cultural gap between the earlier generations of immigrants and their native-born offspring, who now clearly constitute the intellectual consciousness and conscience of Asian American identity talk. The romanticization of legislative prohibition in the sustenance of an insubordinate Asian American identity obscures both the historical constrictions on such an identity and the inadvisability of its total recovery. And, third, it conveniently ignores both the post-1965 new immigrants and Asian Americans, whose origin cannot be located in either the exclusion or the internment and whose presence has dramatically changed the contour of the Asian American community. The blindness of these radical insights will become the nationalist heritage of Asian American identity formation.

III

The dialogue on Asian American identity is intricately linked and indeed concomitant with the concrete tasks of literary excavation and preservation in the 1970s. Regardless of the peculiarity of ideological and aesthetic inclinations, the editors of Asian American literary anthologies all concur on the need for a tradition that can at once disseminate notions of the emergent self, discredit its historical distortions, and enable a paradigm for future production (see Iwasaki 1971 and 1976; Hsu and Palubinskas 1976; Wand 1974; and F. Chin, Chan, Inada, and Wong [1974] 1983). The anthologies seem to constitute a two-step ethnic nationalist's project that begins with a critique of exclusion and is followed by the reconstruction of a lost tradition.

Frank Chin et al., for example, ascribe the absence of Asian Americans from the canon to "the pushers of white American culture" who "forcibly excluded [Asian Americans] from creative participation" (ibid.: vii–viii). Iwasaki charges "the cultural cop/pushers [who] implicitly determine that a bourgeois Anglo-American literary tradition provides the mainline fix for legitimate statements on our society's life and times" (1976: 452). Similarly, Wand traces the literary neglect to "the whites' indifference to or discrimination against ethnic minorities [and] the myth of the melting pot" that renders "any departure from the WASP norm suspect" (Wand 1974: 21). The exclusion of Asian Americans from creative participation is then linked to the history of Asian American sociopolitical oppression. All the anthologies are all heavily prefaced with the narrative of legislative exclusion and Asian immigrant contributions, as if merely writing about an indisputable

Asian American historical presence were sufficient justification for the existence of a parallel literary tradition.

While the focus on the trope of exclusion is in many respects a discursive necessity, it tends to both diminish the distance between lived lives and textual constructs of lives lived, and downplay the material specificities of literary production and reproduction. David Wand seems to come closest to suggesting, when he takes note of "the linguistic and cultural barriers of early Oriental immigrants," that canonical exclusion is just the last stage in an exclusionary process that began with the denial of literacy through residential, occupational, and educational segregation (ibid.: 21). This attention to the relation between English literacy and American literature not only evokes the centrality of language in all arguments about a national literature; it also has practical implications for the ways an Asian American tradition is mediated and becomes representative.[10] The editors all concur that the language of choice in the Asian American tradition is unequivocally English. Hsu and Palubinskas, for instance, qualify "writers [who] established their reputations by writing and publishing in English" (1976: 1), while Wand considers "American English as the lingua franca of Asian-Americans" and his anthology a "showcase of original [English] language works by Asian-American writers" (1974: 6). As the immigrant editors at least bring the issue of linguistic choice to the surface, the U.S.-born ones simply accept English as *the* language without feeling obligated to justify it. All seem to be responding to the historical domination of English as the American language, and all seem to assume that the ethnic community communicates in the official language of the nation.

It is ironic that the formation of a separate canon, with all its subversive energy against the nation that has historically suppressed it, actually works to supplement the national tradition. In this sense, English as the mode of expression for an Asian American cultural body speaks of the language of a minor literature, which, according to Deleuze and Guattari, "doesn't come from a minor language" but rather "constructs within a major language" (1986: 16). English as the Asian American lingua franca exemplifies what those French critics characterize as "the deterritorization of language": in inheriting a language not their own, Asian Americans have so appropriated, challenged, and colored English that it is made into a minority literary agency in the redefinition of the nation (18–19). While Deleuze and Guattari's theory helps reterritorialize the cultural landscape of the United States, the editorial reconstruction of a monolingual English tradition is at sharp odds with the reality of a bilingual, multidialectal Asian American constituency. Such a literary tradition also fails to reflect the reading habits of a significant proportion of the Asian American community, whose subjective interests it intends to incorporate. How does an

English tradition reconcile with the material conditions of Asian American linguistic pluralism? What literary strategies have been developed by Asian American writers to preserve and communicate culturally specific meanings in English? What modes of analysis are deemed appropriate for the evaluation of works in the English language? What attitudes do critics assume toward works in indigenous languages or the babel from ancestral lands? What do Asian American writers of English make of their companion ethnic tradition? What is the presumed audience of the collective English textual assemblage, and what communities are imagined through its canonical reading?

In the early 1970s, when the assumption of an English-language Asian American tradition prevailed, these concerns were by and large swept aside. However, the specter of hybridity embedded in the notion of an English lingua franca keeps hovering over editorial shoulders. To some extent, this forces scholars to recognize the linguistic, generational, class, and cultural split within the community and summons their editorial responses.[11] So, we see in Hsu and Palubinskas the recurrent register of the "bicultural or cross-cultural person" as if to suggest it as the paradigmatic image of an Asian American author, but the unique cultural and stylistic indicators of this biculturalism remain elusive (1976: 2). David Wand moves a step further. In noting the Confucianist, Taoist, and Buddhist influences on Chinese, Japanese, and Korean Americans and the influence of Catholicism on Filipino Americans, he ventures forth with an Asian American "dual heritage," a version of which we saw vehemently rejected by Tong and by Chin and Chan (Wand 1974: 5). "Asian-American identity," Wand contends, has been forged from the material of two cultures: "The language that Asian-Americans use is a synthesis of two worlds: it is not the foreign language of their ancestors, and it is more than the English that is spoken around them. It is idiomatic of the Asian-American life experience, containing Asian influences cultivated in an American environment. It is distinctly Asian-American" (125). Wand has perhaps articulated what is merely hinted in Hsu and Palubinskas, and this short paragraph is for now the clearest and most concrete statement of Asian American aesthetic distinction, a distinction derived from American life experience and expressed through a dual cultural heritage. While such an affirmative synthesis falls short of the rigor and depth of a full-blown ethnic literary theory and is indeed a simple discursive reconciliation of the East and West, it nevertheless is one of the rare comments in the Asian American canonical formation to emphasize aesthetic criteria and to imply, however obscurely, a cultivation of influence through book culture.

Perhaps it is this secret recognition of literary tradition as essentially a dialogue of imaginative experience transmitted through texts that makes

Wand's and Hsu and Palubinskas's parameters of textual selection seem more inclusive. "Writers of Asian origin who have had extensive living experience in America" (Hsu and Palubinskas 1976: 1), "ipso facto Asians . . . on the bases of their ancestry . . . writing mainly in English" (Wand 1974: 4–5) thus characterize the kind of programmatic openness of *Asian American Authors* and *Asian American Heritage*, where both immigrant and native-born writers in English can find hospitable room to cohabitate.[12]

The standard of *Aiiieeeee!* is far more stringent than that of its two precursors. The anthology fleshes out the premises of Chin and Chan's "Racist Love" and debunks the thesis of biculturalism and dual heritage in Wand, and in Hsu and Palubinskas outright. Also disavowed is the generous classification of Asian American writers according to their heredity. It is not that Chin et al. have given up on racial criteria. "Our anthology is exclusively Asian American," the opening page of the preface reads; "that means Filipino, Chinese, and Japanese Americans, American born and raised" ([1974] 1983: vii). The editors try to reconfigure the racial and geographic qualifier so that the conceptualization of an Asian American exclusivity based on nativity can be rationalized without seeming to be partial: "The fact of Chinese or Japanese birth is not enough to distinguish you from being American-born. . . . Between the writer's actual birth and the birth of the sensibility, we have used the birth of the sensibility as the measure of being an Asian-American" (ix). What qualifies the Asian American clearly goes beyond race, geography, or nationality; it is a state of mind that nonetheless can be consciously nurtured, the editors appear to say. This benchmark of sensibility as an earned status would seem to level the playing field between immigrant and native-born writers of Asian descent in search of their cultural ideal—one indeed has the impression that the editors are constructing a collective identity that is free from their own interests and inclinations.

Who, then, possesses the distinguishable sensibility of the true Asian American? He, the editors seem to say, is a "No-No Boy," at once independent from the trap of dual personality and "distinct from Asia and white America" (ibid.: viii).[13] Expanding on the "racist love" thesis, they state: "This myth of being either/or . . . haunted our lobes while our rejection by both Asia and white America proved we were neither one nor the other. Nor were we half and half or more one than the other. Neither Asian culture nor American culture was equipped to define us except in the most superficial terms" (viii). Fearful of excruciating alienation from both cultures and infuriated with the thought of cultural mongrelization, the editors of *Aiiieeeee!* transfigured both their anxiety about native displacement and their homing instinct for "the legitimacy of [their] uniqueness as [an] American minority" into a literary program of roaring repudiation. The objective is to promote a change in the field of perception and to forge codes of a new Asian American culture that will adequately and respectfully authorize their condition of double exile and embody Asian Americans as proper U.S. subjects. Most crucially, the no-no sensibility delineates a specific set of Asian American literary parameters that affirms, first, the nation space of the United States as the symbolic terrain of Asian American writing, and second, the experiences of and on American ground as the subject of the emergent literature. An Asian American aesthetic premised upon the geopolitics of ethnic nationalism is born.

Besides charting a unique ethnic creative space, the sensibility of this double negation instantly necessitates an opposition between the "Asian American" and the "Americanized Asian." "Sensibility and the ability to choose differentiate the Asian American writers," the editors declare, "from the Americanized Chinese writers [who] were intimate with and secure in their Chinese cultural identity in an experiential sense, in a way we American-born can never be. . . . Unlike us, they are American by choice. They consciously set out to become American, in the white sense of the word, and succeeded in becoming 'Chinese-American' in the stereotypical sense of the good, loyal, obedient" (F. Chin et al. [1974] 1983: x). It is here that the originally proposed acquisitive status of Asian American sensibility vanishes. Choice is an immigrant reserve and sensibility a native-born given. The choice does not appear to be much of a choice since it is already denigrated as passive assimilation, while the given sensibility can only be acquired by the chosen few. Although Chin and company accurately note the cultural differences between the immigrant and native-born writing subjects, their no-no program of ethnic nationalism is locked in such a binary frame as to foreclose the possibility of an Asian American diasporic sensibility that the post-1965 immigration and communication technologies have made possible.[14]

Aiiieeeee!'s sensibility hardly entertains the mutability of culture, the multiplicity of identity, and the fluidity of experience. The native-born is said to have been utterly deprived of Asian culture, and the identitarian security of the immigrant is believed to be miraculously unaffected by the dominant American culture. To maintain the antithesis of "Asian Americans" and "Americanized Asians," the editors provide a series of contrastive textual readings from which we cull the following (ibid.: xv). The writing of Americanized Asians is not only "offensive" to Asian Americans, we are told, but also *actively inoffensive* to white sensibilities" (xxii; emphasis in original). It is "culturally" Asian and "monetarily white," confirming the "white point of view" of Asian "cultural superiority" while "serv[ing] white supremacy by keeping [Asians] in their place." And finally, it "respond[s] to racism quietly and privately, not with action" (xxiii). The right Asian American sensibility, one presumes, is resolutely antagonistic toward anything white and deeply suspicious of middle-class values.[15]

The criteria of Asian American sensibility, as this list indicates, is not just cultural but palpably attitudinal: it has become, in other words, a matter of ideology. "The question of point of view is only partially stylistic in the case of minority writing," the editors argue; "it has immediate and dramatic social and moral implications" (ibid.: xxxv):

> Specifically, how does he [the writer] cope with and reflect prevalent white and nonwhite attitudes of the period? How is he affected by the concept of dual personality? By Christianity? How does he define the relationship between his own race, the other minorities, and the white race? How seriously committed to writing and his point of view is this writer? (Ibid.: xxxvi)

Although the passage interestingly and importantly connects textual strategies to social agency, it has a rather confused understanding of the relationships involved. First, consider the relationship between the authorial use of narrative perspective and its practical effects in reception. As implied by the editors, an author is not only incapable of multiple points of view, but he or she also has full control over how a text is read and understood by the reader. Under these circumstances, if the editors dismiss a work as non–Asian American either because it is propagandistically patriotic or because it is exemplary of successful assimilation, the fact that these works could be inspirational to Asian Americans and other ethnic minorities by the virtue of the writing subjects' colored signature is simply lost. Not only is this approach equated with a single objective standard of interpretation, but the evaluation of a work can also be detached from the conditions of its composition. Jade Snow Wong, for example, is labeled an accomplice of racist art. At the same time the editorial mangling of *Fifth Chinese Daughter* and the author's attempt to affirm a different Asian humanity against its historical caricature and demonization are totally disregarded (ibid.: xxix–xxx). She is devalued because she is susceptible to white manipulation and because her family portrait is not typical of the historical male bachelor society that Louis Chu pictures in *Eat a Bowl of Tea* (xxxii). The critical task of examining how Wong's text thematically and formally mediates her discursive pressures—for example, its textual treatments, however unconscious or imperfect they might be, of the many questions Chin and company pose for the minority writer is not really engaged. Neither has the measure of typicality or representativeness received elaboration.

Sensibility, definable as the "right" point of view, has significantly obscured the distinction between textual and social realities. While the *Aiiieeeee!* editors acknowledge that "the distinction between social history and literature is a tricky one," they are quick to conclude that "the subject matter of minority literature *is* social history, not necessarily by design but by definition" (F. Chin et al. [1974] 1983: xxxv; emphasis mine). Despite their objection to "correct English" as "an instrument of cultural imperialism" and their desire for an alternative aesthetics, the editors unwittingly acquiesce to the documentary status of Asian American writing by unwittingly accepting a form of social determinism (xxxvii). By establishing point of view as only partially stylistic and above all social and moral, Chin et al. can pinpoint the role of the "Asian American" writer with a definition of the literature itself:

> The vitality of literature stems from its ability to codify and legitimize common experience in terms of that experience and to celebrate life as it is lived. . . . His [the Asian American writer's] task is . . . [to work] with the imperatives and universals of minority experience . . . to legitimize the language, style, and syntax of his people's experience, to codify the experiences common to his people into symbols, clichés, linguistic mannerisms, and a sense of humor that emerges from an organic familiarity with the experience. (Ibid.: xxxvi–xxxvii)

In this conceptualization, literature becomes the transparent repository of experience, and the author its mouthpiece. The integrity and variety of the art form is reduced to its mimetic function, as is the active and complex role of the writer. Art and artists' creativity do not have lives of their own; rather, they depend on the people whose historical and social interests they are assigned to faithfully reflect and serve. This premise of *Aiiieeeee!* is echoed by the literary manifestos in *Roots* and *Counterpoint*, and a shared new literary agenda seems to have emerged. Recapitulating and reinforcing Chin et al., Bruce Iwasaki states that "revolutionary action" and "the expression of universal [Asian American] experience" cannot be separated: "Literature and change no longer *describe* each other—they become the *same thing*" (1971: 98). Several years later, Iwasaki adds, "The experience of [Asian American] struggle in the broadest sense is the basis; literature is part of the expression of that" (1976: 452).

What we see in these programs of Asian American literature is the conflation between social activism and artistic production, the role of the writer as a mediator of culture and as a political reformer, the work of art as partial expression and partial imagination of experiential lives and as a mirror image of reality and an instrument of social transformation. While the grand promise of literature as the vehicle of social change is both idealistic and unrealizable, *Aiiieeeee!*'s turn to the element of the social in the artistic and its subordination of the artistic to the political are strategic responses to the Anglo-Saxon aestheticization and catholicization of American literature. The exhortation to common experience and Asian American peoplehood, in this context, is nothing but the repetition and reversal of a white universality, a switch of alterity that gives Asian American writers and critics an empowering system of self-reference, through which an identity and a body of culture can be authorized. The rediscovery of texts in *Aiiieeeee!* and the work of the Combined Asian Resources Project (CARP) would be theoretically impossible without their appeal to the experiential, but the vociferous politicization of literature in and by itself does not automatically provide a cogent set of alternative aesthetics.

The experiential determinism of Asian American sensibility subverts the white monopoly of national culture, undermines its appropriation of ethnic artifacts, and establishes, however precariously, an exclusive literary turf not only for whites but also for yellows and browns, whose status of American nativity is considered dubious. While racism is *Aiiieeeee!*'s designated experiential common denominator, and most Asian Americans will agree with the editors that their shared physical characteristics contribute to their psychological, cultural, economic, and political marginalization, it does not follow that individual experiences with racism are necessarily uniform. Instead of figuring out how differently racism affects people of different backgrounds and how their different responses are expressed in writing, the editors of *Aiiieeeee!* clearly favor a single experiential norm that precludes "uncommon" representations.

The privileged hero of ideal Asian American sensibility appears as a victim of blatant institutional racism, a member of the native ghetto who, despite the odds against him, refuses to be pacified through assimilation. Once the ontological centrality of such a hero is determined, the narrative exemplifying his historical teleology is also set in motion: resistance to oppression, rebellion against domination, and rage at alienation naturally follow. Not only have one class position, one ideological perspective, and one generation's peculiarity become the transparent standard, it is also obvious that the editors' sensibility is singularly gendered. "Language is the medium of culture and the people's sensibility," they conclude, "including the style of manhood. . . . On the simplest level, a man in any culture speaks for himself. Without a language of his own, he is no longer a man" (F. Chin et al. [1974] 1983: xlvii–xvliii). In their rejection of "white standards of objectivity, beauty" as "morally absolute," they have paradoxically embraced "all the traditionally masculine qualities of originality, daring, physical courage, and creativity" (xxvii–xxviii, xxx). The canonical sensibility of *Aiiieeeee!* at least gives an impression, that "the 'face' of the race, the 'speaking subject,' is male" (McDowell 1989: 59).

Common experience and representative peoplehood as mediated by the editors reveal ever widening gaps. Most evident of all is the discrepancy between the pluralistic ethos of the actual community and the unifying desire of its presumable intellectual conscience. The editors of *Aiiieeeee!*, with their high moral purpose and revolutionary fervor, have written in the name of the people without really letting the many conflicting expressions of the people's experience enter discursive circulation. The native intellectuals are not obedient servants of the people; neither is their identification with the people seamless. *Aiiieeeee!*'s yardstick of racial sensibility seems to reek of the kind of political authoritarianism that Ernesto Laclau and Chantal Mouffe warned against in reference to proletariat class struggle. When the need for "greater practical capacity for self-organization" ignores the "objective shared by the entire movement," a distinction emerges between the "leader and led." As a result, they argued, the "permanent schism between class identity and the identity of the masses" comes into being (Laclau and Mouffe 1985: 56–57).

Chin et al.'s assumed knowledge of, unproblematic identification with, and representation of the people's historical interests suggest a similar dissociation between the materiality of the Asian American people and their "true identity." Their appeal to an organic familiarity with the universals of the people's experience naturalizes a kind of racial vanguardism and normalizes their intellectual and ideological privilege. Sensibility, not entirely different in function from the previously reigning concept of white "universality," acquires some troubling regulatory power to shape canon and hinder the posing of other questions. The consequence is an overemphasis on how texts measure up to or fall short of *the* ideal, rather than an inquiry into why certain texts appear as they are, departing from the sensibilities of what the *Aiiieeeee!* critics desire.

In *Aiiieeeee!* one cannot but observe the influence from Leroi Jones and Larry Neal's *Black Fire: An Anthology of Afro-American Writing* (1968). The structural affinity between Chin et al.'s introduction and Neal's afterword, "And Shine Swam On," is particularly notable. Writing against Du Bois's famous thesis on the souls of the black folk, Neal sees his literary movement (which is later designated the "Black Aesthetic Movement" or the "Black Arts Movement") as a companion to the Black Power Movement that seeks both a "synthesis of all the nationalistic ideas embedded within the double-consciousness" and "the destruction of the double-consciousness" itself (Jones and Neal 1968: 646–47). The *Aiiieeeee!* editors' rejection of fragmented Asian American "dual personality," which was derived from the orientalist geography of the East and the West, and their intent on producing an integral identity unmistakably parallel the objectives of contemporary black writing, which, according to Neal, are to "consolidat[e] the African-American personality" and to "integrate with *ourselves*" (647, 654; emphasis in original). *Aiiieeeee!*'s "no" to Asia resonates with the refusal of the Black Aesthetic Movement to "return to some glorious African past" (639), and its "no" to white America echoes the understanding that "black people comprise a separate national identity within the dominant white culture" (646). *Aiiieeeee!*'s anti-assimilation position, both in the cultural sense that deplores "'colonized' education" and in the political sense that debunks the "Uncle Tomism of the older generation," is also *Black Fire*'s (642, 647). Such similarities between the two minority literary programs demonstrate the formation of an oppositional bloc, but the ethnic nationalist premise behind this collective articulation of American culture will in time be challenged.[16]

The kind of experiential determinism prevalent in the works of Chin et al. and Bruce Iwasaki, as well as in proclamations of the Black Aesthetic Movement, is now taken to task. Henry Louis Gates has characterized it as a form of "race and superstructure" criticism (1987: 30). When race becomes "the controlling mechanism" in critical theory, he argues, "language and literature" tend to be seen as "reflections of 'Blackness,' [which] are more or less literary according to the ideological posture of the critic" (39). What concerns Gates most is the repression of formal analysis in Afro-American criticism and the danger of insiderism that deems "the experience represented by the author in the text so unique in Western culture that only black critics are able to make normative judgments because only they can gauge how 'true' or 'real to our lives' any particular text might be" (xxvi). While Gates's analysis can benefit our apprehension of *Aiiieeeee!*'s similar tendency and alert us to the perils of essence, regardless of its form, we should also heed the insight of Kwame Anthony Appiah, who notes that racial essence is at the heart of all national literatures (1990a: 274–87), and attend to the warning of bell hooks, who asks why the critique of "the misuses of essentialism" is often centered on "marginalized groups" while the "authority of experience" and its mechanism of exclusion internal to the dominant culture are frequently left out (1991: 175).

For the discourse of political opposition, *Aiiieeeee!*'s essentialist sensibility is at once problematic and inescapable. Its lack of introspection and inclusiveness invokes limits on the individual and historical complexity of identity and appears insufficiently prepared for alternative models of selfhood. Its defiant posture and its performative force, on the other hand, have helped assert a vigorous Asian American presence and enable the possibility of creating, in what Houston Baker says of the Black Aesthetic Movement, an ethnic "reference public" (1981: 7). The "metaphysical rebelliousness," the "willingness" to "postulate a positive and distinctive category of existence and then to read the universe in terms of that category," Baker maintains, is not only "a radical political act" but also "a bold critical act designed to break the interpretive monopoly" of "a white, literary-critical establishment that set a 'single standard of criticism'" (9). *Aiiieeeee!*'s Asian American literary project, against the terms of such evaluation as Baker's, is no less ambitious.

The difference between the Black Aesthetic Movement and its Asian American counterpart, however, is in their alternative reference public and their ethnic reading communities. Although *Aiiieeeee!*, *Roots*, and *Counterpoint* succeeded in creating both, their sphere of influence was limited to the predominantly English-speaking college students, ethnic studies programs, and progressive Asian American intellectuals. Unlike the Black Aesthetic Movement, which in the words of Gates, "single-handedly created a broad community of black readers from the streets of Harlem to the hallowed halls of Harvard, whose purchasing power led all sorts of traditional commercial publishing houses [and others] to reprint and market . . . the past and present works of the Afro-American tradition" (1987: xxvi–xxvii), the Asian American literary movement in the late 1960s and early 1970s did not enjoy such a mass audience within or without its ethnic constituency; neither did it attract mainstream commercial interest in the reproduction and transmission of its texts. Many of the rediscovered works that constitute the past tradition were not reprinted until the 1980s and later, and thus Chin and company's works were largely unpublished till then. It is not a coincidence that *Aiiieeeee!* was initially issued by Howard University Press, the affiliate of a historically black institution; and the other two widely used anthologies with a significant literary component, *Roots* and *Counterpoint*, were the projects of UCLA's Asian American Studies Center.[17]

Aiiieeeee!'s quest for a language that will codify the sensibility and experience of Asian Americans is hopelessly constrained: first because it lacks mainstream literary distribution, and second because its designated constituency is linguistically and culturally diverse. Hampered by institutional oblivion, the English component of the Asian American tradition was at best discontinuous. Literacy in English was not universal among the population but indicative of certain class and educational privileges. The leisure available to browse literary texts belonged to the even more select few. Ghettoized within its ethnic enclaves, the literary tradition of Asian languages was barely communicable to the youthful intellectuals of the emergent movement, and not accessible at all to mainstream reading circles. The supposed linguistic unity galvanizing most national literatures or nationalistic revolts is burdened in the Asian American context by its multiple modes of access, with the older immigrant generations linked by locally published newspapers in their ancestral tongues and the younger native-born generations inevitably shaped by American popular culture. This split and uneven cultural access and power threaten to nullify any attempt at integrating Asian Americans. They equally require that the racial reimagining of an Asian American solidarity invent new ways to disseminate a not-quite-common tradition.

IV

In his study of the politics of language in Africa, Ngugi reminds us of the school's role in "the destruction or the deliberate undervaluing of a people's culture" and "the conscious elevation of the language of the coloniser" in "the domination of the mental universe of the colonised" (1986: 16). The adoption of the colonizer's language, he contends, inevitably results in "the disassociation of the sensibility of that child from his natural and social environment," for the language of the child's formal education is divorced from his spoken language at home. Such disassociation often leads the colonial subject to "look at colonial language as a carrier of culture" (17). For Asian America, postwar school desegregation exposed the majority of its young minds to the equivalent of a colonial education, which was reserved only for children in missionary schools. As products of the public school system, native-born monolingual English-speaking Asian Americans were caught in a linguistic orphanhood. First, while encouraged to celebrate the dominant language and culture, they were denied ownership of both: the races of Asia do not match the pale face of English. Second, they were caught in a Du Boisian double vision, not only examining the world at large with a Eurocentric perspective but also seeing their ethnic world and themselves mirrored in the distorting glass of dominant language and mass media. Third, their adoption of English, while enthusiastically encouraged, was also regarded by their parental culture as a near betrayal; the elders lamented that their children were rapidly losing their Asian heritage and spoke only the language of their historical oppressor. "As a people, we are pre-verbal,—afraid of language as the instrument through which the monster takes possession of us," as Frank Chin summarizes the situation for his generation of writers in "Backtalk"; "we are a people without a native tongue" (1976a: 557).

Chin's earlier works are fundamentally concerned with the effects of Asian American sociopolitical alienation resulting from their alienation of language. The dilemma of the Asian American writer working in a language that is not necessarily his own, struggling both with the master's tongue that mutes his articulation and with the ethnic babel whose meaning is just emerging appears to be the signature of Chin's creativity. Language, for Chin, is not just a means of communication or the medium of culture but also a form of authority. Speaking always midstream in the history of discourse, as we all must, Chin's protagonists must seek approval or else find assurance in their own system of validation. The sons' search for ideal fathers and the blind idolization and violent rejection of paternal figures that recur in Chin's oeuvre, are symbols both of an essential Asian American unease within a nation that rejects their heirship, and of an authorial longing for traditions and origins that will legitimate their existence.[18]

The Year of the Dragon (1974) is perhaps the most pessimistic of Chin's earlier works, and the darkness of its vision can be attributed to the playwright's inability to get his works published. Chin portrays the tension between the dominant stereotype and the ethnic self-image in the person of Fred Eng, whose occupation as a Chinatown tour guide and aspiration as a writer threaten to tear his psyche asunder. The play opens with Fred's affected voice flooding the stage: "We'come a Chinatowng, Folks! Ha. Ha. Ha . . . Hoppy New Year!" He introduces himself to the audience, the tourists, and us: "'We tell Chinatown where to go.' Ha ha ha. I'm top guide. Allaw week Chinee New Year. Sssssshhhh Boom! Muchee muchie firey crackee!" (see F. Chin 1981: 71). The accented speech at once creates an "authentic" atmosphere of local color for voyeuristic Orient hunters and exposes the sham of the dialect for Chinatown insiders. In Fred's stereotypical miming, Chin has uncovered the history of linguistic falsification of Asian American English since Bret Harte's "Heathen Chinee," *Knickerbocker*'s benevolent explication of "Inglis-see talkee," and Charles Leland's *Pidgin-English Sing-Song*.[19]

Fred's imitation of a caricatured fractured English rather than using actual Chinatown street talk invites at least two possible readings. On the one hand, faking conforms to the orientalist political economy. As a Chinatown tour guide, Fred cannot but resemble a nineteenth-century "cheut fann/chu fan," a translator-messenger hired by Chinese organizations to negotiate with whites, literally translated as someone sent "out to the barbarians" (Hom 1987: 29). Acting out the fiction of white fantasy, he plays to the museum mentality of the dominant culture that subordinates the ethnic ghetto community both economically and socially. "They [the white tourists] give me a living," Fred remarks at one point, "I'm God's gift to sluts!" (Chin 1981: 105). At the same time, faking represents Fred's unusual facility with linguistic code-switching and dramatic impersonation, essential abilities for a successful writer. With proper historical awareness, Fred is able, however momentarily, to distance himself from the oppressive circumstances and perform an Ellisonian *Shadow and Act* by "chang[ing] the joke and slip[ping] the yoke" (61).

Whereas the tour guide may be restricted to telling only a profitable tale, the writer apparently has infinite freedom in telling a story. But dropping the "phony accent" proves far easier than writing "just me" (ibid.: 71). Chin leaves his audience little doubt about Fred's talent and attributes his failure to make it as a writer to the same social constraint that traps him in the role of a tour guide: "No one's gonna read the great Chinese American novel," he fumes. But he adds, "I'll write a Mama Fu Fu Chinese cookbook that'll drive people crazy. . . . It's gonna be the first Chinese cookbook to win the Pulitzer Prize" (83). With this, Chin has linked the predicament of the struggling ethnic writer to the doomed destiny of the tour guide, two different storytellers, two different artists of the language, stranded in the same ghetto space not of their creation or choice. Fred could realize his ambition, just as he can earn a living being a guide, if he would write according to the mainstream menu. There seems to be a social contract in which the minority writer is expected to cook up regional flavor or paint local color for the cosmopolitan cultural connoisseur.[20]

The dilemma of Fred brings to the foreground the intricate relationship between the individual use of language and institutional rules about its circulation. In postwar Asian American communities, two attitudes toward the official language were fostered. The first was one of assimilation and acceptance, "look[ing] upon writing as the proof" that the Asian American was "nearing white" (Nee and Nee 1972: 394–95). The second was one of blind resistance that associated writing with white domination and considered it an instrument of oppression that the oppressed did not share. Both reactions were programmed by cultural colonialism to enforce writing as exclusive white property and privilege.

Having portrayed Fred's refusal to write for white approval, Chin orchestrates another scenario. It is here that Chin's favorite father-son pairing takes on a new stylistic and thematic twist. One minute in the play, we hear Fred responding to his white brother-in-law, "You're right, Ross, I don't think of myself as a tourist guide all my life. But my own parents won't read a story I write" (F. Chin 1981: 86). The next moment, we hear Pa entreating Ross to edit his New Year speech without ever considering asking Fred, his son, a writer with a degree in English (104). The father's distrust of the son's language reveals a typical self-contempt that jeopardizes Asian American verbal culture. But more than reflecting a prevailing attitude of the older immigrant generation, Chin has used the conventional father-son dispute to open another dimension: Pa's demand of Fred's filial piety and indifference to his English and writing are metaphors for the relationship between the colonizer and the colonized (137). One recalls that the hegemonic exercise of control over the minority often starts with a consideration of them as childlike, desperately in need of parental guidance. Fred's revolt against his own father can then be likened to an act of resistance to the paternal authority of the dominant culture. In this context, Chin's consistent and scathing satire of the multiple forms of imposed tutelage, from the Lone Ranger through Helen Keller to Charlie Chan, gains added significance.

Although the play concludes with the death of Pa and Fred's apparent liberation from patriarchal pressure, he does not become a famous writer.

When the lights fade on Fred, the audience sees a "shrunken Charlie Chan, an image of death." The stage direction reads: "He becomes the tourist guide" (141). Not until he has given up on being a writer does Fred *become* a tourist guide; the façade, the face, the reflection, and the stereotype are woven into one. Unlike Tam, the protagonist of Chin's *Chickencoop Chinaman*, who is eventually able to earn his natural birthright from orientalist mythologies, Fred has been forced to live someone else's movies without being able to make his own. "I don't wanta be a pioneer. Just a writer. Just see my name in a book by me," Fred Eng soliloquizes in the play; "I just have a few words and they come at me. 'Be Chinese, Charlie Chan or a nobody' to the whites and a mad dog to the Chinamans . . . for what? To die and be discovered by some punk in the next generation and published in mimeograph by some college ethnic studies department, forget it" (117).

With these words, Fred could be uttering his creator's sentiments of literary extinction. Though the historic feat of premiering the first two Asian American plays off-Broadway had earned him mild celebrity in the East Coast literary establishment by 1975, Frank Chin was unable to turn his scripts into published texts. The tension between individual command of language and institutional control of its dissemination that underlies much of *The Year of the Dragon* cannot but be seen as aesthetic formalizations of authorial alienation. Chin refuses Fred's doom, his loss of will and his yielding to forces of disintegration. Just as he abhors Fred's final subsistence as a travel agent in an orientalist economy, Chin also refuses to write a "Mama Fu Fu" Asian American cookbook. But his unhappiness with the severe limitations of ethnic publishing channels and his failure to "operate in the mainstream of American consciousness" leave him with little choice but to make an unceasing "noise of resistance" to institutional silence (F. Chin et al. [1974] 1983: xlviii, xxvi).

Frank Chin's verbal snarl and stampede express a form of self-assured and self-determined Asian American identity, an identity that is, however, still unable to transcend its ghettoized boundaries. Chin's were user-hostile works: in their demand for audience participation in agonizing histories, in their repudiating tone toward anything taken for granted, and in denying to the reader any sort of comfort in his own supposed superiority, they were ill-fitted for the orientalist market. As we leave this chapter on Asian American cultural nationalism in the mid-1970s, in which Chin played such a constitutive role, we are left with a sense of the intellectual exhilaration of the era and as well of a more sober reality. Efforts at Asian American literary self-definition took place both in opposition to the dominant culture and in a location largely external to metropolitan power. The famed integration of personal expression and political action was best accomplished within a fairly closed community of literary production and reception, while the practitioners of this adversarial art were sustained mainly by meager independent or personal resources. Asian American writing was not a professional activity supported by established institutions; neither was its reading a specialized intellectual inquiry buttressed by scholarly discourse and methods. We are, in short, left with a nationalistic cultural legacy that never truly reached the nation.

Can Maxine Hong Kingston Speak? The Contingency of *The Woman Warrior*

A s Frank Chin withdrew to his familiar home base, any point on I-5 along the West Coast, a then Hawaii-based Californian writer made her eastward somersault. Nineteen-seventy-six saw the phenomenal publication of Maxine Hong Kingston's *The Woman Warrior: Memoirs of a Girlhood Among Ghosts*, a book that changed forever the face and status of contemporary Asian American literature. Although it could not claim chronological precedence in the post-1965 Asian American corpus, *The Woman Warrior* remained the first text to both enter the arena of national culture and arrest American public imagination. Its appeal to the shared category of gender produced a heterogeneous readership beyond ethnicity; its postmodern play of the folk fanned commercial interest in the future publication of Asian American texts; and its extensive review and study by critics of legitimate cultural affiliations also enabled the scholarly excavation and preservation of Asian American literary tradition.

The Woman Warrior's historic entry into public culture gave Asian America such an official literary visibility that it is small wonder its reception became controversial. The interpretive differences over the book's meaning, as a matter of fact, became an instant power contestation between the dominant culture and the ethnic community for both the authority and agency of Asian American articulation. Who is qualified to speak about and for Asian America? What is the appropriate language of ethnic artistic representation? How should a minority writer published in a mainstream press negotiate her double audience, and to whom does she owe allegiance? These and related questions that greeted *The Woman Warrior* reveal the representational duress that this single text has had to endure, and their answers also inevitably betray the divergent conceptualizations of an emergent Asian American culture. Central to the debate about *The Woman Warrior* is the definitional struggle, especially between the emergent cadre of ethnic nationalists and mainstream feminist and formalist critics, for the significance of "Asian America."[1]

I

Sometime in July 1976, the bound galleys of *The Woman Warrior* reached Frank Chin through Kingston's editor at Knopf, Charles Elliot. Soon thereafter, Kingston and Chin, two aspiring Chinese American writers, had their first and also last series of personal correspondence. Their epistolary exchange showed their significantly different attitudes about the efficacy of Asian American writing. While Chin, regardless of his admiration of its style, thought of *The Woman Warrior* "as another in a long line of Chinkie autobiographies by Pochahontas yellows blowing the same old mixed up East/West soul struggle," Kingston regarded Chin's writing, despite her appreciation of it, as "the angry-young-man-radical-political screaming." Kingston went on to say:

> The genre *I* am avoiding is the political/polemical harangue, which I dislike because a.) it keeps the writer on the surface of perception; b.) it puts the Asian-Am. writer on the same trip as the racist; we provide the other half of the dialogue, the yin to his yang, as it were, c.) the blacks already wrote that way in the '50's; all we'd do is change black faces to yellow, no furthering of art.[2]

In brief, Kingston neither held Chin's confrontational politics to be effective nor believed that adversarial art had worked historically for ethnic writers, either African American or Asian American.

The approaches of Chin and Kingston appear to differ in two principal ways: first in their positioning of Asian American writing relative to the dominant American culture; second in their choice of Asian American subjective space and symbols. Although Kingston vocally disapproves of Chin's ideology of opposition because of its likelihood of reproducing racist paradigms, she does not address his apprehension of the "East/West soul struggle." She also appears unaware of *Aiiieeeee!*'s ethnic nationalist program, which rejects ancestral Asia and white America as the source of an Asian American symbolic and locates a unique Asian American cultural sensibility in the history and body politic of the United States. The ideological and aesthetic differences between Chin and Kingston seem to first converge on the conceptualization of Asian American geocultural space.

If *Aiiieeeee!*'s no-no maneuver was a way of claiming an ethnic national space that resolutely refutes the dominant orientalist social geography, Chin's own creative efforts also show the difficulty of fully articulating a distinctive Asian American aesthetic space. In *The Woman Warrior*, Kingston seems to have formally avoided Chin's approach not by simply saying "yes-yes" to Asia and America (for that would mean giving her "yin to his yang, as it were"), but by first accepting the East/West apartheid and its hold on the popular mind and then attempting to mediate within this age-old dual geography. Kingston's rejection of Chin's repudiative racial self-inscription and her breakthrough into mainstream American culture, one may argue, seem to have begun with her deliberate accommodation, adaptation, and appropriation of the familiar orientalist geopolitical imagination.

We can expand on this interpretive suggestion by comparing the openings of *The Woman Warrior* and its predecessor, Lawrence Yep's 1975 novel *Dragonwings*:

> "You must not tell anyone," my mother said, "what I am going to tell you. In China your father had a sister who killed herself. She jumped into the family well. We say that your father has all brothers because it is as if she had never been born." (Kingston 1976: 1)

> Ever since I can remember, I had wanted to know about the Land of the Golden Mountain, but my mother had never wanted to talk about it. All I knew was that a few months before I was born, my father had left our home in the Middle Kingdom, or *China*, as the white demons call it, and travelled over the sea to work in the demon land. There was plenty of money to be made among the demons, but it was also dangerous. My own grandfather had been lynched about thirty years before by a mob of white demons almost the moment he had set foot on their shores. (Yep 1975: 1)

Both paragraphs are told from an adolescent's point of view, both episodes have a mother who is unwilling to break the taboo subject, and both stories involve the death of a kins[wo]man. Though Yep's narrative begins in China, he directs the audience's gaze westward to America—in other words, toward their home. America, in the narrator's perspective, is at once a land of plenty and a land of prohibition, where immigrants of color had to endure racial violence. As the line between the ethnic subject and the dominant/demonic Other is drawn, so is their antagonistic relationship set within the unfolding narrative space. Such a narrative deployment may create cognitive dissonance among white American readers who feel somehow implicated in the discursive landscape—after all, the lynch mob is specified as white. Kingston's narrative takes a different trajectory. The narrative hand guides the audience eastward to China, into what is at once unfamiliar geography and secret family lore. China is a repressive space for the Chinese, but the white American reader, an outsider to that land and culture, is invited both to enter the fictional space and to pry into the mysterious death of an Other. By virtue of being comfortably ensconced in another country, the reader is granted not only an absolute narrative alibi but also the power and privilege of imaginative travel and epistemological control. If Yep's America asks the reader to confront the devil, Kingston's China allows the reader to avoid such a task, for China, as a spatial and metaphysical alterity, will remain an enigma as long as it serves the Western subject.[3]

Gayatri Chakravorty Spivak's analysis of Derrida's original formulation of "Chinese prejudice" proves helpful here. The term describes the mechanics of appropriation that use China as a blueprint, and a blueprint only, for Western philosophical writing. "Chinese prejudice" is an ideological self-justification for a Western imperialist project that sublates Chinese into an easy-to-learn script and in turn supersedes actual Chinese. (Ezra Pound's creative use of the Chinese ideograph is a modern example, and Kingston's use of the Poundian ideograph in the "White Tiger" chapter is an interesting reappropriation.) The result is a Western hallucination that consolidates "an inside, its own subject status" by producing the Chinese Other (Spivak 1988a: 292–93). In this way, China, whether represented by its language, culture, geography, or any other feature, is detached from its own history and made to conform to American orientalist discourse, ultimately compensating for occidental desires.

It is toward these desires and the power of their imposition that Edith Eaton [Sui Sin Far], the nineteenth-century Asian American author, directs her satire. Writing in *Leaves from the Mental Portfolio of a Eurasian*, she remarks:

> They [the "funny people who advise me to trade upon my nationality"] tell me that if I wish to succeed in literature in America I should dress in Chinese costume, carry a fan in my hand, wear a pair of scarlet beaded slippers, live in New York, and come of high birth. Instead of making myself familiar with the Chinese Americans around me, I should discourse on my spirit acquaintance with Chinese ancestors and quote in between the "Good Mornings" and "How d'ye dos" of editors,

> "Confucius, Confucius, how great
> is Confucius,
> Before Confucius, there never was
> Confucius,
> After Confucius, there never came
> Confucius,"
> etc., etc., etc.,
> or something like that, both illuminating
> and obscuring, don't you know.
>
> (Eaton 1982: 90)

For an Asian American writer to make her mark, she has to write and act with the kind of cultural intelligibility required of an Oriental. "Chinese costume[s]" and "spirit acquaintance with Chinese ancestors" and Confucian analects, rather than knowledge of the Chinese Americans around her are deemed appropriate aesthetic subjects. Hilarious as Sui Sin Far's anecdote is, it painfully exemplifies a historical dilemma that arises time and again, for the discursive need of American orientalism never fails to tempt (as in the above instance) or coerce (as in denial of publication).[4]

That Asia is a socially created space in American orientalist discourse and in the discourse of Anglo-Saxon nationalism has a special impact on Asian American writers. First, Asia has historically occupied the position of the Other in Western imagination, whether civilizational or colonial, that has to be subdued or converted. Second, Asia is the superimposed homeland of Asian Americans, whose allegiance to the United States, whether political or cultural, is perpetually doubted. Unlike Americans of European descent, Asian Americans are conflated with Asians, whose presence in the United States is not equated with their belonging to it. Third, by the spatial logic of the previous two points, Asia is the proper site of Asian American imagination. For Asian American writers finally, Asia no longer represents a physical space, a geopolitical entity, a cultural resource, an ancestral home base that can be differentially incorporated into the immediacy of their American experience; it is supposed to epitomize and embody *the* natural experience and essence of Asian Americans.

In light of this analysis, Kingston's recourse to China indicates her tentative loop back to a predetermined discursive site and a predetermined geocultural relationship as well. The choice was timely: China, one recalls, was suddenly of great currency after the 1973 signing of the U.S.-PRC communiqué in Shanghai, a watershed event for the normalization of diplomatic relations between the two countries. But the public Sino-frenzy was only the top of the upward swing of benevolent orientalism since the heyday of the 1960s counterculture and its revival of similar nineteenth-century transcendentalist yearnings for Eastern mysticism. Literature produced between the years of the Shanghai communiqué and the publication of *The Woman Warrior* exhibited a marked public curiosity about China.[5] Period fashions, from cotton loafers to Kung Pao chicken and Kung Fu movies, also indicated a general receptiveness to Asian products in American markets. All these were not possible, however, without the fundamental shift toward "late capital" on the transnational playing field, which not only gave "the Asia-Pacific" region its unprecedented American significance but also gave rise to the articulation of "Asian America" in the first place. In this context, Kingston's selection of China as the beginning of an Asian American imaginary seemed also to correspond to, if not anticipate in the literary realm at least, the nascent development of a transnational diaspora to which Frank Chin et al.'s version of ethnic nationalism was essentially antagonistic.

II

As soon as *The Woman Warrior* hit the market, opposing camps tried to claim it. In *Ms*, Sara Blackburn called the book "a psychic transcript of every woman I know—class, age, race or ethnicity be damned" (1977: 39). "In the vivid particularity of her experience, and with the resource of considerable art," wrote Diane Johnson for the *New York Review of Books*, "Kingston reaches to the universal qualities of female condition and female anger that the bland generalities of social science and the merely factual history cannot describe" (1977: 19). Such white feminist affirmation of *The Woman Warrior* ignited the book's instant rejection by some Asian American critics. Jeffery Paul Chan called Johnson yet another "Pearl Buck shaping converts in the oriental orphanage of her imagination. Never mind history, Johnson has uncovered a feminist" (1977: 41). Ben Tong agreed: "Maxine Hong Kingston's *Woman Warrior* is a fashionably feminist work written with white acceptance in mind" (1977: 6).

The conflicting reviews probably tell as much about the parties in contention as they do about the text. For the feminist reviewers, the book offered yet another testimonial of female suffering that urged sisterly solidarity. *The Woman Warrior* is good, we were assured, because it transcends "class, age, race or ethnicity" and achieves "the universal qualities of female condition." In place of a male omniscience is now a female universal that not only cancels the specificity of ethnic womanhood but also validates it in white feminist terms. While such stamps of approval elevated the status of the book for mainstream readership, they severely limited other possibilities of interpretation. The condescension of cultural colonialism in the rhetoric of acclaim had serious repercussions for the future reception of the text. Both Chan's and Tong's attacks, we note, were aimed first at the reviewer; their quarrel with the text was only a *related* response. The priorities and opinions of the initial feminist reviewers likely affected the motivations and opinions of later readers. Consequently, the reception of *The Woman Warrior* involved not only the simple writer-reader relation but also the power relations among different groups of critics whose status depended, in this instance, on their interpretation.

Let us return to Johnson, Chan, and Tong to see how the text of *The Woman Warrior* became a battleground between the dominant culture and the ethnic culture. After likening *The Woman Warrior* to many Western feminist classics, Johnson made a shocking observation: "The Chinese-Americans are a notably unassimilated culture. It is not unusual in San Francisco to find fourth- or fifth-generation American-born Chinese who speak no English. Generations have not eased their mistrust of American culture, and they will not tell Americans certain things about theirs" (1977: 20). In what Chan called her "utter stupidity" and "button-popping arrogance," Johnson blatantly denied the existence of Asian American English and reinforced the orientalist displacement of Asian American culture onto its ancestral origin. While Johnson could still have been under the narrative spell of the revealed "forbidden tale," without bothering to check her prejudicial racial slip, the indignant Jeffery Chan, a coeditor of *Aiiieeeee!*, was led to wonder why "[a] white reading public will rave over ethnic biography while ignoring a Chinese American's literary art," with Chin's *The Chickencoop Chinaman* particularly in his mind. This "engenders the feeling," Chan proceeds sardonically, that "perhaps Chinese-Americans have no authority over the language and culture that expresses our sensibility best" (1977: 41). Meanwhile, Tong takes Johnson's equation of "recently immigrated folks from Hong Kong and Taiwan" with all Asian Americans as an attempt to erase their diversity and reduce them to "foreigner Asians except for those few exceptions that prove the rule who write in white for whites" (1977: 6).

If Chan is especially sensitive to Johnson's lack of knowledge of Chin and *Aiiieeeee!*, Tong resents both the representative status Johnson awards Kingston's text and the persistent racialization of Asian American foreignness that her review betrays. As these criticisms show, *The Woman Warrior* is caught amid the crucial conflicts of an emerging Asian American literature. Among those are the struggle between the mainstream and the marginal "interpretive communities" for the appropriate (re)production of Asian American voices (see Fish 1980: 303–72), as well as the disagreements among Asian American writers and intellectuals over who should constitute the mainstay of their culture: the new immigrants with their diasporic sensibility or the native-born generations whose sensibilities are formed by a colonial education and the structures of exclusion.

For the moment, however, the nationalist and transnationalist conflict that became intense two decades later was largely submerged. The contest over the right to speak for an emerging culture pivoted on *The Woman Warrior*'s textual validity. In her open letter to Kingston, Katheryn Fong blamed the author for her "distortion of the histories of China and Chinese America," her failure to give historical causality to her narrative, and her "over-exaggera[tion]" of Asian American female oppression (1977: 67–69). Poet Nellie Wong, however, offered her personal testimony to back up the accuracy of Kingston's work, arguing that the text "supports [her] own explorations of Asian women's relationships to each other" (1978–79: 46–48). These mixed reviews, with their shared interest in the truth value, showed not only the ascending representative status of *The Woman Warrior* but also the suggestive power of the book's generic classification.

"Genres," in Fredric Jameson's view, "are essentially literary *institutions*, or social contracts between a writer and a specific public, whose function is to specify the proper use of a particular cultural artifact" (1981: 106). Clearly, the reviews responded to the generic cue of *The Woman Warrior* as nonfiction. What they did not seem to realize is that genre could be assigned after the fact. Literary classification is equivalent to the packaging of a final product, which is not always determined by the producer or author. Explaining why *The Woman Warrior* was designated as nonfiction, Charles Elliot, Kingston's editor at Knopf, is reported to have said: "Well, first novels are hard to sell. I knew it [*The Woman Warrior*] would stand a stronger chance of selling well as nonfiction autobiography. It could have been called anything else."[6]

Profit motive aside, the editor's decision about the generic category in effect controlled how the work was likely to be experienced. Generic definition involves therefore not only economic interest but political interest as well. It is to this latter interest that Frank Chin has been especially sensitive. The history of Asian American works published as autobiography is to him a history of manipulation and suppression of "yellow art" by "white American publishers." So, after reading the galleys of *The Woman Warrior*, Chin expressed to Kingston his strong reservations not about the book but about classifying it as autobiography. He wrote, "the yellow autobiography is a white racist form, . . . an insult to our writing and characterizes us as freaks, anthropological phenomena kept and pampered in a white zoo and not people whose world is complete and complex." He then advised Kingston to "go for fiction with this book if you can and dump the autobiography. As fiction, I can like your stuff without necessarily liking or agreeing with the narrator or any of the characters and credit you with subtleties and knowing lapses I can't give to an autobiographer."[7]

Chin's objection to autobiography in Asian American production hinges not so much on its inherent properties as on the function it is intended to perform for the reading public. Once *The Woman Warrior* was labeled nonfiction, it was understood by convention to be a narrative of real events. The consequence is actually twofold. On the one hand, it invites the audience to identify it as a real account of life. On the other hand, it discourages the possibility of interpreting it as a symbolic act. Therefore, the generic definition can have the effect of depriving Asian American expression of its credibility as imaginative art and reducing it to some subliterary status, serving the role of social scientific data, an encompassing reflection of Asian American totality.[8]

The unease about the authenticity of *The Woman Warrior* in the reviews by Fong and Wong now make sense. Faithfully responding to the generic signal of the text, the reviewers held the book up as a mirror to see if "the people" were truly reflected in it. The distinction between artistic image and existential actuality vanishes and the problems of representation haunt us again. Representation, we recall, has both aesthetic and political functions. An artistic object may either "stand for" something and someone or "act for" something and someone. In fact, the two functions are hardly distinguishable in the process of eliciting a reader's response. The reason that representation is of such paramount importance for Asian Americans, however, must be explained through the history of their "under-representation" and the history of their "involuntary representation." While the former indicates their general artistic and cultural absence from American culture, the latter, paradoxically, refers to the abundance of stereotypes heaped upon them without their consent. This history of iconic oppression has made the minority community in question particularly sensitive about the limited exposure it does get, and has ironically increased the representational capacity of existing artistic expressions and images. That a piece of ethnic literature is deemed exemplary and its author designated a community spokesperson provides the basic context in which works of minority art are received. The advantage of such a context is that it enhances the affective or persuasive power of an ethnic text, whose writer suddenly finds herself in a position to alter the conceptions the majority of readers have about another ethnic group. Meanwhile, however, simply because it is only through the chosen few that members of the dominant culture learn about an ethnic life, the representational power of ethnic works as a whole are automatically restricted.

Two immediate consequences thus follow. First, the work of ethnic art inevitably shoulders, as historical circumstances obligate it, the burden of representing the whole humanity of its people in culture and politics, a task no single work is capable of. Second, ethnic writers are unwillingly caught

in the struggle for the hard-to-obtain position of the community representative. It is at these constraints of ethnic representation that Kingston's
blast in her review of her reviewers is directed:

> Why must I "represent" anyone besides myself? Why should I be denied an
> individual artistic vision? And I do not think I wrote a "negative" book, as the
> Chinese American reviewer said; but suppose I had? Suppose I had been so
> wonderfully talented that I wrote a tragedy? Are we Chinese Americans to
> deny ourselves tragedy? If we give up tragedy in order to make a good im-
> pression on Caucasians, we have lost a battle.

"Oh, well," we almost hear her heaving of a heavy sigh but turning optimistic in the end, "I'm certain that some day when a great body of Chinese
American writing becomes published and known, then readers will no
longer have to put such a burden on each book that comes out. Readers can
see the variety of ways for Chinese Americans to be" (1982: 63). With this,
Kingston proposes a solution to the problem of representation, which is yet
to become a reality.

III

The material imperatives surrounding the issue of representation raised by
The Woman Warrior are again addressed in Chin's "Afterword," which con-
cludes his 1988 collection of short stories, *The Chinaman Pacific & Frisco R.R.
Co.* Calling the autobiographer "Mei-jing" (Chinese for "American dollar")
and her book "The Unmanly Warrior," Chin points his spearhead right at
Kingston in a parody of the critical standoff over *The Woman Warrior*:

> The old French people of Frenchtown on the edge of Canton didn't like the
> book. They didn't have Smith Mei-jing's grasp of the Chinese language, the
> Chinese who loved her book said. The people of old Frenchtown said her
> book falsified history. They are conservative and old-fashioned and don't ap-
> preciate good writing, the Chinese who loved the book said. . . . The French
> girl is writing not history, but art, the Chinese who loved the book said, and
> continued: She is writing a work of imagination authenticated by her per-
> sonal experience. . . . The French people of Frenchtown said, her own expe-
> rience is an insane, paranoid distortion of basic knowledge common to all
> French. . . . And the Chinese who loved her book said, her personal experi-
> ence was authentically French and her unique understanding of both the
> French and the Chinese views of life brings the Chinese the closest, most hu-
> man understanding of the French ever produced in the Chinese language. . . .
> Sour grapes, the Chinese who loved her book said, She's not writing history
> or about history, therefore the accuracy of any of her history is irrelevant to
> the question of her artistry, authenticity, or psychological reality, her Chinese
> admirers said. (Chin 1988: i–ii)

If "the people of Frenchtown" are Asian American community critics, "the Chinese who loved her book" must be establishment critics. If the former denigrate the book on historical grounds, the latter defend it on artistic grounds. Besides arrogating to himself the role of a "real" community representative, thus invalidating Smith Mei-jing's (Kingston's) claim to truth, Chin does raise important issues about the artistic use of ethnic folklore and folk idiom.[9]

What Chin argues through "The Unmanly Warrior" story of Joan of Arc is that Kingston has conflated the Chinese legends and deviated, in her narrative re-presentation, from the proto-text of Mu Lan. It was Yue Fei (A.D. 1103–1141), for example, a male general of the Sung Dynasty, not Mu Lan, whose mother tattooed his back to remind him of his loyalty. Kingston's textual transplantation is thereby to Chin a concoction of Chinese misogyny, meant to distort Chinese history. In the same vein, both Jeffery Chan and Ben Tong charge Kingston with mistranslating the key term of *The Woman Warrior*, "*kuei*," into "ghost," to court white readership (J. Chan 1977: 41; Tong 1977: 6). For the sake of comparison, one may again look at Laurence Yep's *Dragonwings* in which "*kuei*," is consistently rendered as "demon." This is not to indicate, however, that "ghost" is linguistically impossible; rather it is a common translation, as Kingston's narrator innocently finds in the dictionary (Kingston 1976: 103). Even Yep's protagonist Moon Shadow is fully aware of "*kuei*"'s ambiguities:

> The Tang [Chinese] word for demon can mean many kinds of supernatural beings. A demon can be the ghost of a dead person, but he can also be a supernatural creature who can use his great powers for good as well as for evil, just like dragons. It is much trickier to deal with a demon of the Middle Kingdom [China] than an *American devil*, because you always know that the *American devil* means you harm. (Yep 1975: 10)

The issue here is how ethnic linguistic practice is appropriated in the English context and what its manner of appropriation attempts. Missing from *The Woman Warrior* are the etymological history and the colonial contexts of Asia and Asian America in which the word is uttered. The translation of *kuei* as "foreigners" became common in the mid-nineteenth century when Western imperial powers invaded the Manchu Empire of China with guns and opium. For the first time in history the citizens of the "Central Kingdom" were decentered, and they strove to retain their centrality by defining their oppressor as the other, "*fan-kuei*" or "*yang kuei-tzu*," foreign devils of white peril (Fairbank 1983: 163).[10] The usage is so prevalent that even a non–Asian American writer like Tom Wolfe is privy to its import: "*bok gooi* meant not simply *whites*," he notes, "but *white devils*" (39). Such negative connotations associated in the English language with Satanic forces are more or less dropped as Kingston opts for the word "ghost," which accentuates the insubstantiality of a specter while diminishing the adversarial context in which "kuei" is cursed under one's breath. In an effort to relieve the white man's historical burden, the world of the memoir is turned phantasmic and its atmosphere phantasmagoric.

Kingston's use of "kuei" is evidence of the regulatory pressure of the dominant culture on Asian American articulation, as old as in Sui Sin Far's anecdote and as recent as in Fred Eng's lament. Rather than abiding by "the Frenchtown" perspective, which views history as a handful of unchanging facts and the artist's job as its faithful transmitter, Kingston seems to suggest that history cannot activate itself and the act of translation should have to accommodate the interpretive interests of the translator as well as the interests of her imagined audiences. Any pursuit of historic purity at the expense of the historic present is futile, Kingston seems say; that echoes Frank Lentricchia, who remarked: "to proceed with the illusion of purity is to situate oneself on the margin of history, as the possessor of a unique truth disengaged from history's flow" (1983: 36). The "Frenchtown" view of history seems to have succumbed to just such purist temptations; not only does it imply *the* way of approaching historical reality but in so doing it also confirms that the faithful reflection of facts is *the* gauge of the ethnic text, ostensibly contradicting the belief of Chin et al. that Asian American texts ought to be treated as "works of art" (Chin et al. [1974] 1983: xxii).

One notes that Kingston's mediation of "kuei" shows her grasp of the historical currents that govern (despite the individual's aversion to them) the production of ethnic literature. Ben Tong is certainly right when he links Kingston's textual strategy with the Chinese American tradition of *jaw jieh* (catching pigs), "a time-honored practice of bullshitting white people into buying up whatever junk we dig out of basement attics . . . [of] pushing abalone shells, 'beggars chicken,' tour guides, cookbooks and all the rest, both in the name of economic survival *and* revenge" (Tong 1977: 6). Though Tong will not credit her with such intentionality, Kingston doubtless operates within the tradition of *jaw jieh*, which she comes by through either praxis or intuition. Nowhere are Houston Baker's comments on Ralph Ellison's "creativity and commerce" more appropriate than in this context of our discussion: "if the folk artist is to turn a profit from his monumental creative energies (which are often counteractive, or inversive, *vis-à-vis* Anglo American culture)," he says, "he must, in essence, sufficiently modify his folk forms (and amply advertise himself) to merchandize such forms as commodities on the *artistic* market. The folk artist may even have to don a mask that distorts what he knows is his genuine self in order to make his product commensurate with a capitalist market-place" (Baker 1984: 244). Maxine Hong Kingston, like Ralph Ellison before her, is a master of such strategies.[11]

IV

What is truly a marvel is the way in which the author of *The Woman Warrior* prophetically enshrines her work in the "Masterpiece Theater" of American literature. At the end of the book, Kingston strategically revises yet another Chinese legend, the capture of the second-century Chinese woman poet Ts'ai Yen by the barbarians, and transforms it into a superb meta-narrative for entry into the canon. In her autobiographical verse, Ts'ai Yen expressed ever so poignantly her anger and humiliation at being made slave and wife by the invading nomadic tribe. The tone of fury and despondency so pervasive in her poetry is, however, notably absent in Kingston's version (You et al. 1964: 51). We see instead a baffled Ts'ai Yen living among the noble savages, receiving gifts from the barbarian chieftain after he impregnates her and riding on his horse when he charges into villages and encampments. One day, Kingston tells us, Ts'ai Yen is so struck by the music of barbarian reed pipes filling the desert that she starts to sing:

> out of Ts'ai Yen's tent, which was apart from the others, the barbarians heard a woman's voice singing, as if to her babies, a song so high and clear, it matched the flutes. Ts'ai Yen sang about China and her family there. Her words seemed to be Chinese, but the barbarians understood their sadness and anger. Sometimes they thought they could catch barbarian phrases about forever wandering. Her children did not laugh, but eventually sang along when she left her tent to sit by the winter campfires, ringed by the barbarians. (Kingston 1976: 243)

The poet in exile is no longer alienated. In both sound and image, the passage creates a mythic vision, "cross[ing] boundaries not delineated in space" and transcending differences in discourse (ibid: 9). Not only is her music in tune with the barbarians' but her words are perfectly comprehended: the apparent opposition dissolves when the Chinese and the barbarians reach a truce. In a leap toward universal harmony, the poet is integrated into the "ring" that used to marginalize minority groups. In the round aura of the "ring" is no longer an other but one of us, the center that holds.

Kingston remarks, "I do believe in the timelessness and universality of individual vision. It [*The Woman Warrior*] would not just be a family book or an American book or a woman's book but a world book, and at the same moment, my book." The book will also be one, she adds, "for my old English professors of the new criticism school in Berkeley, by incorporating what they taught about the structure of the novel" (1982: 64–65). Indeed, the traditional humanist vision, the singular autonomy of the text, and the romantic cult of genius all play their parts in the hermeneutic ring of literary canonization. Trained in the school of New Criticism, with all its paradox, irony, and seven types of ambiguity, Kingston was able to appeal to formal excellence, to which both the traditional reviews and the newer forms of textual theories—structuralism and poststructuralism, for example—would be responsive. With this, *The Woman Warrior* was also able to mobilize the journalistic reviews that decidedly set the canonical process in motion.

John Leonard, then *New York Times* book review editor, was reportedly responsible for the first stampede of its publicity (1976). His praise and that of others like him in such major publications as *Time*, *Newsweek*, and *The New York Review of Books* spurred a tide of additional journalistic reviews in smaller publications and had a ripple effect on academic reviews as well. The first printing of 5,000 hardcovers sold out virtually overnight. Within months, another 40,000 copies were sold before the book was tapped for the 1976 National Book Critics Circle award for nonfiction (Horton 1979: 49–50). Other book awards from *Mademoiselle* and Anissfield-Wolf soon followed; it made the bestseller lists of the *New York Times* and the Book of the Month Club, among others; and in 1979 *Time* rated *The Woman Warrior* among the top ten nonfiction works of the decade (Currier 1980: 235). It is not insignificant to note that Kingston's institutional recognition predated that of Alice Walker and Toni Morrison, making her the most prominent female ethnic writer in the 1970s and 1980s.[12] In almost no time, *The Woman Warrior* popped up on class reading lists and in departmental curricula—one year it was simultaneously adopted as a text in twelve departments at the University of California, Berkeley (Chun 1989). Before long, it entered prestigious literary anthologies and college readers, got included in literary histories and critical biographies (*Columbia Literary History of the United States* and *Contemporary Authors*, for example), and became the subject of scores of journal articles, a host of scholarly books, and conference papers too numerous to list. The body of criticism on it is still growing steadily, and according to recent Modern Language Association statistics, *The Woman Warrior* "is the most widely taught book by a living writer in U.S. colleges and universities" (Talbot 1990: 8).

Among the agencies of authority that helped secure *The Woman Warrior* in the canon and drew the work into the orbit of a population of potential readers, the academic critics were unquestionably the most powerful. How they maintained, transmitted, and reproduced the meaning and significance of the book in academic institutions, and how they served Asian American subjects with their critical practice, was crucial.[13] The theoretical sophistication with which critics credited *The Woman Warrior* elevated the book to a status no Asian American text has hitherto enjoyed. Attention to the book's "paradoxes of autobiographical enunciation" (Kemnitz 1983), "fictivity" of "speech act" (Myers 1986), "bridging of autobiography and fiction" (Homsher 1979), and "the metaphysics of matrilinearism" (Demetrakipoulos 1980) all enrich *The Woman Warrior*'s formal complexity. But the lack of attention to autobiography's generic suggestion for ethnic minority writers also confirmed the initial anxieties of some that the book would be "misread," which were prompted not only by its misclassification as autobiography but also by its gender depiction and geopolitical location.

Misreading can be not so much the effect of critical cultural illiteracy as an effort to forcibly fit textual analysis into a dominant feminist motif, say, "from silence to voice." "Even as a child," Linda Morante observes, "Kingston realizes the *cultural roots* of her reticence" (1987: 78). Since the "cultural roots" she refers to are Chinese, it begs the question whether the narrator's silence *is* inherently Chinese. Kingston is not ambiguous about this point in *The Woman Warrior*: at the Chinese school, she says, "we chanted together, voices rising and falling, loud and soft, some boys shouting, everybody reading together, reciting together and not alone with one voice. . . . The girls were not mute. They screamed and yelled during recess" (1976: 194). Elsewhere in the text, the narrator tells us, "I have tired [sic] to turn myself American-feminine. Chinese communication was loud, public. Only sick people had to whisper" (13). Does this say that the Chinese culture suppresses voice? Or does the critic purposely ignore the dialogical nature of the narrative, which is in Kingston's own words, "not alone with one voice"? The vicious patriarchy that presumably silences female expression is by itself nowhere to be heard in the text: the mother is the "champion talker" while the father is almost inaudible (235).

Morante is right to point out that "the Chinese keep secrets, they conceal their names, they withhold speech," and Brave Orchid "demands the silence that is self-obliteration" (1987: 78, 80). But she does not acknowledge the cause of this imposed silence, despite the fact that she quotes the following passage:

> "Don't tell," advised my parents. . . . Lie to Americans. Tell them you were born during the San Francisco earthquake. Tell them your birth certificate and your parents were burnt up in the fire. Don't report crimes; tell them we have no crimes and no poverty. Give them a new name every time you get arrested; (Kingston 1976: 214)

She could have cited a few more sentences but she did not. However, I will: "the ghosts won't recognize you. Pay the new immigrants twenty-five cents an hour and say we have no unemployment. And of course, tell them we're against Communism. Ghosts have no memory anyway and poor eyesight. And the Han people won't be pinned down" (214–15). It is the aftermath of the exclusion law and the fever of the Red Scare that silenced Chinese Americans. To conceal "the unspeakable" (6) is a strategic response to institutional racism, an act of survival, and not at all an immutable Asian cultural trait.

Failure to be informed about Asian American history is frequently coupled with a colonialist benevolence. "Establishing herself [the narrator Maxine] as a talker in opposition to her mother—as American instead of Chinese, a truth teller instead of a liar—makes it possible for her to define herself as separate from her mother," Suzanne Juhasz remarks in her reading of *The Woman Warrior*: "Leaving home at this stage means leaving China, and her mother's Chinese way of talking" (1985: 183). Sure enough, the mother's immigrant way of lying can hardly be deemed American, while the daughter's acquisition of English has enabled her to depart China. That metaphor may be too subtle for very literal minds to grasp: the narrative protagonist has never been to China, and neither has the author, but still, the critic willingly assigns her an alien status. No wonder Juhasz thinks Kingston's command of English commendable: "Its style, as *correct* as it is exquisite, seems to make acceptable to *literary* people the most *sophisticated criticism* in its themes" (1980: 236; emphasis mine). Well, the hope of salvation for the Asian American female subject lies in the power of English language, or rather, as Juhasz tries to convince us, in Sister Critic's rescue mission.

What we have here is a tragic repetition, this time in the critical realm, of the exercise of power by American orientalist discourse. Now, when the West again decides to know the East, the only epistemological means available, it seems, is to automatically assume a speaking part for the East—thou China, still unravished bride of quietness. Gayatri Spivak's critique of Julia Kristeva's wishful representation of China in *About Chinese Women*, I believe, sheds light on the interested position of so many of Kingston's feminist critics as well:

> The pioneering books that bring First World feminists news from the Third World are written by privileged informants and can only be deciphered by a trained readership. . . . This is not the tired nationalistic claim that only a native can know the scene. The point I am trying to make is that, in order to learn enough about Third World women and to develop a different readership, the immense heterogeneity of the field must be appreciated and the First World feminist must learn to stop feeling privileged *as a woman*. (Spivak 1981–83: 156–57)

The orientalist nature of scholarship on *The Woman Warrior* also characterizes the criticism by men, with only a slightly different turn of the screw. While the female critics stress their shared gender oppression with Asian American women despite cultural difference, the male critics could not help deploring the wretched fate of "Chinese women" wrapped in "the double bind that would limit them to the maggot nonidentities of wife and

slave" (Eakin 1985: 275). The horrifying "village patriarchy" thus func-
tioned to compromise Western sexism and consolidate the Euro-American
male subject. Eakin proclaimed: "The violent consequences of the aunt's
assertion of her individuality balance in searing intensity the depth of the
villagers' commitment to cultural determinism and conformity. The quest
for selfhood, so familiar in the literature of the West, unleashes a rush toward annihilation in this stark and somber tale from the East" (257–58).
He seems to have forgotten the puritan patriarchy that branded the scarlet
letter on Hester Prynne and the Creole patriarchy that limited Edna Pon-
tellier's choices to the bottom of the sea. Only in the despotic Orient, as his
cathartic reading goes, are men capable of such inhumane cruelty.

When "the attempt to deconstruct the hegemony of *patriarchal* discourses through feminism is itself foreclosed by the emphasis on 'Chinese'
as a mark of absolute difference," Rey Chow remarks, and "when the West's
'other women' are prescribed their 'own' national and ethnic identity, they
are most excluded from having a claim to the reality of their existence"
(1991: 163). As Asian American women's oppression is displaced onto their
ancestral cultural origin, what the white critical benevolence accomplishes,
in addition to elevating the status of *The Woman Warrior*, is precisely the
reinforcement of racial and cultural incommensurability between ethnic
and dominant populations within the same nation. One is left to wonder
whether the book's prominence is derived from its occupation of a barbarous periphery away from the civilized metropolis.

Though perhaps politically unconscious, the desire to appropriate by
way of assimilation prompted reductive and essentialist readings that made
the "No Name Woman" chapter almost the canonical elect of *The Woman
Warrior*. That chapter is included in Gilbert and Gubar's *Norton Anthology
of Literature by Women* (1985), McQuade et al.'s *Harper American Literature*
(1987), Henry and Myrna Knepler's *Crossing Cultures: Readings for Composition* (1983), X. J. and Dorothy M. Kennedy's *Bedford Reader* (1985), Shrodes
et al.'s *Conscious Reader* (1985), and Hetternan and Johnston's *Harvest Reader*
(1991). Paul Lauter et al.'s *Heath Anthology of American Literature* (1990) is a
notable exception to this pattern. None of these anthologies contains an
editorial note to a date that Kingston uses to catch the reader's attention
early on. The third sentence of *The Woman Warrior* reads,

> In 1924 just a few days after our village celebrated seventeen hurry-up wed-
> dings—to make sure that every young man who went "out on the road"
> would responsibly come home—your father and his brothers and your
> grandfather and his brothers and *your aunt's new husband* sailed for America,
> the Gold Mountain. (1976: 3; emphasis mine)

So, we know that "no name woman" aunt was just married and did not accompany her groom to America. What we do not know from the text and

what I think the editor should have made known is the context that *may have* given rise to the aunt's act of "extravagance" (7). Nineteen twenty-four was the year in which the 1882 Chinese Exclusion Act was expanded to exclude all Asians from entry as immigrants, including Chinese alien wives of U.S. citizens (Lai and Choy 1971: 93; Yung 1986: 42). Can we afford to neglect the history of the era in which Kingston stages her narrative, a narrative about marriage and estrangement, deviation and discipline that occurred under the shadow of legislated racism against Asian Americans? While not to advocate a view of literature as social documentation, a historical note could have prepared the uninformed audience for a more meaningful reading. The editors screened out the context of the other chapters, which might otherwise have provided a sense of history. With the benefit of some context, the reader would probably be less likely to make sweeping judgments about "Chinese repression of women" if she realized that this atrocious scene of gender oppression in China was in part occasioned by the racial exclusion of Asians in America.

"The Immigration Act of 1924," as Laureen Mar's poem of the same title tells us, enthralled both ethnic male and ethnic female subjects. Like Kingston, whose imaginative exploration of the law's inhumanity led her to "devote pages of paper" to the no-name woman aunt (Kingston 1976: 19), Mar's verse commemorates the no-name man who attempted suicide because he was unable to unite with his wife in America:

> I've taken the police squad outline from where you fell,
> you remember, years ago, you heaved yourself up on the
>   window edge
> of a run down hotel and jumped? Well, they traced you
>   on the sidewalk
> in chalk. The figure vaguely resembled you, a little
>   amorphous
> and anonymous, the way they liked you.
>
> (Mar 1983: 181)

But the poetic persona decides to "[peel the man] off the sidewalk as carefully / as [she] could," and restored his life in verse. Though his wife has been "stranded years in China," she comforts the man, "You won't go crazy, there are / plenty / of men like you for you to drink tea with. / Get down off the / window!" (ibid.).

"No Name Woman" may be the only Asian American text that many college students are ever exposed to; and the fact that my students of American literary survey unfailingly respond to the chapter as a Chinese story poses a serious challenge to the reading and writing of Asian American literature. Besides bringing Asian America into the national consciousness and activating the quest for the ethnic anecdote, lore, and myth, *The*

Woman Warrior's enduring contribution lies perhaps just in its foregrounding of representational issues that have accompanied the growth of Asian American creative and critical production. The deployment of geocultural space, generic convention, and gender characterization, and the dilemma of individual and collective delineation between the ethnic and dominant cultures that Kingston's debut text intensified, were strategically revisioned by the author in her later works; they also remain central to the construction and contestation of an Asian American cultural imaginary.

Claiming America

Whether the political formation of the United States hinges on an exclusive correspondence between race and culture constitutes the main query of this part and the next, which juxtapose the Asian American quest for national membership with the orientalist spatialization of absolute values and collectivities. "Claiming America," to borrow Maxine Hong Kingston's phrase, deals mainly with appropriative maneuvers for an Asian American integrity in the historical, cultural, and ideological formation of the United States.

Chapter 3 follows Kingston's improvisation of recent Asian American literary history in *Tripmaster Monkey*, which combines celebration with travesty to make the contentious construction of Asian American literary tradition the center of the 1960s U.S. countercultural revolution. Chapter 4 compares *Jasmine*'s narration of liberty and mobility through the conventions of the "American romance" with *Typical American*'s negotiation with "possessive individualism," to note Bharati Muhkerjee and Gish Jen's departure from a colored Asian American alliance and their proposal of a Jewish alternative for Asian American allegiance. Together, the authors help illuminate and complicate the questions of canon and cultural capital in the context of emergent Asian American nationalist discourse and the discourse of (universal) European American assimilation.

Canon, Collaboration, and the Corporeality of Culture

The interpretive history of *The Woman Warrior* illuminates two particular problems for Asian American cultural (re)production. First, it shows the persistent performative power of an orientalist epistemology in the geopolitical alienation of Asian Americans. Second, it demonstrates the pressure of a "minority metonymical collectivity," as an individual writer from the group suddenly finds herself shouldering the representative burden of the whole. Both problems are intrinsic to Asian American entry into the literary culture of the United States because they reflect the hidden mechanism of a "canonical quota," which dictates that only one Asian American text or author is granted institutional recognition at a given time, and that the canonical token should be symbolic of Asia, however conceived.[1]

The existence of a quota may be an evolutionary advance from historical cultural erasure, but it effectively reduces Asian American difference to a supposed uniformity that is self-evident in a single text. The token slot as the definitive space of Asian American representation obscures the contestation for the means of cultural production between cultures. It effectively reduces cultural contestation to intra-ethnic literary rivalry. The writers within the group are caught in a struggle for representative authority; command of the quota slot will ensure a writer publication and continued distribution, while the denial of that slot will mean minimal exposure or total oblivion.

The Asian American canonical quota has significantly blurred John Guillory's rigid distinction between the canon's supposed democratic legislative function and the canon's indication of access to the means of literary production. While Guillory's emphasis on the acquisition of literary capital has led him to deny the legislative effect of the canon, the very existence of the quota calls his dismissal of it into question. Since the quota system rests upon its representative value (a single Asian American writer is designated to speak for her community/race) *and* limits minority access (only one writer is heard at a particular point in history), the struggle for representative authority and for the means of cultural (re)production become virtually indistinguishable.[2]

Confronted with the adverse effects of the quota and the hierarchical nature of the traditional canon, one may be prompted to disavow the canon altogether. However, doing so would ignore the effects of the canon as a social institution; the disavowal of the canon might also imply a forsaking both of the necessity of minority cultural representation and of the need for access to the national culture. Because the canon is not just "something we study" but "something we live, and live through," argues Henry Louis Gates, "how effective and how durable our interventions in contemporary cultural politics will be depends upon our ability to mobilize the institutions that buttress and reproduce that culture" (1992: 34). It is precisely in this sense that Maxine Hong Kingston's project of "Claiming America," evident in such later works as *China Men* (1980) and *Tripmaster Monkey* (1989b), begins to show her determination to break the quota system and her strategic subversion of its terms (Pfaff 1980: 1).

Caught in what Aijaz Ahmad calls "the lonely splendor of a representative," Kingston now lends the authority of her voice to the muted communal stories beyond her individual self (1992: 98). Applying the autobiographical mode that ensured her breakthrough and continuing with the feminist aesthetics that secured her renown, she turned her inventive narrative of America in *China Men* (winner of the 1980 National Book Award) into nonfiction truths that the public ought to know. The book's reconfiguration of "Asian America" within the geocultural and historiographical confines of the United States is not only symptomatic of Kingston's responsiveness to the controversies surrounding her first book, but it also signals her conscious and sympathetic alignment with the program of Asian American ethnic nationalism.[3] The crucial thematic shift and critical stylistic turn that began with *China Men*'s celebration of Asian American heroic ventures culminated in her most ambitious work to date, *Tripmaster Monkey*, an improvisational performance of contemporary Asian American cultural emergence.

I

While turning the pages of *Tripmaster Monkey* when it first came out, I could not help being astounded and amused by a sense of déjà vu, a feeling Le Anne Schreiber suggested in her review in the *New York Times*, though in a rather different way, that "Maxine Hong Kingston is writing with a monkey on her back, a chattering, squeaking monkey-hero named Wittman Ah Sing" (1989: 9). My sentiments were matched by the book's reviews, which, though generally favorable, were bewildered by the protagonist's belligerent and brash voice. In her review "Manic Monologue," Anne Tyler wrote, "*Tripmaster Monkey* is a novel of excess—both the hero's and the author's" (1989: 44–45). A *Times Literary Supplement* piece stated that "there is a self-indulgence in the way she [Kingston] contrives increasingly bizarre situations to show off her character's exuberant love for words and literature" (Ong 1989: 998), while *Publishers Weekly* called Wittman "hyperkinetic, hypersensitive and hyperverbal" (1989: 97).

The tone and impressions of these *Tripmaster Monkey* reviewers in 1989 were curiously reminiscent of the reviews that greeted Frank Chin in 1972 when Edith Oliver of the *New Yorker* commented on Tam's "furious and dazzling eruption of verbal legerdemain" (1972: 46), Jack Kroll of *Newsweek* likened Tam to "Lenny Bruce . . . pouring out a nonstop 'ragmouth' stream of rococo riffs, invective and fantasy, a fragment of words" (1972: 53), and Clive Barnes of the *New York Times* was turned off because of "an ethnic attitude [he] had never previously encountered" (1972: 55). Only Bharati Mukherjee, in the *Washington Post*, linked Wittman Ah Sing to "a young man angry in the tradition of Frank Chin" (1989b: 1), and in the *Seattle Weekly*, S. E. Solberg called Kingston's text "a sadly flawed roman a clef" of her literary arch rival (1989: 47).

My juxtaposition of these reviews is not to suggest simplistically that Wittman Ah Sing is Frank Chin; rather the novel's protagonist is Kingston's textual mediation of the Asian American literary context of which Frank Chin is unquestionably a constitutive part. The parallel attention to an actual literary figure and his linguistic re-presentation help illuminate the process by which Kingston both consciously translates facets of her immediate social milieu into anatomies of language and deliberately exercises her representative agency. Her first novel, *Tripmaster Monkey*, seems to embody the "fundamentally anticanonical" impulse of the genre, which as Michael Holquist writes, "insist[s] on the dialogue between what a given system will admit as literature and those texts that are otherwise excluded from such definitions of literature" (see Bakhtin 1981: xxxi). Kingston's appropriation of the novel interestingly complements and complicates the Bakhtinian novel in that it embraces both the canonical space and the anti-canonical impulse, thus accentuating the dialogical tension within: the narrative recognition of Chin is an inclusive act of an excluded figure, at once a jazzy improvisation and a kung fu challenge of his fake book / original score.

In contrast to Chin, who sees the canonical quota as impermeable except by force, Kingston seems to suggest a strategic way of turning such a limitation into a liberating advantage. Given that Chin had no books to his credit yet when *Tripmaster Monkey* was published, the publishing/publicizing of his voice was Kingston's novel way of using her already established canonical position both to reveal its artificial limits and to test its holding power.[4] The dialogical imagination of *Tripmaster Monkey* is Kingston's intuitive textual practice of Benedict Anderson's theory of nationhood as an imagined community. "Communities are to be distinguished," Anderson writes, "not by their falsity/genuineness, but by the style in which they are imagined" (1983: 15). If Anderson's contribution lies in his consideration of the role played by the print media in the production of national styles, Kingston's work shows the power of literature in the affective construction of the nation. Her discursive re-membering of Chin / Ah Sing is to draw him from the ghettoized channels of expression into the canonical space of a national forum in which an Asian American subject can be meaningfully debated and defined, not as a separate ethnic entity but as an integral part of American national culture.

With *Tripmaster Monkey*, Kingston has moved beyond the celebratory heroics of survival in *China Men* to a revisionist mapping of Asian American experience as a preeminently cultural odyssey. "The difference between us and the other pioneers," says the novel's protagonist, Wittman Ah Sing, is that "we did not come here for the gold streets. We came to play" (1989b: 249–50). In having Ah Sing both echo Walt Whitman's "Song of Myself" and repudiate "Ah Sin" of Bret Harte's "Heathen Chinee," Kingston began transforming the stereotype of an Asian American laborer into her prototype of an Asian American artist and proposed an alternative goal of Asian American trans-Pacific migration. Crediting Asian Americans with carving agricultural fields, building the transcontinental railroad, or linking contemporary commercial America in cyberspace, she seems to suggest, may not be adequate affirmation of their subject status. Only in the enacting of the fabulous Asian American artistic imagination can a true identity of the people be validated. In this emphasis, Kingston has clearly subscribed to the ideology of nationalism informing the dominant U.S. culture and to its vehement counterformation—ethnic nationalism in the 1960s and 1970s.

On the one hand, Kingston's nationalist rejoinder in the 1980s recognized the centrality of nation-space for Asian American articulation, and on the other shrewdly brought back the crisis of identity in such ethnic nationalistic projects as *Aiiieeeee!*[5] In many respects, *Tripmaster Monkey* does not so much raise the question of Asian American identity as problematize the relationships in its construction. The novel is not only an interruption of such orientalist alterities as "Asian" and "American" but also an imagining dialogue, in both the Bakhtinian and Andersonian senses, of the mutually constitutive differences between gender and generation, and between language and culture, in the writing of Asian America.

II

"Maybe it comes from living in San Francisco, city of clammy humors and foghorns that warn and warn—omen, o-o-men, o dolorous omen, o dolors of omens—and not enough sun," intones the opening line of *Tripmaster Monkey*, "but Wittman Ah Sing considered suicide every day." In a moment of youthful fancy, he "actually crooked his trigger finger—bang!—his head breaks into pieces," "brains, mind guts" scattering all over, accomplishing, as it were, his "Hemingway" exit from the universe (Kingston 1989b: 3).[6] Ah Sing regretted that "he hadn't been in on building any city," having missed the empire-building days of the westward expansion in which his ancestors participated and having been born a trifle too late for the clamor and commotion of being on the road. It seems natural that he would be plagued by the Shakespearean question via Laurence Olivier: "To be or not to be?" (4, 3).[7]

Foregrounding Ah Sing's existential dilemma from the beginning, Kingston sends her protagonist roaming San Francisco. A stroll through the Stockton Street tunnel, a ride on the municipal bus, a visit to City Lights on the Beach, and the heart-wrenching declaration of purpose to the beautiful Nanci Lee all foreshadow in the first chapter the novel's theme of "quest," reflecting the classic bildungsroman or story of initiation. Most intriguing, however, is her variation on the predictable plot of her protagonist's growth. Though Ah Sing's suicidal impulses at the beginning of the novel turn by the chapter's conclusion into a sign of resurrection, his affirmation of life is pronounced less in personal terms than in the terms of culture. Thus, in his passionate speech to Nanci Lee, he says:

> What theater do we have besides beauty contests? . . . Do we have a culture that's not these knickknacks we sell to the bok gwai [white devils]? . . . Where's our jazz? Where's our blues? Where's our ain't-taking-no-shit-from-nobody street-strutting language? I want so bad to be the first bad-jazz China Man bluesman of America. . . . What I'm going to do, I've got to wrest the theater back for you. (27, 25)[8]

Wittman Ah Sing's individual rebirth, Kingston seems to suggest, may not be sufficient unless it is conceived in the mode of his native tradition's revival. If the newfound mission to "wrest the theater back" indicates the protagonist's willful self-integration, it too becomes a symbolic gesture for the assembly of a disintegrated cultural body. *Tripmaster Monkey*, therefore, is not just another coming-of-age story, because Wittman Ah Sing's trip is an embodiment of Asian American tradition's rite of passage, a transformation of death into the resurrection of an ethnic nationalistic culture.

Recovering from the "loud takeover" of suicidal thoughts, Wittman Ah Sing swaggers down the tunnel, "his cowboy boots, old brown Wellingtons, hit[ting] its pavements hard" (3). "Heading toward him from the other end came a Chinese dude from China" (4). The "tall and thin" Wittman, fifth-generation native Californian, with "moustache [falling] below his bearded jawbone, hair braided loose, very hip, like a samurai" (14), contrasts sharply with the visages of those "fresh off the boat," their "hands clasped behind, bow-legged, loose-seated," also "out on a stroll" (4). Here is how Kingston renders the scene:

> As luck would have it, although there was plenty of room, this dude and Wittman tried to pass each other both on the same side, then both on the other, side stepping like a couple of basketball players. Wittman stopped dead in his tracks, and shot the dude a direct stink eye. The F.O.B. stepped aside. Following, straggling, came the poor guy's wife. She was coaxing their kid with sunflower seeds, which she cracked with her gold teeth and held out to him. "Ho sick la. Ho sick," she said. . . . Next there came scrabbling an old lady with a cane. She also wore one of those do-it-yourself pantsuit outfits. On Granny's head was a cap with a pompon that matched everybody's sweaters. The whole family taking a cheap outing on their day off. Immigrants. Fresh Off the Boats out in the public. Didn't know how to walk together. Spitting seeds. So uncool. You wouldn't mislike them on sight if their pants weren't so highwater, gym socks white and noticeable. F.O.B. fashions—highwaters or puddlecuffs. Can't get it right. Uncool. Uncool. (5)

If we are to view Wittman Ah Sing's trip in the opening chapter as the epitome of the allegorical journey of the entire novel, this meeting between the F.O.B. and the A.B.C. (American-born Chinese) deserves our scrutiny.

The encounter is most probably Kingston's fictional version of the actual published debate in 1972 between Frank Chin and Frank Ching, the managing editor of *Bridge*, on the tradition's value for different Asian Americans. "As far as I'm concerned," Chin wrote in his letter to the editor, "Americanized Chinese who've come over in their teens and later to settle here and American born chinaman have nothing in common, culturally, intellectually, emotionally. And it's the racist admonition that all Chinese be alike . . . because of skin color" (Ching and Chin 1972: 30). In reply, the *Bridge* editor charges that "the arrival of more Chinese immigrants only aggravates your [Chin's] fear of being identified with them in white minds. In wishing to be accepted and recognized as American—albeit Chinese-American—you [Chin] try to put as much distance as possible between yourself and the new immigrants. It is sad to see a person so insecure that he has to turn his back on the people of his ancestors in order to affirm himself" (34).

In her narrative reworking, Kingston has turned this heated theoretical exchange into a scene of virtually no contact, except for Ah Sing's "stink eye"/"I" at his "mislike[d]" mirror other. Yet the silence of her characters is accompanied by a loud clash of visual signs, between Ah Sing's rugged Western outfit and the immigrants' homemade dress, between his solitary wandering and their gregarious generational trot. With these divergent manners of conduct, Kingston effectively backs up Chin's statement about the real cultural differences between the two segments of the Asian American population and questions, as Chin does, the validity of racial lumping by skin color. She resonates with Ching, on the other hand, by equating Ah Sing's dismissal of the F.O.B. with his secret wish that they remain in the ghetto spaces of Chinatown and not "out in public" to ruin his "self-image." Though not a single word is spoken between them, the presence of the immigrants does compel Ah Sing to think momentarily "in Chinatown Language," which the narrator wryly interprets as an attempt "just to keep a hand in, so to speak, to remember and so to keep a while longer words spoken by the people of his brief and dying culture" (6). Kingston's voice-over reinforces the opening scene of Ah Sing's imaginary death or the tradition's stasis, and links it once again to Chin's pessimistic commentary on the Asian American as "a dying people . . . who failed to generate an identity and culture attractive and compulsive enough to make our people attractive to each other and survive as a people and grow as a culture" (1977: 44).

However, by linking Ah Sing's external detachment from and internal connection with the F.O.B., however grudging the latter may appear, Kingston presents a more nuanced description of the obstacle to intraethnic commerce. Attributing Ah Sing's revulsion at his racial self-reflection to an internalization of dominant cultural values proves ultimately unsatisfactory, because such an explanation holds the ethnic subject entirely responsible for his own social marginalization, and consequently blames him for his exercise of exclusionary tactics. Kingston uses Ah Sing's awkward utterance to reveal the precarious maintenance of the ethnic tongue within the dominant culture, where the language's social rewards are minimal at best. His self-conscious muttering "in Chinatown Language" thus correlates the loss of a shared linguistic medium with the loss of the immigrant and native-born Asian American connection, losses that were largely the result of exclusion-era social and educational policies.

Such restrictive historical conditions led to "the tunnel" encounter, in which Ah Sing and the immigrant Chinese man are compelled first to duck and then almost to bump against each other. In this instance, the tunnel becomes Kingston's luminary image of a barriered passage, the orientalist discursive given of Asian American racial foreignness, that neither party can possibly escape. The consummate irony of the tunnel is that while it traps both the immigrant and the native-born within the stifling space of sameness, this space is actually where their incommensurable cultural differences are most pronounced. Ah Sing and the Chinese dude's near collision thus symbolizes how the Chin/Ching dispute is an exacerbated effect of the orientalist discursive irony to which both are subjected: both are struggling with the burden of racial alienation while attempting to find an "I," at once individual and social, with which to transcend it.[9] If Ching's definition of Asian American is the expression of a desire to form a racial coalition by virtue of similar ancestry, Chin's sensibility-oriented definition tries to keep ancestry irrelevant so that his "Mayflower complex" may survive.[10] By conjuring their confrontation in the tunnel, Kingston deftly exposes the arbitrary fiction of racial uniformity while accepting it as an inevitable Asian American collective destiny. The only way to reach the end of the tunnel, Kingston hints, is perhaps to reconsider its foundational blocks. Going beyond *China Men*'s revision of America's European origins, Kingston now questions both the colonialist's *and* the immigrant's invention of nativity not merely as a justification for their American presence but as an instrument of exclusion. She makes us wonder if national self-legitimation based on ancestry and nativity is fundamentally at odds with America's promise of democratic consent.

By recollecting the Chin/Ching argument in the 1970s, when the native-born Asian American majority was joined, as the result of 1965 immigration reform, by new Asian immigrants to America, Kingston is attending to the moment in the 1980s when the Asian American population became overwhelmingly immigrant.[11] She seems to be emphasizing the need to renegotiate generational differences because the Asian American community is radically changing its composition. Ah Sing's walk down the tunnel may start off as an individual adventure but it is quickly implicated, through virtual visual contact, in the familial venture of the immigrants. His stream of consciousness in fragmented Chinese seems also a linguistic awakening prompted by the surround-sound of the new immigrants. Their walk together has begun, as the narrator of *Tripmaster Monkey* puts it so well: "Community is not built once-and-for-all; people have to imagine, practice, and re-create it" (306).

If the tunnel signifies a barriered Asian American passage where race and nativity must intersect, Ah Sing's date with Nanci illuminates the gendered nature of tradition's recuperation. To prepare for this scene, Kingston first sends Ah Sing on the Muni bus. The cityscape of San Francisco through the bus window and the mindscape of Ah Sing through his meditations on American authors reflect each other. Ah Sing simply does not figure in the architectural monuments or the writers' stories. Those who put California on the American literary map and whose spirit flows in his veins—Steinbeck, Kerouac, Twain, Stevenson, Atherton, London, Bierce, and Norris—did not care to register his racial experience (Carlos Bulosan was the only exception). The horror of having no place in the white Western scheme of things, Kingston makes it unequivocal, is what prompts Ah Sing's resort to an Asian American tradition. However, she is equally concerned whether this imposed inadequacy within the dominant culture will overcompensate for itself in masculine self-fulfillment.

That September afternoon unwinds pleasantly enough when Ah Sing and Nanci talk about the arts over a cappuccino in North Beach. Their shared social alienation has led them to exchange personal histories, but soon the conversation becomes strained. Ah Sing's incessant talk about himself, his birth backstage in vaudeville, his showbiz credits, his "building worlds, inventing selves," have not produced the expected adoration from Nanci (19). Instead, she is getting impatient for "*her* turn to talk about *her* kiddiehood": "You're not the only one, Wittman, who fooled with magic, and not the only one who refuses to work for money. And also not the only one to talk" (16, 17). As if to provide a footnote, the narrator informs us that in those days "women did not speak as much as men. Even among the educated and Bohemian, a man talked out his dreams and plans while a girl thought whether she would be able to adapt herself to them" (17).

While the picture of Ah Sing conjures up that of Joe Starks in *Their Eyes Were Watching God*, who "loves obedience out of everybody under de sound of his voice" (Hurston 1990: 46), Kingston is specifically debating *Aiiieeeee!*'s rather skewed definition of Asian American culture as "the style of manhood" (Chin et al. [1974] 1983: xlviii). She attempts to reveal how the figure of woman has been omitted in this cultural nationalist program, and how such a bold omission can be traced to the manner and mode of verbal intercourse. Ah Sing's monopoly of the conversation is conceived as an act of domination that silences and erases the woman of interlocution. Nanci's disappointment with Ah Sing's exclusive interest in his own auto-biographical narrative and his denial of her participation in *their* conversation are fictional defamiliarizations of both actual and potential troubles associated with Asian American ethnic nationalism. Kingston is questioning whether such ethnic nationalism is an androcentric articulation of a "collective" identity that subsumes female interests, unwittingly subordinates women to listening or servicing roles, and is yet another appearance of the macho male who provides the cause and performs the feats to win her heart and achieve his integrity (Wei 1993: 75–81). Nanci is more than a narrative counterpoint to Ah Sing, a return of the repressed feminist perspective at the moment of ethnic emergence; she creates the tension between the "mellow yellow" and the "militant yellow."[12]

After visiting his favorite hangout, the City Lights, where Nanci fails to find the magazine that includes a scene from his play, Ah Sing takes her to his apartment to read from his poem box. The "ineluctable goingness of railroad tracks" wins Nanci's compliments of "lovely" and "sweet," but her response is not what Ah Sing intended (31). To impress her and present his true self, Ah Sing gesticulates "in the manner of Charles Laughton as the Hunchback of Nortre Dame" and "like Helen Keller," stuttering out, "'Wa-wa-wa-water? Gabble gobble, one of us'" (32). One only needs to re-member Chin's Chickencoop Chinaman, Tam, his obsession with the rail-road, his parody of Helen Keller as the epitome of the model minority who conquers her "birth defect" with will power, and his Afro-style of speaking and strutting to realize the purpose of Kingston's pastiche. "You sound black," Nanci says, "I mean like a Black poet. Jive. Slang. Like LeRoi Jones," to which Ah Sing can only respond with helpless rage. "He spit his genuine China Man spittoon," laughing with mockery, "Goot and angry." "Angry." "Angry." "Imitation of Blacks." . . . "Angry too muchee" (32–33).

This exchange between Ah Sing and Nanci functions on several levels. It is a general reference to affinity politics in the 1960s, when racial minorities formed a colored coalition against the white establishment. It points to a particular mode of minority discourse wherein repudiative rage is not just a preferred but a privileged expression. And, it occasions a reassessment of the limits and possibilities of the novel of protest, whose generic boundaries *Tripmaster Monkey* is doubtless testing. Above all, it evokes the fundamental difference between Frank Chin and Kingston, as noted in Chapter 2. The analogy Nanci draws between Ah Sing and LeRoi Jones is doubly interesting because Ah Sing's change from "sweetness" to "anger" recapitulates the radical break of the Afro-American poet's career as signified by his name change to Imamu Amiri Baraka (Wallace 1978: 62–63). But Kingston is not just echoing Chin's self-awareness of a potential derivativeness of

Asian American art. She seems deliberately to have conflated Ah Sing's verbal aggression with the violent manifestations of the Black Power Movement in order to resituate the Kingston-Chin opposition of "art versus politics" in a more ideologically charged context of "pacifism versus militancy," a rhetorical polarization that will prove difficult to resolve.

Through a series of narrative maneuvers in the opening chapter, Kingston constructs Wittman Ah Sing as a problem protagonist, a nativist with an acquired "Mayflower complex," a chauvinist with thinly disguised macho heroism, an ethnic nationalist with a Western education but bent on recovering an Asian racial consciousness, and possibly a militant with a tendency toward violence. Far from making him a mere caricature of negativity, a figure of folly to be forgotten, and a historical relic whose rightful place remains in the unmediated past, Kingston rescues Ah Sing as an agent of history. The re-presentation of Ah Sing / Chin serves both to recapitulate and revise the nationalist trajectory of the previous quarter-century of literary Asian America with which Kingston may not personally identify and toward which her feelings are still ambivalent.

That ambivalence is exemplified in Kingston's consistent double troping. If her recreation of Ah Sing vis-à-vis Frank Chin's work is an act of pastiche in which to play with his texts, re-presenting them as her tribute to their value, her gesture is also unmistakably parodic because of her unrelenting critique of Chin's methods and messages. In a succession of scenes, Kingston sets her protagonist against either the omniscient narrative voice or a character's commentary so that the unifying impulse of an ethnic nationalistic narrative is sometimes contested, at other times consolidated, and at still other times suspended by the discrete interests that wish neither to be nominally included nor to be totally excluded. With her consistent narrative doubling, Kingston refuses to see nation and self, native and immigrant, male and female, East and West as either sacrosanct or necessarily oppositional; rather, she regards them as mutually constitutive relations that need perpetual interruption. Such a narrative of interruption as *Tripmaster Monkey* ultimately rejects the notion of Asian American tradition as a "one-man show" and reconstructs it as an intersubjective and collaborative "revue."

III

The end of Wittman Ah Sing's staging of an Asian American tradition and the denouement of the narrative is in many ways a revue, but first, let me offer a quick sketch of the novel. *Tripmaster Monkey* is an episodic work whose plot is driven by Ah Sing's quest. Soon after he makes his promise to

Nanci to revive the Asian American theater and mount his mammoth play, he is fired from his job. But at a friend's party, his idea to start "the Pear Garden Players of America" is a winning proposal. "Not because lonesome Wittman was such a persuader," the narrative reads, but because "anybody American who really imagines Asia feels the loneliness of the U.S.A." and can decide to "do something communal against isolation" (141). The immediate solution to Ah Sing's isolation came from Tañia De Weese, whom he met at the party and married via an ordained minister of the Universal Life Church, both because he loved her and because he wanted to avoid the draft. The novel then alternates between two lines of development, one concerned with the writing and production of the play and the other with Ah Sing's family obligations. The description of the play-making process provides occasions to showcase Asian folk tales, mythology, and classics and to excavate Asian American historical events and personages, both of which mark Wittman Ah Sing's conscious re-orientation. At the same time, his visits with Tañia to his own parents, Ruby Long Legs and Zeppling Ah Sing, and his search for Popo offer comic relief that balances the seriousness of tradition formation and creates the image of Ah Sing as a responsible family man.

But to write and perform Asian American theater, Wittman Ah Sing is first and foremost "whammed into the block question":

> Does he announce now that the author is—Chinese? Or, rather, Chinese-American? And be forced into autobiographical confession. Stop the music—I have to butt in and introduce myself and my race. "Dear reader, all these characters whom you've been identifying with—Bill, Brooke and Annie—are Chinese—and I am too." The fiction is spoiled. You who read have been suckered along, identifying like hell, only to find out that you'd been getting a peculiar, colored, slanted p.o.v. "Call me Ishmael." See? you pictured a white guy, didn't you? If Ishmael were described—ochery ecru amber umber skin—you picture a tan white guy. Wittman wanted to spoil all those stories coming out of and set in New England Back East—to blacken and to yellow Bill, Brooke and Annie. A new rule for the imagination: The common man has Chinese looks. (34)

Blocking Ah Sing's writing is his shock that within the dominant discourse he is an imagistic nullity. In a dialectic between reality and representation, he is an entity without a proper name. The only way for him to circulate in a significant cultural production is to disrupt the identification of whiteness with humanity, to "introduce his race," and to turn his material being into signs of language; but even doing that, as he becomes increasingly aware, is fraught with difficulty and irony.

Peter Brooks contends, in his thesis on modern narratives, that the "semioticization of the body" will have to be "matched by a somatization of story," that the "body must be a source and locus of meaning, and that stories cannot be told without making the body a prime vehicle of narrative significations" (1993: xii). The problem with Wittman Ah Sing is that he has a body that is no-body because it is deprived of the capacity to register meaning. Kingston more or less concurs with Chin here on the inevitability of race, color, and "look" in literary representation and reception. The void that is the Asian American body, its absence and abjection, she seems to conclude, contributes to an Asian American identity crisis as well as a crisis of its inscription in the mainstream culture, crises that can only be resolved, according to nationalist cultural politics, by resorting to an alternative body politic, the ethnic tradition. With Ah Sing's question, Kingston has made relevant Henry Louis Gates's critical assessment that "the ideology of tradition has long been in the service of minority legitimation. . . . If minority discourses in America seem to embrace the ideology of tradition, it is because they remain at a stage where the anxiety of identity formation is paramount" (1992b: 311). Kingston's special contribution to this understanding of minority discourse lies in her integration of the Cartesian mind-body split: abstract identity and concrete self, in her view, are never actually separate. The physical body, the race and the look, and the cultural body, the symbols and the praxis, always mirror each other to constitute the integrity of the Asian American body. To bring that body into the field of the signifiable entails an embodiment of its tradition that will in turn, to borrow from Wittman Ah Sing, get "embodied in physical characteristics, such as skin colors" (312).[13]

The tradition's self-embodiment begins with Wittman Ah Sing's imaginary trip from "the ass end of China," on "the song boat" where "[a] company of one hundred great-great-grandparents came over to San Francisco during the Gold Rush" (37–39, 249). Kingston uses the lost "long play" as a recovered Asian American theatrical form upon which her hero Wittman Ah Sing can improvise. She also designates the scripts of the nineteenth-century Asian troupes as the textual base upon which to perform the rite of Asian American selfhood. Seen in this light, Ah Sing's enactment of Gwan Goong, the Cantonese American hero from *Three Kingdoms*, "the man of action [who] aggressively reads and talks" (134), his presentations of the Monkey from *The Journey to the West* and the Black Tornado from *Water Margins* (256–60), are Kingston's purposeful means of locating Asian American sources of meaning in Asian classic and folk texts.[14] With this specification of an Asian cultural corporeality, Kingston both counterbalances Ah Sing's Western cerebral composition and collaborates with Frank Chin to reclaim an Asian American self through romantic retrievals of radical individuality.

The following citations from *Tripmaster Monkey* and "The Eat and Run Midnight People" demonstrate Kingston and Chin's conceptual consensus:

They [our brave theatrical ancestors] were flimflammers of tourists, wildcat miners, cigar makers without the white label, carriers of baskets on poles, cubic air breathers, miscegenists, landsquatters and landlords without deeds, kangaroo jurists, medical and legal practitioners without degrees, inconvertible pagans and heathens, gamblers with God and one another, aliens unqualified to apply for citizenship, unrelated communalists and crowders into single family dwellings. . . . Unemployment-check collectors, dodgers of draft of several countries, un-Americans, red-hot communists, unbridled capitalists, look-alikes of japs and Viet Cong, unlicensed manufacturers and exploders of fireworks. Everyone with aliases. More than one hundred and eight outlaws. (Kingston 1989b: 301–2)

I tell her being a Chinaman's okay if you love having been outlaw-born and raised to eat and run in your mother country like a virus staying a step ahead of a cure and can live that way, fine. And that is us! Eat and run midnight people, outward bound. Chinaman from the Cantonese, yeah, I tell her, we were bad asses of China, the barbarians, far away from the high culture of the North where they look down on us Southerners because we do not have the noble nose, because we are darker complected, because we live hunched over, up to our wrists in the dirt sending our fingers underground grubbing aftereats. We were the dregs, the bandits, the killers, the get out of town eat and run folks, hungry all the time eating after looking for food. Murderers and sailors. Rebel yellers and hardcore cooks. (F. Chin 1988: 11)[15]

Like undulating waves, the two passages push toward the same shore: both authors seem to agree that rebelliousness is the prevalent strain of the Asian American character, inherited from peasant insurgents of Asian antiquity, and practiced by their pagan descendants in the American West.

While Kingston shows little hesitation either in resonating with Chin's "Chinaman 'I'" or in incorporating his irascibility into her description of the Asian American, she is distinctly uneasy about his equation of the "I" with the "recognized style of Asian-American manhood" (xxxviii). When Ah Sing speaks about their "taking the 'I' away from us," or "cutting off our balls linguistically," Kingston makes us wonder if his recuperation of the self is unapologetically phallocentric and if the tradition's newly embodied vocality has excluded Asian American women (318). Seizing upon her protagonist's obsession with the penis and challenging his repeated association of discursive dispossession with male castration, Kingston provides a series of scenes that investigate the process through which the reconstruction of Asian American tradition and identity is equated with the chain of penis, voice, and race. The close readings that follow illustrate Kingston's feminist interruptions of that chain.

The first comes after Ah Sing and Taña make love:

Taña thought about complimenting Wittman on how nice and soft his penis is. But he was such a worrier over masculinity, he'd take it wrong. Men don't understand that a penis is the loveliest softness to touch, more tender than a baby's earlobe, softer than a woman's breast. And after fucking is the best time to touch and touch, but you can't do that for too long, or they feel bad they're not getting hard. Wittman was not the one you could praise for softness. Taña saved up her acclaim. (157)

Kingston's revisionist reading of the penis is accomplished through a feminist reversal of patriarchal values. Instead of considering "hardness" the celebrated masculine virtue, she redeems "softness" as "the loveliest" and the most cherished quality of being human.[16] Taña's fondness for postejaculatory fondling when the penis is loved just for being soft is perhaps Kingston at her most humorous. Here she reminds us of Richard Dyer when he notes the striking discrepancy between penile symbolism and "what penises are actually like." "Male genitals are fragile, squashy, delicate things," he remarks, "even when erect, the penis is spongy, seldom straight" (Dyer 1993: 112). Kingston's exposure of the male mystique of being big and hard, like Dyer's, has deflated penile potency of all its tough and dangerous exaggerations. Her returning the penis to its normal form, its original "softness," reinscribes manhood as both nonaggressive and vulnerably charming.

If such a redefinition is an instance of questioning male/penile physical drive, in the next passage Kingston takes to task the penis's exclusive metaphysical claims:

He [Wittman Ah Sing] sat on the footboard, his sword between his knees. In the shining steel handguard, his penis reflected huge. Behind it, his pinhead peeped out a long ways off. How odd, his head, the container of his mind, which contains the universe, is a complicated button topping this gigantic purple penis, which ends in a slit, like a vagina. (221)

Wittman Ah Sing's contemplation on the penis is really Kingston's questioning of the arbitrary elevation of the male instrument to the position of super signifier. Although Lacan tried to distinguish between the penis as a biological organ and the phallus as a signifier, "the Lacanians' desire clearly to separate *phallus* from *penis*, to control the meaning of the signifier *phallus*," argues Jane Gallop, "is precisely symptomatic of their desire to have the phallus, that is, their desire to be at the center of language" (1988: 126). From what appears to be a diametrically opposite direction, Kaja Silverman maintains that the "specular image of the penis" always signifies "wholeness and sufficiency" and that "the Name-of-the-Father also requires the anatomical support of that organ" (1992: 92, 104).

While sharing Gallop and Silverman's concern with the phallocentricity of the symbolic order, however cleverly camouflaged, Kingston sets out to rewrite this particular origination of language and meaning. The "head" that "contains" both intelligence and the "universe," the erect penis that expresses, we learn, is at its best "like a vagina." The Kingstonian simile has a couple of implications. It suggests a secondary order of the penis, that it is possibly a copy of the vagina, its "slit"/lips apparent only when turgid. It divests the penis of its mythical properties, its power both to fill a vaginal orifice or metaphoric lack and to regenerate lost plenitude. And last, the penis in the vagina or the vaginal penis is a version of the Taoist "yang" in the "ying" and vice versa. We need only recall Jane Gallop's statement that "as long as the attribute of power is a phallus which can only have meaning by referring to and being confused with a penis, this confusion will support a structure in which it seems reasonable that men have power and women do not" to realize how crucial is Kingston's alteration of the phallic specular image (1988: 127).

The Kingstonian vaginal "head" is a structural revision that disrupts what Silverman calls "the smooth transition from the phallus as penis or penile image, to the phallus as a representative of 'being,' and, finally, to the phallus as a signifier of privilege" (1992: 99). Kingston's vaginal head puts the *phallus* and *logos* equation into serious jeopardy. And it provides an alternative image that does not so much enshrine the mother in place of the father as it does ensure a new frame of cultural representation in which mother/daughter can both generate meaning and be meaningfully referred to. Subjects of neither gender, Kingston says with her novel image, should be exclusively designated to possess either ontological wholeness or lack. Rather, both women and men are entitled to presence, voice, and fullness in the symbolic order of language and law.

With these insights, we can return to the moment when Wittman Ah Sing's preoccupation with castration occasions Kingston's last extensive reconsideration of the penis, particularly its relationship with voice, sex, and race:

> I ought to unzip and show you—one penis. Large. Star Quality. Larger than this banana. Let me whip out the evidence that belies all smallness. Nah. Nah. Nah. Just kidding, la. I'd only be able to astound the front rows; the people in the back will tell everybody they didn't see much. I've got to get it up on the big screen. The stage is not the medium for the penis or for the details of this face. For the appreciation of eyelids, double eye or single eye, we need movie close-ups. So you can love this face. (316)

Ah Sing's bravado situates the issues of signification and sexuality in an instant dialectic of veiling and unveiling. On both issues, however, his posture runs paradoxically counter to the patriarchal grain of salt. First, if we take Kingston's cue to read "unzip[ping]" as the opening of the mouth, the letting out of a voice, we must note with irony that such a gesture will indeed "whip out the evidence that [betrays] all smallness"; for it is Lacan, we remember, who asserts that "the phallus can play its role only when veiled, that is to say, as itself a sign of the latency with which any signifiable is struck, when it is raised to the function of the signifier" (Silverman 1992: 88). In other words, the omnipotence of patriarchal knowledge is directly attributable to the masking function of language in a symbolic order dominated by the name of the father. The sign of latency comes precisely from its concealment. Second, the attempt to flash the penis contradicts the patriarchal convention of sexual representation as well. While women's sex has been generally deemed acceptable for public display, men's is not. The penile spectacle will not only expose the inadequacy of an inflated masculinity; it will also demystify and therefore undermine the veiled basis of patriarchal power. Furthermore, such revelation can result in undesirable "instabilities" that are likely to fracture the male subject's phallic gaze and to reify him as a specular object.[17]

Ah Sing's deviation from the rules of phallocentric signification and the norms of dominant male sexuality is symptomatic of his uneasy relationship with both. The veiling metaphor of the Lacanian phallus works effectively with the simultaneous "there and not there" structure, a structure by, for, and of the subjects of the center. In this system, the invisibility of the penis is not an absence but a sign of hidden potency. Ah Sing, the racially marked subject, however, is unable to share this system of power. To drape his penis is to concede to common sense that it is literally "not there" and that the Asian man really does not "have" it despite its being there.[18] It is to admit a permanent lack, an emptiness that cannot produce. In a similar vein, however, "unveiling" cannot be a willing solution, either. Wittman Ah Sing realizes soon enough that though he might "astound the front rows" with his magnitude, he will never even come close to the fantastic projection of the Master's veiled super phallus. So, to cloak Ah Sing in Prufrock for the moment, "how should [he] then presume? / And how should [he] begin?"[19]

Kingston has pointed out with Wittman Ah Sing's example that the power of signification is as presumed as sexuality is symbolized in the dominant culture. But being Asian Americans as we are, historically silenced and desexualized, we cannot take for granted what we actually are because what we assume to be true about ourselves is seen as an absence of proof to the contrary. Our lived experiences are rarely able to be translated into public awareness while American orientalist discourse determines the contour of our face and consciousness. "Do I dare / Disturb the universe?" (Eliot 1973: 450) and "Do I dare reveal my face?" are Ah Sing's overwhelming questions. In a sense, these are questions of the Asian American self that he intends to champion. Do I dare to "celebrate myself, and sing myself / And what [you] assume [I] shall assume / For every atom belonging to [you] as good belongs to [me]"?[20]

It is in the spirit of the democratic bard where the self is always multiply incarnated that Kingston endows her protagonist with a new sense of mission. The song of Ah Sing from this point on takes a notable turn from the desire to "show you—one penis" to showing "the details of this face," and to cultivating "the appreciation of eyelids, double eye or single eye. . . . So you can love this face." Although Ah Sing begins his presentation of the Asian American "I" by presuming a blatant phallic image, tense and recalcitrant against castration, he re-members midway the dismembered or cosmetically cut female eyelids and concludes with an exhortation of self-love, a self transformed from the singular "I" to the plural "we," from the gender-exclusive "penis" to the collective racial signifier of "this face."

With her shifting imagery, Kingston revises the historical bias of ethnic nationalism and transforms as well Walt Whitman's revulsion against the puritanical prohibition of the body into an indictment of the dominant culture's repression of the Asian American body. It is perhaps this racial advocacy, this incorporation of color into the body that sets her protagonist Ah Sing slightly apart from his poetic progenitor, for "We are Golds" (326) is not an evocation of generic men and women, Whitman's Children of Adam, but more a response to its contemporary call, "Black is beautiful." The Asian American "I," in light of this connection, is primarily a colored body, consanguineous with other colored bodies that are conspicuously missing from the Republic of Letters.

IV

Here then is Kingston's ambivalence toward her hero. On the one hand, she endorses Ah Sing's linking of race and culture, agreeing with him that tradition, identity, and people are never shapeless and color-blind. Though she may not concur with Ah Sing's conclusion that "history being trapped in people means that history is embodied in its physical characteristics" (312), she does realize the provisional value of coloring consciousness not as an end in itself but as a transitional tactic to forge the uncreated conscience of the race. On the other hand, Kingston is apprehensive about the consequences of racialist thinking when its boundary with racist discourse gets blurred, for race talk is essentially at odds with her other views of human fluidity (88, 103).

Although for the most part Kingston keeps this contradictory tension from exploding with her narrative pastiche and parody, and her publisher tries to ease it by pitching *Tripmaster Monkey* as a book about San Francisco in the sixties, about the "life of youth and art," Ah Sing's political harangue nevertheless takes on a life of its own and threatens to ruin the authorial good credit of poetry that the "average" American reader of Kingston has become accustomed to. As determined as Kingston is to make *Tripmaster Monkey* a rehearsal of Asian American consciousness, therefore, she cannot be impervious to the risks that accompany her progressive leaning toward "ethnocentric" discourse. For this reason, the device of identification and repetition—i.e., pastiche—will have to take a back seat so that a clear distinction between the narrator's and the protagonist's point of view can be drawn.

The abrupt stylistic shift occurs in the last chapter, when Kingston abandons Wittman Ah Sing by simply remarking, "Let him get it all out, and we hear what he has to say direct" (306). From that moment on, the editorial voice of Ah Sing seems to preside over the authorial voice of his narrator. Enclosed in direct quotation marks for pages at a stretch, Ah Sing's "solo screams," not unlike those of Frank Chin, "AaaaaAAAaah! Aaaaaieeeeee!" (324), bombard the audience (320–28). The use of direct speech and the withdrawal of narrative mediation for Ah Sing's most belligerent monologue clearly betrays an urge for authorial detachment. Kingston, the narrator, wants to ensure that Ah Sing, the character, takes off as the author of his own meaning and becomes accountable for its import. Unlike her parodic moves on the phallus, for example, where ironic distancing is tinged with authorial sympathy and amusement, the literary mother of Ah Sing has gone so far in this last chapter as to disown her son in order to secure ideological distance between them.

Ah Sing's comment on the popular wisdom of Asian inscrutability as the product of white "willful innocence" may well illustrate my point (310). Two solutions to the perversion of willful innocence are proposed. First, Ah Sing recollects a passage from James Baldwin's *Notes of a Native Son* in which the black author says, "People are trapped in history and history is trapped in them . . . and hence all Black men have toward all white men an attitude which is designed, really, either to rob the white men of the jewel of his naiveté, or else to make it cost him dear" (1984: 310).[21] Second, Ah Sing recalls the Chinese classic text *Three Kingdoms*, saying, "We have a story about what to do to those who try to hang on to the jewel of their naiveté. Cho Cho will get them" (311). General Cho Cho, having lost one of his military campaigns, hid out with a well-meaning village family. To demonstrate their hospitality, the family planned to kill a pig for a surprise feast. Fearing they had plotted on his life, Cho Cho killed all three generations in the household before the banquet was ready.

It is noteworthy that Kingston has threaded her references in such a way that the twentieth-century Baldwin and the fourteenth-century Luo Guan Zhong automatically become spokespersons for Ah Sing's unqualified endorsement of racial violence. In Kingston's reworking of her sources, Ah Sing's lesson becomes simple: people of color will revolt and retaliate with random violence if the dominant white culture continues either to fail them or to feign innocence. But this is hardly what Luo Guan Zhong or Baldwin meant in their writings. In the Chinese epic novel, for instance, Cho Cho is consistently characterized as a scheming pretender to the throne. His massacre of innocent people, far from validating the use of violence, is almost always understood as an example of despotic paranoia. "Stranger in the Village," on the other hand, addresses the conceptual and institutional enforcement of racial segregation and the reality of an "interracial drama" that "has not only created a new black man, [but] has created a new white man, too" (Baldwin 1984: 175). The half-sentence that precedes Kingston's quotation and that she does not include in Ah Sing's speech reads: "What is crucial here is that, since white men represent in the black man's world so heavy a weight, white men have for black men a reality which is far from being reciprocal" (ibid.: 166). The cost of white man's "jewel of naiveté" is not his life but "the indispensable value to us in the world we face today," as the concluding line of Baldwin's essay makes explicit, this intertwined "black-white experience" (175).

Baldwin has taken a distinct integrationist stance that argues for nothing but a recognition of black contribution and humanity, a stance that Kingston has strategically turned, as she did the Cho Cho episode, into one of militancy and separatism. Kingston's misappropriation of Baldwin particularly demands our attention, for it cleverly covers the least-suspected spiritual kinship between them. Here, the fateful epistolary exchange between Chin and Kingston again haunts us. What appears curious about Kingston's judgment on Frank Chin is the fact that it is largely informed by Baldwin's pronouncement on Richard Wright. Kingston's argument against Chin's "polemic" genre (see full citation in Chapter 2) essentially echoes Baldwin's critical scrutiny of *Native Son* and the "protest novel" in *Notes of a Native Son* (1984: esp. 22–23 and 33–45).[22] "The failure of the protest novel," Baldwin writes, "lies in its rejection of life, the human being, the denial of his beauty, dread, power, in its insistence that it is his categorization alone which is real and which cannot be transcended" (23).

But like Baldwin, whose recognition of Bigger Thomas's "fearful image" to register attention does not prevent him from critiquing the genre's "overwhelming limitation" (ibid.: 34), Kingston wants to prevent Wittman Ah Sing from repeating Bigger's destiny and Baldwin's sentence on the genre's failure. It is precisely for these reasons that tailoring the tales of "willful innocence" becomes a narrative imperative. Kingston needed to fracture her commentary about race into poles so that her work would not be conceived as an exact replica of Wright/Chin or become the unwitting sacrificial object of her own parody and pastiche. "The listeners did not applaud this [Cho Cho's] tale of paranoia," the narrator intrudes briefly before letting her protagonist resume his direct speech; "they were not ready to slaughter innocents. The white people were probably getting uncomfortable" (312). With such omniscient framing, Kingston has created her ideal reader, one whose sympathies clearly lie with the author. She succeeds not only in excommunicating her creature from her own consciousness; she has also condemned his incitement of mindless violence, conveniently paving the way, as it were, for her final solution to the erected contraries of race and racelessness, violence and peace.

The last pages of *Tripmaster Monkey* thus predictably transform the warning of violence into a message of love. Wittman Ah Sing confesses to the audience his romance with Taña and his commitment to their marriage, and he initiates a "kissing contest," a "love-in" that drew even the "Caucasians who had tuned out during the racial business" (329). Conjugal bliss has obviously assuaged Wittman Ah Sing's belligerence by the book's end, and Kingston can reassure us, by suddenly reclaiming her narrative omniscience, that her protagonist has been re-formed:

> [He] had made up his mind: he will not go to Viet Nam or to any war. He had staged the War of the Three Kingdoms as heroically as he could, which made him start to understand: the three brothers and Cho Cho were masters of war; they had worked out strategies and justifications for war so brilliantly that their policies and their tactics are used today, even by governments with nuclear-powered weapons. And they *lost*. The clanging and banging fooled us, but now we know—they lost. Studying the mightiest war epic of all time, Wittman changed—beeen! into a pacifist. Dear American Monkey, don't be afraid. Here, let us tweak your ear, and kiss your other ear. (340; emphasis in original)

The transcendent force of love has mitigated Wittman's feeling of antagonism and led to his commitment to peace. "The motley people of Hawai'i teach Wittman that a Chinese American is a *pake*," writes Kingston in a *Mother Jones* article following the novel's publication, as if to make explicit its unspoken intentions. "Forget territory," she advises, "Let's make love, mate and mix with exotic peoples, and create the new human being. . . . Because he has married Taña De Weese, blond and Caucasian, Wittman, who invents philosophies to catch up with his actions and vice versa, recommends interracial marriage as the way to integrate the planet" (Kingston 1989a: 38).

Interracial conjugal union has finally been proposed to ease the racial tensions that Ah Sing's program of ethnic nationalism foregrounds. This is fascinating not only in the immediate necessity of narrative resolutions but also in the way it broadens our understanding of race, romance, gender, and nation within a specific Asian American context. Kingston's coupling of Wittman and Taña, Asian male and Caucasian female, seems a fictional effort against "the demographics of love," which led, as San Francisco County's marriage records showed, to "four times as many Asian women as Asian men marry[ing] whites" (Walsh 1990: 12). Moreover, it complicates the critical theory of *Nationalisms and Sexualities* by questioning the editorial judgment on nationalism's universal subordination of women. "No nationalism in the world has ever granted women and men the same privileged resources of the nation-state," Parker et al. contend; "their claims to nationhood frequently dependent upon marriage to a male citizen, women have been subsumed only symbolically into the national body politic" (1992: 6). While gender inequality within nationalism is generally true, Parker and company's generic use of "women" and "men" has precluded the consideration of race and the way it would inevitably alter the stability of meaning of conjugal union in relation to nation. Ah Sing's marriage to Taña, other than manifesting an authorial desire both for racial reconciliation and for the multicultural consolidation of her imagined nation, is also Kingston's deliberate resumption of her query in *China Men*.

In that book, Tang Ao's arrival on the Land of Women / America results in a literal divestiture of his male status. With this central metaphor, Kingston points out the historical gendering of race and its intricate relation to nation that Parker and others are ultimately unable to account for. The Asian men's landing on the shores of America brings about a forcible feminization of the race that is qualitatively different from the subordination of white women within. Unlike white women, whose idealization speaks at once of their marginalization *and* their symbolic inclusion in the American national body politic, the Asian man is practically outside this body and its symbolic order. Kingston's matchmaking of Ah Sing and Taña, read in this context, illuminates a gender reversal in national matrimony. To stake claims in their national identity, and to gain access to the privileged resources of the nation-state, Kingston appears to argue, Asian American men will have to be "women": they must do what white women do, though with considerable ironic removal, not courting white men but marrying white women.[23] In this way, Kingston seems to offer a version of Asian American feminism that considers dialectically the workings of both race and gender within nation, and to intersect if not suture the positions of some Asian American male writers who have made the latent desire for miscegenation their particular literary subject.[24]

Although Kingston refuses to reify white women either for Asian American male vengeance or for their symbolic mastery over the nation, she does not fundamentally question the iconization of America as a white woman. Taña, with her "movie-star eyes and movie-star hair and movie-star lips" exemplifies the "blonde power" of the white goddess: "All she has to do is regard me, behold me like that," Wittman confesses, "and I won't be able to leave her" (336). The unambiguous whiteness of Tañateña conflates with nationality and sexuality in two ways. First, it maintains the racial hierarchy of desirability, and second, it reinforces whiteness as a synecdoche of nation. As Richard Dyer has it, the dominant race imagery of the twentieth century has its origin in the "offer[ing]" of "the white woman as the most prized possession of white man, and the envy of all other races." This discursive coding, he argues, has led to the infamous "exploit[ation of] the rape motif in *The Birth of a Nation* and countless films and novels since" (1986: 43). While Kingston has turned this racist paranoia about miscegenation into a celebration of a motley nation, she accepts, without much misgiving, white middle-class femininity as the genuine article for Asian American men. The attainment of Tañateña, narratively speaking, represents Ah Sing's pinnacle achievement, and their interracial marriage is her blueprint of a nation in perfect union.

The formal wedding of Wittman Ah Sing and Tañateña De Weese reflects Doris Sommer's insight on the foundational fictions of Latin America. The political need to "reconcile and amalgamate national constituencies," Sommer argues, is often expressed in the rhetorical "strategy to cast the previously unreconciled parties, races, classes or regions as lovers who are 'naturally' attracted and right for each other" (Sommer 1990: 81). Though the two authors' works are geographically and politically dissimilar, Kingston's *Tripmaster Monkey* and Sommer's designated genre of "irresistible romance" have an affinity that is more than just apparent. The metaphor of interracial wedlock is Kingston's attempt to dissolve if not make totally moot *Tripmaster Monkey*'s narrative tensions between the militant and the pacifist, the male and the female, the East and the West. She would have her readers believe that her protagonist has finally realized the futility of war, and hence developed a life-affirming philosophy; the equality of gender, hence a loving relationship; and the suspicious value of a pure tradition, hence the celebration of hybridity.[25] The interracial conjugal tie officially terminates Wittman Ah Sing's status as an alienated loner and signals his unquestioned social acceptance. No longer a separatist and no longer a threat, he is now eminently safe and potentially productive (for after all, he has applied for a position in Tañateña's insurance company, willingly submitting himself, Wallace Stevens–like perhaps, to domination by material concerns, which he had resisted in his hippie lifestyle [331]). Kingston invests considerable energy in these last pages of the novel to convince us that her rebel with a futile cause has at long last been incorporated into the nation.

The final conviction of *Tripmaster Monkey*, that love shall prevail over all social divisions, reorganizes the differences within Asian American identity formation into a promotion of the most familiar brand of liberal humanism. This use of interracial romance to suggest Ah Sing's social acceptance also betrays an unconscious authorial approval of the fact that Asian Americans must depend upon whites for their national identity. Their birthright and legal certification no guarantee for their citizenship, Asian Americans will have to marry whites, their second chance, as it were, of "naturalizing" once again into nation. This particular pairing of white and yellow also reveals the limitation of interracial romance for national coherence. Ah Sing does not marry, for instance, an African American, a Latino American, or a Native American, even though all those choices are more than fictionally possible in his greater San Francisco. The dominant racial hierarchy, it seems, has not entirely lost its grip on *Tripmaster Monkey*'s interracial imagination.

The trope of interrace presents Kingston not only a safe and sound ideological proposition but also an expedient aesthetic measure to avoid dealing with intra-ethnic gender troubles. The book opens, remember, with the tantalizing romantic possibilities between Ah Sing and the attractive Nanci Lee, their love-hate relationship a metaphor for the conflict and convergence between Asian American women and men. But the hope of this first chapter and a trial relationship in the second (between Ah Sing and Judy Louis) are aborted in the third chapter to introduce Taña De Weese, whose steady gaze at Wittman and whose recitation of Robert Service, we learn, "melt" his "loneliness" (113). This narrative deployment has the advantage, on the one hand, of retaining some of the dynamics of gender bending; it enables the teasing out of phallus and voice, for example. On the other hand, it decenters the set of intra-ethnic gender problematics and conveniently transfers it across the border. Although Nanci and Judy do participate in Ah Sing's final dramatic extravaganza, theirs are only guest appearances, sidebars to the central plot of the male protagonist's nationalistic quest for tradition and its hurried resolution in the interracial romantic union.

The interracial gender relationship has replaced the intra-ethnic gender relationship both for critical analysis and for narrative excitement. As a result, the disparity between the Asian American socialization into the gender roles of the dominant race and the reality of being that race's Other, the dialectic between intra-ethnic romantic frustration and the gender norms that are not designed for Asian American benefit, seem to have escaped Kingston's extensive engagement. *Tripmaster Monkey*'s narrative of nationalistic cultural politics is made independent of the relationship of Asian Americans with each other, their recognition of the experiences engendered by their racial existence, and their commitment to the erotic pleasures generated within, which both create and procreate life. Though well-intended, the proposal of interracial conjugal bliss seems to imply a need to melt difference through the mingling of blood. Race is ultimately conceived not so much as a cultural, political, and economic concept but as a biological one; the solution to its rifts is to erase it. But the confirmation of Wittman and Tañas marriage in the final pages of the novel also makes clear that the project of interracial romance for race's disappearance and for the arrival of raceless harmony is also projected outside *Tripmaster Monkey's* text proper: the project becomes a register for the future, a utopia to be fulfilled in the day after.

Despite its weak ending, *Tripmaster Monkey's* willingness to engage the intricate relationships of individual interest and communal concern in contemporary Asian America remains a daunting challenge for other writers. The best way to reevaluate its significance is to approach Kingston's own statements after the novel's publication:

> Asian Americans are so cautious about saying that my work speaks for them, they give it a lot of weight. They make it take on many responsibilities. (Quoted in M. Chin 1989: 17)

> I am nothing but who "I" am in relation to other people. In *The Woman Warrior*, "I" begin the quest for self by understanding the archetypal mother. In *China Men*, "I" become more whole because of the ability to appreciate the other gender. (Kingston 1991: 23)

These remarks are radical rethinkings of her position in "Cultural Misreadings," which holds the "idea about the role of the writer" as something deeply "disturbing" to the "personal" self (Kingston 1982: 63). While an earlier Kingston was seduced by "the myth of the original writer," the later Kingston reached a conclusion via fictional narrative that Trihn Minh-ha arrived at through her theoretical prose: "I can let neither light nor air enter me when I myself close up and exist as a crystalized I, be this feminine or masculine, female or male. Woman (with capital W) may therefore kill women if she loses the contact and speaks of Herself only according to what She wants to hear about herself" (Minh-ha 1989: 29, 28). Both ethnic American women writers seemed to have concurred, at the decade's close, with Gayatri Spivak's consistent critique of Western feminism's myopic individualism and converged on the task of reevaluating the notions of authorship, authority, and agency (Spivak 1987: 241–68).

"Relation" and "responsibility" are Kingston's keys to an understanding of both *Tripmaster Monkey's* brilliant strokes and its misfired strategies. By no means jettisoning the subjective side of self-formation, the expansion of an authorial "I" from its sacred autonomy to the incorporation of its social dimension explains Kingston's commitment to community, in its lexical root of *comuneté* or "relations" (Williams 1985), now enumerated in its intra-ethnic, interracial, male, female, regional, national, and above all cultural matrix, and coalesced in the performance of her Whitmanesque/Wittmanesque theater. No other Asian American writer to date has taken such a Joycean venture, encoding Asian American cultural concerns in modernist density as well as in postmodern playfulness, and translating them into a canonical American language. She has channeled the burden of collectivity, notably her writing's speaking *for* effect, into new avenues of creativity. By firmly anchoring herself in multiple subjective positions *from* which to speak, she is able to speak *to* constituencies past, present, and future, at once preserving and imagining communities of memory.

Particularly remarkable about Kingston's narrative feat is its simultaneous fulfillment of the speaking *for* and *against* functions that help predeliver, through her "credentialed speech" on a respectable national literary podium, what Frank Chin and others have prepared for publication.[26] *The Big Aiiieeeee!*'s deferred materialization after *Tripmaster Monkey*'s debut is forever framed and modified by its fictional antecedent, which is, one is tempted to say, a derivative, a fake, a copy that is also indisputably a true prelude to the "real" "fake book," this original score and that famous scream.[27] In the fashion of the Chinese intertextual warfare known as "the brush and ink battle," or to use Chin's preferred term, the "Sun Tzuian commentary," *Tripmaster Monkey* sets up the discursive stage on which the Asian American tradition of verbal culture has been performed and transformed.[28] But the war is staged to end wars, as the tripmaster narrator contemplates: "Whatever there is when there isn't war has to be invented" (306). Judging the novel at this level, it is Kingston's signal of reconciliation with Chin's ethnic nationalism, and her articulation of a more inclusive literary community. "We don't want to be divisive," she remarks when the subject of Asian American contention comes up in her interview with Marilyn Chin (M. Chin 1989: 7). "I think the best feeling in the world is understanding between two people," Kingston has commented elsewhere; "I think that is probably the whole point of sense and everything, just to get communication between two human beings in all of time and space. . . . I think that is why writers write" (Klein 1989: D10).

4

American Romances,
Immigrant Incarnations

*T*ripmaster Monkey's preoccupation with ethnic cultural identity as a means of claiming America is not shared by Bharati Mukherjee's *Jasmine* (1989a), which came out the same year. Though equally motivated by a desire to make America its own, *Jasmine* is the singular Americanization of a former village girl who has the astounding capacity to make her own ideal republic and to live the many lives of reincarnation.[1] Born Jyoti, the Punjabi Indian peasant woman never had the luxury of finishing elementary school. However, untrammeled by poverty and defiant of destiny, she chooses to become Jasmine upon her secret marriage to Prakash, who both rescues her from village feudalism and initiates her into his American quest. But before Prakash can make it to Florida to complete his engineering degree and establish "Vijh & Wife" in America, he is killed in a Sikh terrorist bombing. Undeterred, Jasmine purchases false papers and travels as a stowaway halfway around the globe to Florida, determined to burn Prakash's new Western suit as well as herself in a ritualistic consummation of their American dream. But her brutal rape by the man she has paid to smuggle her into the country forever alters her plan to carry out sati. To avenge herself, she slits the throat of the smuggler "Half-Face" and with the help of a Quaker lady finally makes it to New York. It is there, babysitting for the Hayes family, that she experiences the epiphany of "becom[ing] an American. . . . Jase the prowling adventurer" comes into being (146, 157). Though Jasmine will become Jane Ripplemeyer, the unwed "wife" of an Iowan Mr. Rochester, the end of the novel finds her with Taylor Hayes, her original and renewed American love, heading for California, that new horizon of her infinite self-transformations.

The Indian immigrant's incredible American saga has already aroused much critical suspicion. Anindyo Roy, for instance, has pointed to the novel's fabrication of an "epic truth" by "circumventing and suppressing the historical exigencies of Third World immigration" (1993: 128). Alpana Sharma Knippling blames *Jasmine* for its homogenization of "ethnic minority immigrant subjects" through an authorial "will-to-power" (1993: 145, 152). Gurleen Grewal is perhaps most perceptive in noting both the novel's "classic recipe of assimilation" and demonstrating its hypocritical "silen[ce] about the conditions that make such assimilation possible" (1993: 182). In unison, the critics seized upon the fissure between a historically plausible immigrant and its fictional correspondent, but the intimate relation between the novel's dual impulse of immigration—one belonging in the text proper to Jasmine and the other to the framing consciousness of Mukherjee—has escaped attention. The ritualistic Americanization of Jasmine from Hasnapur to California can not be set apart from Mukherjee's own artistic migration from Calcutta to Canada to America. To be oblivious of this parallel journey is to miss not only the mutual constitution of the character's exuberant idealism and its author's own romanticism but also the integral link between Jasmine's assimilation of American culture and Mukherjee's conscious appropriation of American literary traditions.

If *Tripmaster Monkey* is Maxine Hong Kingston's double engagement of Asian American nationalist cultural politics and the conditions of the American canon, *Jasmine* is Bharati Mukherjee's simultaneous fictional exploration of reputed American cultural values and the Asian American immigrant writer's place in the changing cultural landscape of the nation. Mukherjee wants to reexamine the fabled spirit of American individualism, manifest both in the personal conviction of self-transformation and in the political promise of social mobility. By engaging this ubiquitous American narrative and reenacting its potential through her immigrant everywoman, she also wants to assure herself of a role in the expanding republic of American letters.

I

Shortly after the publication of *The Middleman and Other Stories* (1988b), which won her the 1989 National Book Critics Circle award for fiction, Mukherjee wrote "Immigrant Writing: Give Us Your Maximalists!" An authorial manifesto, the essay both articulates her aesthetics and anticipates the composition of *Jasmine*: "While American fiction was sunk in a decade of minimalism, an epic was washing up its shores. . . . Characters in this [Maximalist] world have the density of 19th-century presences; like creatures out of Balzac or Dickens, they pass before me leaving real footprints" (Mukherjee 1988a: 28). "But where, in fiction," Mukherjee asks, "do you read of it?" (1). The "disguis[ed] nativist social agenda" of "minimalism" that "speaks in whispers to the initiated" has so precluded the cultural presence of recent American initiates (28) that it leads Mukherjee to ask, "Who . . . speaks for *us*, the new Americans from nontraditional immigrant countries? Which is another way of saying, in this altered America, who speaks for *you?*" (1; emphasis mine).[2]

Against what she regards as the nativist literary exclusion of immigrant letters of color, Mukherjee "claims America" by anchoring her writing in the white ethnic tradition. In evoking Eastern European immigration and its flourishing in the Jewish American renaissance, she draws an irresistible analogy to the literary emergence of her "nontraditional immigrants" in an era of transnational capital.[3] In so doing, the objections to minimalism's inchoate nativism begin to function as self-legitimating acts of reinscribing the nation: the artistic absence of "Bionic Men and Women among us" becomes for her a touchstone of American representative democracy, and immigrant writing a quintessential signature of the American character (ibid.: 28).

Mukherjee's recourse to American demography's imaginative correspondent also anchors the new immigrant experience in the mode of realism in the tradition of Balzac, Dickens, and Malamud, she says, and against the aesthetics of Naipaul and Salman Rushdie. She argues that "in literary terms, being an immigrant is very déclassé. . . . There's a low-grade ashcan realism implied in the very material. . . . Exiles," [on the other hand,] "come wrapped in a cloak of mystery and world weariness." Although the "mordant bite" of her fellow Indian expatriates in the West "is a great comfort. . . . Lacking a country, avoiding all the messiness of rebirth as an immigrant, eventually harms even the finest sensibility" (ibid.: 28).

As in her association of minimalism with nativism, Mukherjee's use of realism similarly conflates the ideological and the aesthetic. Immigrant writing is superior not simply because of its earthiness, its realistic espousal of the common multitudes, but also because of its unwavering engagement with the host culture and its implicit commitment to the new homeland. If her disaffection with the white suburban canon of contemporary American writing comes from its perceived nativist foreclosure of literary immigrants, her disassociation from the emerging canon of postcolonial writers is an expression of her impatience with the extolled virtues of postmodern migrancy. The maximalist project of Mukherjee turns out a unique brand of immigrant cultural nationalism that rejects both diasporic noncommitment and nativist exclusion. While striking resonant chords with Asian American ethnic nationalism in its rooting impulse, its politics of identity and recognition, the immigrant focus of Mukherjee does not seem devoted to either the pursuit of a specific racial consciousness or the realization of an Asian American solidarity. (Mukherjee's characters are exceptionally global in origin, though their destination is distinctively American.) The maximalist project is thus a deliberate restoration of the American "melting pot" myth (against the Canadian "mosaic" as Mukherjee puts it), with a "nontraditional" color coating. It is Mukherjee's recharacterization, both in casting and description, of the nation's celebrated ideals of democracy and mobility. It is small wonder that the personal ceremony of Mukherjee's naturalization at the Federal District Court House in Manhattan should turn "Immigrant Writing" into a political as well as literary statement of her American allegiance.[4]

II

While maximalism's epic theme and realism's credible detail are self-proclaimed markers of Mukherjee's throbbing new Americanism, their ideal formal wedding in *Jasmine* has, as has been noted earlier, become a point of intense contention. There is no denial of Mukherjee's acuteness of observation and her ability to capture in precise language Jasmine's shifting settings. The marshlands of Florida with "Eden's waste" (96), the hustle and bustle of multiethnic Flushing, the "naturally blond [Elsa] county," Iowa, and the tapering off of yeoman farmer America are all evoked with poignant atmosphere and vivid verisimilitude (29). However, the very assets that supposedly enable Jasmine's mobility, her comprehension of the multiple registers of American English, her discernment in fashion and furnishings, her ease of conversation and command of Western culture, her references to George Bernard Shaw and the Brontë's as well as Dick and Jane, though rendered lifelike, are indisputably out of character. In her attempt to inscribe a survivalist immigrant epic, Mukherjee has enthusiastically universalized her own autobiographic ascent in the narrative of Jasmine, her immigrant everywoman; the result is a liberal fusion of authorial

class confidence and educational privilege with the rather limited consciousness and condition of the character. Its realistic façade poised against
its fantastic plot, *Jasmine* appears not a novel in the European tradition that
its author invokes but a quintessential "American romance" with its inescapable contradictions.

Taking up Lionel Trilling's suggestion that "American writers of great
genius have not turned their minds to society"; "[they do] not write novels
but romances" (1950: 212), and building on Hawthorne's theory of the
"neutral territory," Richard Chase defines the American romance as a "border fiction" whose "field of action is conceived not so much as a place as a
state of mind" (1957: 18, 19). Hospitable to "melodrama and idyl," romance
is characterized by its "willingness to abandon moral questions" (ix). Close
in spirit to "epic," it "does not confine itself to what is known, or even what
is probable" (16). The essence of romance, according to Chase, is its fundamental "freedom from the conditions of actuality" (x), its breaking of the
"Jamesian circuits" of social relations (28), and its exhortation of "the dis-
connected and uncontrolled experience" (25). Summoning Tocqueville to
turn the phantom influence of Trilling to his advantage,[5] Chase attributes
romance's "mythic ideality" to the "solitary position" of man in "the very
institutions of democracy" (15, 11), where, he contends, "it will not matter
much what class people come from, and where the novelist would arouse
our interest in a character by exploring his origin." With this assertion, romance's "abstract[ion]" and "ideal[ization]" of character become a literary
or perhaps literal realization of American democracy's demolition of class
hierarchies (13), and Chase, like Perry Miller, designates "romance" as the
unique generic expression of European American literary nationalism, typ-
ifying it as the vehicle of "an American imagination" and "the originality
and 'Americanness' of the novel" (19, vii).[6]

The apparent asocialness of the "romance" has thus come to confirm,
through an explicit denial of its connection to society and politics, both an
essential American freedom of individual autonomy and a political system
that makes the freedom possible. Such apparent ideological neutrality has
been faulted by critics of the American romance, among them Russell Reising, who charges that this antimimetic model has "resulted in a circular
conception of American literature. Since that majorness is frequently defined as either the rejection or the transcendence of social concerns, the
many authors, texts, and genres which *do* express a frank and explicit in-
volvement with social questions are either domesticated to the prevailing
critical paradigm, or they are excluded from study altogether" (1986: 36).
What Reising illuminates is the integral correspondence between the
generic requisites of the American romance and the constitution of the traditional American canon. What affinity we see between *Jasmine*'s maximal-

ist extravaganza and American romance's spectacular detachment from "conditions of actuality," however, is Bharati Mukherjee's astute access to the conditions of canonicity. In light of this argument, *Jasmine*'s endless ventures toward the limitless frontier not only repeat the basic romance plot but reiterate the grand narrative of American democracy, which, as is commonly believed, endows the individual, regardless of race, gender, class, or creed, with equal opportunities for mobility.[7] The story of a poor Indian village girl making it in America seems uniquely positioned, precisely because of its new immigrant perspective, to retell the reigning truths of an old mythology. *Jasmine*'s thematic and generic correspondence with the tenets of the American romance therefore make the novel both original and unmistakably American.

One may object to labeling *Jasmine* a romance by noting its attention to squalor and violence. Jasmine's rape by a white man on landing, Professorji's professional displacement, Bud Ripplemeyer's maiming, and Darrel Lutz's suicide seem examples enough to show the novel's social concern. However, what makes the novel a true romance is not its lack of concern with the material universe but the way in which the material universe is made to be either ineffectual or indifferent. Muhkerjee consistently removes experiences of suffering to the periphery of Jasmine's existence and projects, if necessary, both her internal pain and external obstacle onto some form of Other. Not surprisingly, the misfortunes of people upon whom Jasmine's livelihood happens to depend remain theirs, and even the violation of her own female body can be displaced onto a persona of the past. Like the refugees' "old clothes balled up and tossed into the ocean," cumbersome events and circumstances in Jasmine's life can as easily be discarded and disregarded, with no impact, no impediment, and no strings attached (96).

It is with this transcendent defiance that *Jasmine* makes a mockery of material actualities. The Balzacian or Dickensian matrix of social determination that propels their individual characters' struggle has outlived its usefulness for Mukherjee. In Jasmine's fictional frontier, negative reactions to the racialized class demotion of immigrant professionals, either from the medical doctor turned cab driver or professor turned supplier of wigs, are translated as "bitterness" or "nostalgia." Such regressive attitudes are deemed tangential to Jasmine's own development or made to foil her more progressive and healthier American responses (124, 165). "I would not immure myself as [they] did," the narrator says; "I changed because I wanted to. To bunker oneself inside nostalgia, to sheathe the heart in a bulletproof vest, was to be a coward" (165). External reality finally recedes before the adventurous immigrant; F. Scott Fitzgerald's "willingness of heart," or more aptly perhaps, the kind of romantic American claim captured by Carlos Bulosan, takes over Mukherjee's fictional universe as well—"America is not merely a land or an institution. America is in the hearts of men that died for freedom . . . all of us, from the first Adams to the last Filipino, native born or alien, educated or illiterate—*We are America!*" (189).[8]

"I'm aware of the brutalities, the violences here," Mukherjee admits, "but in the long run my characters are survivors. Like Jasmine, I feel there are people born to be Americans. By American I mean an intensity of spirit and a quality of desire. I feel American in a very fundamental way, whether Americans see me that way or not" (quoted in Steinberg 1989: 47). Once again, the author has generously incorporated her character into her own psyche, and America is no longer experienced as a set of circumstances that "immures" but as a set of pure and undetermined individual choices that frees. America is more than anything else a feeling and an idea, a mental construct independent of social constraints, and an expression of the inner self, that "intensity of spirit" and "quality of desire." Such belief and make-believe should rank *Jasmine* as probably the most ardent of contemporary American romances, not just in Chase's classical definition but in that of popular romance as well.

The structural distinction of romance, states John Cawelti in *Adventure, Mystery, and Romance*, is not that it "stars a female" but that "its organizing action is the development of a love relationship, usually between a man and a woman" (1976: 41). The basic narrative of "the ideal romance," Janice Radway argues in *Reading the Romance*, usually "explains the heroine's transformation from isolated, asexual, insecure adolescent who is unsure of her own identity, into a mature, sensual, and very married woman who has realized her full potential and identity as the partner of a man and as the implied mother of a child" (1985: 134). Popular romance's coupling of love's magical property and the evolution of its heroine's identity seems to claim *Jasmine* as one of its own. Not only does Jasmine's radical reincarnation significantly correlate with if not entirely hinge upon love; such love is also a form of transmuted gratification for its author's "clear-eyed but definite love for America" (Mukherjee, quoted in Steinberg 1989: 47). Jasmine's romantic awakenings and heterosexual liaisons, in other words, are artistic vehicles for Bharati Mukherjee's own disguised patriotic passions. Similar in function to Wittman Ah Sing's conjugal romance in *Tripmaster Monkey*, the love affairs of Jasmine are performances of an authorial nationalistic erotics, which, as we shall see, never belongs to the realm of the pure libido but rather subjects itself to the demands of the lover/America.

With sheer artistic ingenuity, Mukherjee has replaced Kingston's feminine image of the nation with one of masculine indulgence, protection, and authority. In this metaphoric arrangement, Jasmine's relationships with a series of men begin to suggest the degrees of her American absorption and integration. Although Prakash, Jasmine's Indian husband, has the "intensity of spirit" and "quality of desire" characteristic of Mukherjee's definition of an American, and although he is the person who starts Jasmine off on her American quest, his hesitant English disqualifies him as her authentic American beau.[9] It is Taylor Hayes, the Columbia University professor, who has, with his "crooked-teethed smile . . . admitted her [Jasmine] to the broad democracy of his joking" (146, 148). "The love I felt for Taylor that first day had nothing to do with sex," Jasmine confesses; "I fell in love with his world, its ease, its careless confidence and graceful self-absorption" that America represents (151). While the arms of Bud Ripplemeyer, "the pillar of Baden," become for her a temporary haven, Jasmine will subsequently reject both Bud and the bankrupt Jeffersonianism of heartland America that he symbolizes to rejoin Hayes, a version of American urban sophistication, professional security, and class comfort (178).[10] "I am not choosing between men," Jasmine reassures us toward the end, refusing to be downed by dreary dailiness and Bud in the wheelchair; "I am caught between the promise of America and old-world dutifulness" (213–14):

> Adventure, risk, transformation: the frontier is pushing indoors through uncaulked windows. . . .
> "Ready?" Taylor grins.
> I cry into Taylor's shoulder, cry through all the lives I've given birth to, cry for all my dead.
> Then there is nothing I can do. Time will tell if I am a tornado, rubble-maker, arising from nowhere and disappearing into a cloud. I am out the door and in the potholed driveway, scrambling ahead of Taylor, greedy with wants and reckless with hope. (214)

With California beckoning, Mukherjee has made her last appeal to the fabled geography of the American frontier and included Jasmine's journey in the meta-narrative of "westering," to use John Steinbeck's term. It is the identification with this expansionist narrative and the conception of America as the territory ahead, to be explored by *any* adventurer willing to light out, that *Jasmine* has reenacted the American ideal of free individual enterprise and American romance's most typical fictional resolution of perpetual promise. It is not ironic but prophetically American perhaps that Jasmine, "arising from nowhere and disappearing into a cloud," should consummate her American romance in a "neutral territory" where origins and existing conditions do not matter. After all, this place called America is for Mukherjee not marked with geopolitical boundaries and does not require passports or residence cards: it is a limitless inner space, "an intensity of spirit" measured by "hope" and "a quality of desire" defined by "wants."

III

Mukherjee's narrative affirmation of individual choice as a unique American construct echoes the most recent theoretical reincarnation of the American romance, the influential and controversial *Beyond Ethnicity* by Werner Sollors: "The conflict between contractual and hereditary, self-made and ancestral definitions of American identity—between consent and descent—[constitutes] the central drama in American culture" (1986: 5–6). What distinguishes and binds Americans as Americans, however, is for Sollors their jettisoning of the "descent language" of "hereditary liabilities and entitlements" and their subscription to the "consent language," which "stresses our abilities as mature free agents . . . to choose our spouses, our destinies, and our political systems" (6). The definition of America as both a covenant and a choice makes possible Sollors's critical (de)coding of immigrant rites and rituals and Mukherjee's creative (en)coding of the same compatible projects.

What is most valuable about their contribution is their undermining of national legitimacy determined by birth and their simultaneous validation of naturalized citizenship as equal if not superior to ascriptive forms of American allegiance.[11] Such a language of consent and self-construction may give Americans of non-European origin an overdue centrality in the cultural formation of the United States, but this idealistic line of American consent also overlooks, as Alan Wald has pointed out, the "color line" of "material" and "social domination" (1987: 23). As I noted in the Introduction, the forcible removal of Native Americans, the conquering and annexation of Latino Americans, the enslavement of African Americans, and the exclusion and internment of Asian Americans are all too evidently descent-targeted breaches of democratic consent that only a willing suspension of history can ignore. What Sollors's "volitional allegiance" and Mukherjee's "rehousement" have in common, besides their liberating capacities, is their consensual disregard of race in American consent.[12]

With her emulation of Bernard Malamud, Mukherjee has enacted an Asian American immigrant ritual in the primarily European American mode of ethnic ascent with which Sollors has staked his claim. But her optimistic account of Jasmine and discount of the role of race in her journey present a radical revision of the Asian American immigrant corpus. The poetry of detained angels in *Island*; the *Songs of Gold Mountain* from the era of exclusion; Carlos Bulosan's narrative of miserable migrant workers and Bienvenido Santos's bitter *Scent of Apples*; Royong Kim's *Clay Walls* about the strife of life; the concerted and constrained communication between the *issei* and the *nisei* in Hisaye Yamamoto's *Seventeen Syllables* and in Toshio

Mori's *Yokohama, California* all refute the exuberant indifference to race that *Jasmine* has come to signify. The immigrant tradition, far from overdetermining a uniform trope of racial discrimination, is keenly attentive to the multiple accents of American racial actuality and honestly accountable for its influence in the varied experience of Asian Americans. The chosen matrimony with America in those texts is a far less happy and frequently more abusive relationship than Mukherjee would allow.

One may justify *Jasmine*'s departure from that tradition by observing the historical differences in Asian American immigration. But the text's conformity to romance's dictates seems to raise doubts about whether the new immigrant could indeed become the architect of her own wants. The stylistic requisites for Jasmine's successful Americanization, the erasure of race, class, and other real conditions, are in this sense indicative of the tangible material limits even on today's "nontraditional" volitional allegiance. To make her protagonist a free agent, Mukherjee, as the true agent of that message, cannot practice at will, say, the realistic credo of Balzac or Dickens; yet her resort to romance at the same time betrays its generic irony. As Myra Jehlen puts it in "The Novel and the Middle Class in America":

> However far away into the wilderness American romances take us, ultimately they find it an impossible situation and, whether out of commitment or by default, lead us back to society. For the self-reliant individuals, Natty Bumppo, Hester Prynne, Captain Ahab, Huck Finn or Isabel Archer all fail in the end to create their private worlds and their failure sounds dire warnings of the dangers of isolation and solipsism. Typically the American romance is the story of a *defeated*, a downed flight. (Jehlen 1987: 125)

Although Jasmine's America has an even "weak[er] gravity" than that of her romantic predecessors, and Mukherjee is less willing to suspend her heroine's flight, the text's return to society in Jehlen's sense is perhaps unavoidable (158). "Texts are worldly," Edward Said maintains, "even when they appear to deny it, they are nevertheless a part of the social world, human life, and of course the historical moments in which they are located and interpreted" (1983: 4). In the spirit of this "secular criticism," we can now return to the novel's formal arrangement to address a pair of related questions, the first being whether Jasmine has indeed become an autonomous subject and the second whether the artistic interpellation of her subjectivity has subjected Mukherjee to the dominant political unconscious about American racial formations.

Although the end of the novel impresses us with a self-determining Jasmine ready to reposition the stars, she remains dependent upon the paternalistic approval of the white republic for her American identity. Mukherjee seems to have liberated Jasmine from the feudal Indian practice of an arranged marriage to suggest not just the freedom of American romance but its superiority based on individual choice, superiority made most apparent, one may add, with the admitted social inferiority of the undocumented Asian immigrant.[13] In affirming Jasmine's mating choices, Mukherjee once again concurs with Sollors that "American allegiance . . . was—like love—based on consent, not on descent, which further blended the rhetoric of America with the language of love and the concept of romantic love with American identity" (Sollors 1986: 112). Paradoxically, however, Jasmine's spiritual American citizenship—she still has no papers when the novel ends, though this is beside the point in an otherworldly romance—is attained only with her carnal consent. The terms of her American contract, her willingness to sign on regardless, are not cost-free. Though textually muffled in general, the givens of Jasmine's descent—her gender, her sexuality, and her Asian body—are voluminous commentary on the kind of American allegiance she is able to pledge and the form of American identity she is able to assume. Despite the incantation of Emersonian self-reliance, Jasmine's reincarnations through romance have not meant fundamental changes of her self but a recycling of her roles as caregiver, homemaker, and temptress in the process of patriarchal recuperation and nationalistic incorporation.[14]

However, this is not the way Jasmine would have seen herself, for Mukherjee's textual apparatus has endowed her with such an illusion of structural openness that Jasmine cannot see otherwise. But the text's representation of Jasmine's Americanization is an already compromised reality. It is reflective of, if not complicit with, the dominant American ideology, not a set of political ideas but murmurs of feeling about licensed partnerships and undesirable unions. The success of Jasmine's American romance is contingent upon her disrupted and unfulfilled passions; the premature death of Prakash is the case in point. The termination of the Vijh marriage is for Mukherjee a fictional necessity, for not until Prakash/India is metaphorically murdered, according to the author's aesthetic of "unhousement" to "rehousement," can Jasmine become an eligible American bride. But Prakash's graceful exit betrays ever so miserably an authorial failure of imagination that can conceive neither an Asian male version of Jasmine's epic evolution or an Asian American joint venture, like the half-aborted Vijh & Wife that equally illustrates the volitional aspects of American allegiance. Such potentially imaginable American wedlock and such palpably "real" engagement are, however, eschewed. Jasmine's narrative of mobility will be an improbable journey without her professed "beauty"; coupled with Prakash's debilitating sexuality in the American national eros, her free choice to become American is even more impossible.[15] It seems that the reality of race, gender, and Asian American sexuality in the dominant social network is after all felt at the "romance" kingdom's periphery of difference. The sovereign subject status of nontraditional immigrants, however, remains an article of faith. *Jasmine* is an inspiring work of fancy; reservations about it are perhaps best expressed via Gandhi's famous response to "American Democracy": "I wish it were true."

IV

The opening words of Mukherjee's maximalist manifesto, "I'm one of you now," are echoed in the first sentence of Gish Jen's 1991 novel, *Typical American*: "It's an American story: Before he was a thinker, or a doer, or an engineer, much less an imagineer like his self-made-millionaire friend Grover Ding, Ralph Chang was just a small boy in China struggling to grow up his father's son" (Jen 1991: 3).[16] Like Jasmine's transcendence of her social confinements and her transformation of self on American grounds, Ralph Chang's American journey is foreshadowed as one of radical change and self-becoming. Both Mukherjee and Jen insist on treating the narrative of Asian American immigration as one of the many analogous narratives of national consent, not an exception to but typical of the American spirit. To say "I'm one of you now," or "to see Asian Americans as 'us' rather than 'other'" (as Jen would) (quoted in Brown 1991: 13), is to posit a new relation to the dominant culture and to create a fiction beyond the negative embodiments of race and ethnicity.

In their deliberate move toward the mainstream, Mukherjee and Jen are shepherding a new Asian American homesteading narrative very different from that of the ethnic nationalists.[17] Yet, in their reworking of what Myra Jehlen identifies as *American Incarnation*, "an archetypal conjunction of personal identity and national identification coming together in the very earth of the New World" (Jehlen 1986: 2–3), the authors themselves also take divergent paths. If Mukherjee is preoccupied with "notions of individual autonomy defended by natural inalienable rights," Jen is more keen on such individual autonomy's sanctification through "individual self-possession" (3). The idealist definition of the sovereign spirit in Mukherjee's kingdom of romance is in Jen a novel subject of materialist self-possession.[18]

Jen's protagonist, Ralph Chang, came to the United States on a Chinese government scholarship to study for his doctorate in engineering. The Communist takeover of the mainland and America's refusal to let him return to serve the communists left him stranded. He fell into the limbo of "no-status," descending into a Chinatown basement slaughtering chicken for a living, before he was rescued by his sister Teresa, now a U.S. medical student, married her best friend, Helen, and finally obtained his Ph.D. "Bound together by some old rope—their overlapping history, their parents' relationship" (52), the Changs cultivated a "family feeling, that tremendous, elemental solidarity" against encroaching alienation (140). Though the apartment they shared had a crack so big that "actual slivers of sky shone through it, lustrous and white," the house had held with its own invisible "turnbuckle" to "keep its corners from falling" (120).

But like "the language of *outside the house*" that "had seeped well inside," the ideas and practices of the external world flood in to make a mockery of the flimsy family compound (124). Ralph would be stung by a bee before his clandestine meeting with Grover Ding. "He could hardly see. His whole brow was swelling as though with a third eye" (89). The addition and inflation of Ralph's eye/I, the narrative wryly implies, will prevent him from seeing clearly. The Faustian bargain he strikes with Grover to purchase a rundown fried chicken joint, is the result of this impaired vision. Since then, the once self-sustaining simplicity of family feeling no longer appears adequate, and the crying need for self-expansion takes a materialistic turn. While Ralph clicks his cash register in the upstairs bedroom producing false receipts to evade taxes, Helen turns her new loveseat into her "deepest pleasure" zone for Grover, "[a] man with monogrammed shirts, a maid and a mansion" (214). If the prelapsarian bliss of the Chang family was noted for its tender gestures and sharing moments, such happiness was dashed once Grover entered their household. The simple pleasures of daily life and concrete human interaction were now replaced by monetary mediation and gold worship. The house of Chang, with its lawn of "unearthly green," begins to see its "structural weakening" (159, 175). The chicken palace will sink, too, because Grover has sold Ralph "a pit, into which someone had dumped trees . . . the land, therefore, was unstable and unbuildable" (244).

The house metaphor that is so central to Gish Jen's characterization of the Chang family's American settlement, was, as we recall, Bharati Mukherjee's as well. Unlike her predecessor, who portrayed the process of "unhousement" to "rehousement" as an affirmative process of "murder[ing] who we were so we can rebirth ourselves in the images of dreams" (Mukherjee 1989a: 25), Jen not only questions the vision of individual autonomy achieved at the expense of historical affiliations but also uses the Changs' immigrant transformation to expose the dilemmas of American liberal democracy, a house built on "possessive individualism." As C. B. Macpherson instructs us, the foundation of American democracy is composed of a set of self-possessive assumptions underlying both the individual human subject and his or her relation to society. First, the subject is conceived as one who is the sole proprietor of his or her own person, owing nothing to society but capable of selling his or her capacity to labor. Second, the subject is one who is essentially independent from the will of others and free from any relations with people except those entered into willingly and in self-interest. Third, as the logical consequence of the foregoing notions of self, human society is seen as consisting of no more than a series of market relations (Macpherson 1962: 263–64).

In this context, Ralph Chang's Americanization entails less a forswearing of old political allegiances than an active consent to new cultural definitions of self. What this means in practical terms is that he abandons the precapitalist mode of production, in which kinship relations play a major role, and adopts the capitalist mode of production, in which market relations dominate all forms of human exchange. Gish Jen illustrates this modal change through a subtle comparison of Ralph Chang's two lists of resolutions. Earlier in the novel, while still on the trans-Pacific steamship bound for America, Ralph sets his goals to paper: "I will cultivate virtue" / "I will bring honor to the family" top his American mission (6). With the list, Jen both cross-references Franklin's *Autobiography* and Fitzgerald's *Great Gatsby* and couches her protagonist in the *Typical American* narrative of rational self-aspiration. Moreover, she wants to reveal that the ascetic virtues these characters cultivate—discipline, self-abnegation, and self control—have very different objectives.

If Franklin's and Gatsby's lists invariably lead them to pursue freedom from the will of others so that a sovereign self can stand, Ralph's is designed to fulfill a collective destiny so that the entire family can rejoice. In Ralph Chang's list is thus the ideological unconscious of a "Confucian individualism" that contrasts sharply with the American "possessive individualism" from which Franklin and Gatsby draw their inspirations. If, as Bellah et al. argue, "the cramped self-control of Franklin's 'virtues' leave little room for love, human feeling, and a deeper expression of the self" (1986: 33), Confucian individualism demands that the subject claim his or her rights and status within the social scene and define the self in "a web of reciprocal obligations" (Fairbank 1983: 71).[19] Ralph's struggle to get his degree and then a tenured professorship, and Teresa and Helen's sacrifice to make this possible, exemplify the reciprocal commitment and communal spirit of Confucian humanism. However, feeling "lightly hitched to society" and inspired by his millionaire friend Grover Ding, Ralph would soon embark on a new course of "imagineering" (87, 88) that satirizes his old habits of the heart: "ALL RICHES BEGIN IN AN IDEA" / "YOU CAN NEVER HAVE RICHES IN GREAT QUANTITY UNLESS YOU WORK YOURSELF INTO A WHITE HEAT OF DESIRE FOR MONEY" (198–99). Ralph has embraced possessive individualism in its most materialistic form.

Although sister Teresa was "outraged" at his "money worship" (201), she is helpless against her brother's march of self-possession, which turns love and loyalty into dinosaur notions and will also drive her out of their house and eventually put her into a coma. Before long, Grover stands ready to foreclose on the home and the chicken house, and with both, the American Dream that he peddles to Ralph. With soggy foundations and tumbling houses, Gish Jen attributes the decline and disintegration of the Chang family to both individual weakness and structural deficiency, putting on trial both their altered personal ethics and the deep-seated American national ethos of possessive individualism. Ralph Chang and Helen are indeed typical Americans reminiscent of such classic figures as Willy Loman and Sister Carrie, but Jen's deft combination of individual tragedy and social drama also add a particular spin to the perennial story of American individual autonomy.

Ralph's self-actualization by all economic means necessary is not a mystical expression of transcendental impulse impelled by either his Emersonian namesake or Norman Vincent Peale. Rather, it is his answer to the social cues of America as summarized in Grover's astounding one-liner: "That's what you are in this country, if you got no dough, a singing Chinaman" (106). Teresa Chang agrees: "To be nonwhite in this society was indeed to need education, accomplishment. . . . A white person was by definition somebody. Other people needed, across their hearts, one steel rib" (200).[20] Grover and Teresa, moral enemies and rival guardians of Ralph's soul, are two individuals with little in common besides their Chinese heritage, but they have concurred on the racial hierarchy of this nation and the Asian American stake in it. "Country," "dough," and "Chinaman" are Gish Jen's key words to the interrelations of nation, class, and race in the determination of her protagonist's Americanization. If Grover's motto has professed the link between money and identity, Teresa's observation has pronounced the connection between identity and race. Both have unveiled, revising Sollors's binarism, the undeniable limitations of racial descent on individual American consent.

Ralph Chang's appropriation of possessive individualism as the self-made King of Fried Chicken, therefore, is not merely an assimilation of core national values but a measured social response to racial disregard as well. His unironic cautionary tales to his daughters, "you have no money, you are nobody. You are Chinaman!" (199) are as much a realistic admission of some "innate racial depravity" as they are an expressed desire to overcome it through class respectability. Acquiring the "white heat of desire for money" could be in this context both a symbol of Ralph's race envy and Jen's cryptic critique of American democracy's inequality. The fervent proprietary pursuit of her protagonist appears at once a psychosocial compensation for the historical denial of Asian American land ownership and a reflection of the contemporary Asian American professional exodus from the corporate world to self-employment.[21] To reincarnate himself as an

American, Ralph seems to conclude, he must be the proprietor of his own person as well as a man of Grover's "commanding presence" in the white world (214). To be a self-made *man* is also to be the "father of the family" (140). Economic self-possession against ethnic tarnish is thereby for him a simultaneous remasculation of self.

It is small wonder then that Ralph's possessive individualism has, in the American culture of masculine ownership and feminization of poverty, developed its competitive, predatory, and masculine edge, leading eventually to the loss of his humanity. In a scene evocative of *The Great Gatsby*, Ralph knocks his sister down with his car. Recalling the moment:

> He sees himself at the wheel. He pictures Arthur Smith [his neighbor] and his gun, and knows what it means to be armed—that one's house is one's own. In China, one lived in one's family's house. In America, one could always name whose house one was in; and to live in a house not one's own was to be less than a man. In America, a man had need of a weapon. He ought to have killed Grover Ding, that other intruder. Instead, a shadow slid from the wall.
>
> How he felt humanity squeeze his hand, and how he let that hand go— shook himself free of it, even, like a young boy confronted with an ardent admirer.
>
> Sudden glare. Teresa's body thumped the bumper, gently. (282–83)

Economic emasculation (the foreclosure of the house) and symbolic castration (Helen's infidelity) drive Ralph Chang to mindless violence. Helpless before Grover, the America that seduces and then swindles him of his self/house, Ralph vents his defeat and dispossession on Teresa, the China that mortgages and nurtures his house/life.[22]

Unlike Fitzgerald's reckless drivers who can retreat into their vast money, Ralph loses not only the house that he can call "his own" but also his "family's house." By distinguishing between the two kinds of houses, one characterized by the mode of possessive individualism that Ralph has come to embody, and the other by the ascriptive communalism that he has rejected, Jen manages to resolve the many cultural tensions upon which her tale of immigrant incarnation center. Seeing himself in "the curved glass" of the TV screen, an American Dream "as still as the others had been antic" (292), Ralph realizes "that a man was as doomed here as he was in China. . . . America was no America" (296). The exercise of free will finally awakens him to determinism's hold on reality, collapsing the orientalist dichotomy of Western freedom and Asian bondage; he is also seized by a moment of irresistible nostalgia. The "simplicity of childhood" returns to warm the chill of the bitter winter, and Ralph cannot help reminiscing the jettisoned values of a "terraced society," where "relationships count so heavily that to say something *has no relationship* in Chinese—*mei guanxi*— is to mean, often as not, *it doesn't matter*" (265, 140, 177–78). Although Jen does not seem to advocate a return to older "integrated civilizations," where each one knew himself or herself for a part of an organically cohesive whole (Lukacs 1971: 29), she does use Ralph's desperate loneliness to question his eagerness to assimilate himself as a self-possessive American.

The symbolic return of Teresa at the end of the novel, who almost always represents the family principles, "reunification, that Chinese ideal," hints at a hopeful recuperation of domestic ties that materialism and possessive individualism had eroded (265). In this respect, Jen not only allies herself with the tradition of nineteenth-century American "woman's fiction," which views loving family life as an alternative to the domination of money and market (Baym 1978: 27); she also echoes, however intuitively, the current Asian cultural challenge to Western capitalism, which refuses to sacrifice familial reciprocality and responsibility to the contractual exchange of the market.[23] Ralph Chang's American consent may have led ultimately to anomic alienation and the severing of kinship ties, but it also heightens the cultural contradiction of the nation built on the pursuit of happiness and demonstrates the true unnaturalness of an American naturalization compelled by possessive individualism. For Asian Americans to integrate with the land and the nation, the author of *Typical American* seems to caution, they will have to both contest the emblematic freedom of American individualism and construct enduring relations of human interdependence. It is only through this fundamental American cultural reinscription that an Asian American homecoming and the national well-being of the United States can be ensured.

Whither Asia

If "Claiming America" marks a willed Asian American possession of the United States, "Whither Asia" conceives the nation in difference. Responding to the rising importance of the "Pacific Rim" discourse and its dissemination through market multiculturalism, the host of narrative "Orientations" in this part broach the contradictory effects of transnational theories on the foundational premise of ethnic nationalism, particularly its coupling of territorial affiliation with Asian American subjectivity.

"Whither Asia" approaches the nature of Asian American geopolitical allegiance and affective attachment from a number of angles. Chapter 5 considers *The Joy Luck Club*'s reconfiguration of *The Woman Warrior*'s transpacific dual geography and its tactful translation of an Asian symbolic into an unconditional surrender to maternal ancestry. It then analyzes *The Big Aiiieeeee!*'s programmatic geopolitical reversal of *Aiiieeeee!* and its nostalgic return to the fountainhead of ethnic culture. Though Amy Tan and Frank Chin are methodologically and ideologically at odds with each other, their reliance on genetic tropes and the racial subconscious at once enlivens the discourse of cultural essentialism and emblemizes an Asian American subjectivity whose supposed uniqueness risks self-segregation. What is the relation between the structures of Asian American feeling and the institutions of American cultural reproduction is therefore the question to which Chapter 6 turns. There, the re-Orientations toward cultural Asia are discussed through an interlocking reading of *Donald Duk*, *Bone*, and *Turning Japanese*. By examining the dynamics between the local place and the living community, school and family, and nation and ancestral origin, the chapter both investigates how social geography and human subjectivity interact, and questions whether they indeed form some essential equivalence.

Genes, Generation, and Geospiritual (Be)longings

T

ripmaster Monkey and *Jasmine*'s narrative claiming of America is almost entirely overshadowed by the meteoric success of Amy Tan's *Joy Luck Club* (1989).[1] A book about mother-daughter relationships and cultural displacement and recuperation, *The Joy Luck Club* harks back to the familial rifts and reconciliations of *The Woman Warrior* and departs from Kingston and Mukherjee's preoccupation with Asian American integration. If her fellow writers choose to substantiate the individual in terms of the national, situating their protagonists in the reimagined community of the United States, Tan manages to limit the trials and tribulations of her characters to the genealogical family, apparently independent from the larger society.

The focus on the filiality of the "club" rather than the consent of the "country" is an amazing act of narrative "privatization." In identifying family breakdown as the source of all forms of social disarray, and family unity as the floating signifier "for all manner of social ties," *The Joy Luck Club*'s treatment of female familial experiences exemplifies Tan's active participation in the dominant privatization of social problems (Stacey 1994: 67, 54). Once the biological family is privatized as the essential unit of social coherence and the exclusive locus of her narrative, Tan also finds a common affective denominator that can effectively appeal to her targeted audience of white female "baby boomers," who may not otherwise identify with her Asian characters (Somogyi and Stanton 1991: 29). Although the privileging of the family serves to appropriate both the dominant neoconservative discourse and the white reading community, Amy Tan will have to address the questions that the specific ethnic content of her book raises: whether the Asian values of her book are exemplary of American values, and whether her Asian American families are a metaphor for the national community at large. In approaching these issues of cultural intelligibility and membership, *The Joy Luck Club* both implicitly engages Kingston and Mukherjee's nationalist claiming of America and anticipates Frank Chin and David Mura's diasporic revision in "Whither Asia."

I

The structure of *The Joy Luck Club* reflects Amy Tan's conceptions of the family. The novel's sixteen chapters of first-person female narrative are divided into four sections with four stories each. Except for the first and last stories, in which Jing-mei Woo substitutes her own voice for her mother Suyuan Woo's, the American daughters' stories are neatly sandwiched by the autobiographical tales of the novel's Chinese mothers. This maternal enclosure of the daughters' stories is strengthened with local framing by a vignette at the beginning of each section. There, in a quasi-language of myth and fable, the mothers would impart their life lessons to the daughters, whose American ears, for the moment, seem deaf to Chinese accents. At a practical level, the symmetry of Tan's narrative scheme seems intended to fit a cluster of short stories into the novel form, but it also serves thematically to anchor the foundational categories of Tan's family. If its diachronic "mother-daughter plot" echoes *The Woman Warrior* and invokes the feminist fictional alternative to Freud's Oedipal "family romance" (Hirsch 1989), *The Joy Luck Club*'s woman-centered family trope is also juxtaposed with the synchronic movements of the East and the West, China to America and vice versa. Gender, generation, and geography are thus interwoven and transcoded to exemplify Amy Tan's ideation of an Asian American family amid the familial relations of ethnicity and nation at large.

The novel's opening vignette, "Feathers from a Thousand *Li* Away" illustrates Tan's method. Elaborating on a classic Chinese idiom, which literally translates, "Sending a goose feather from a thousand *li* [about 0.5 km] afar, the gift is light while the affection is heavy," Tan writes:

> The woman and the swan sailed across an ocean many thousands of *li* wide, stretching their necks toward America. On her journey she cooed to the swan: "In America I will have a daughter just like me. But over there nobody will say her worth is measured by the loudness of her husband's belch. Over there nobody will look down on her, because I will make her speak only perfect American English. And over there she will always be too full to swallow any sorrow. . . . Now the woman was old. And she had a daughter who grew up speaking only English and swallowing more Coca-Cola than Sorrow. For a long time now the woman wanted to give her daughter the single swan feather and tell her, "This feather may look worthless, but it comes from afar and carries with it all my good intentions." And she waited, year after year, for the day she could tell her daughter this in perfect American English. (Tan 1989: 17)[2]

The vignette is both deeply moving and troubling. Tan speaks effectively of the pain of familial incomprehension, the loss of the "mother-tongue," and the unarticulated desire for generational understanding. But the geocultural gap between China and America creates such a division of social spaces that it immediately revives the figment of orientalist imagination with an apparent Chinese authenticity. In an extraordinary demonstration of Tan's artistic ingenuity, the mother in the vignette concocts a "familiar" saying about the worth of a Chinese woman that is found nowhere in Chinese idiom.[3] China, the readers are led to believe, is replete with male chauvinist pigs whose pot bellies rest on their wives' empty stomachs, while in bountiful America those who speak English are automatically well fed and respected. The invention of the authentic-seeming idiom not only effortlessly implies that the Chinese culture has consecrated its sexism in language, it has also erased, through the Coca-Cola and Sorrow contrast, gender inequality from the civilized liberties of America. It is small wonder that the barbarous and backward East should stretch its neck toward the progressive and blissful West.

Helena Michie has concisely argued that "dominant metaphors of feminist critiques of society are familial in origin; the word 'patriarchy' itself . . . locates power in literal and metaphorical fatherhood and defines the family as the scene, if not the source, of women's oppression. . . . The struggle of *many* sisters with a *single* father. . . . disrupt[s] the Oedipal triangle . . . by the introduction of politics and community as they enter onto the familial stage embodied severally as 'sisters'" (1991: 58). Although Michie's analysis suffers from a universal conception of both patriarchy and its feminist alternative, it is precisely to this conception that *The Joy Luck Club* appeals. The narrative's explicit attempt at mother-daughter communication is an implicit attempt to enter the community of white women readers. To this end, the gallery of Asian and Asian American women in the novel must provide points of identification for white female generational anxieties, while the group of Asian and Asian American male characters must function as textual "pawns," not only "for bringing up the conflicts between the mothers and daughters," as Tan puts it, but to so particularize patriarchy as well (Somogyi and Stanton 1991: 29).[4]

Since the majority of the men in the novel are Chinese and its baby-boomer audience is largely white, the racial and geocultural specificity of Amy Tan's gender references are unambiguous. As the oppressor of women, the Asian male begins to epitomize the Eastern origin of patriarchy, which is of course genetically transmittable only to Asian American men. The move has both racialized gender oppression to read exclusively Asian and deflected attention from the practice of domestic sexism. It significantly downplays the important contribution of Asian American feminism, which recognizes the dominant cultural differentiation of Asian American gender roles within the racial hierarchies of the United States (E. Kim 1990: 68–75). What appears to be a frontal assault on the patriarchal system finds a figurehead father either in the remote Orient or the distant ethnic ghetto, leaving the white American patriarch unscratched and unscathed.

Tan's racialization of Asian sexism helps figuratively invoke white women's experience with patriarchy but ultimately precludes any geopolitical solution to it. Likewise, the novel's characterization of Asian American mother-daughter experience helps foster affective bonds among women of different backgrounds while deferring the question of transracial female solidarity. This effect is achieved through a double maneuver. As is evident in the novel's structural arrangement of mother-daughter conflict as a China-America split, generational difference is diagnosed first and foremost as a geocultural chasm. But just as sexism is biologized, both generation gap and geocultural fissure can be miraculously synchronized with genes. The novel masterfully executes this maneuver by elaborating the maternal fables of oriental wisdom and oriental suffering in the vignettes and extending these generational lessons into the main chapters.

Rose Hsu Jordan's doomed marriage, for example, is traced not just to her neglect of her brother but also to the fate and failure of her grandmother's widowhood and concubinage (130, 215). "Even though I taught my daughter the opposite," An-mei Hsu reflects, "still she came out the same way! All of us [mothers and daughters] are like stairs, one step after another, going up and down, but all going the same way" (215). Similarly, daughter Lena St. Clair's marital woes are attributed to her mother Ying-Ying's abuse in her first marriage and the loss of her tiger spirit in the second. Until Ying-Ying recovers her "fierceness," Lena will "ha[ve] no *chi*," the spirit to stand on her own. "I will gather together my past . . . and hold [my] pain . . . to penetrate my daughter's tough skin and cut her tiger spirit loose," Ying-Ying decides; "I will win and give her my spirit, because this is the way a mother loves her daughter" (165, 252). As Lena becomes the beneficiary of Ying-Ying's spirit, daughter Waverly Jong absorbed her mother Lindo's "invisible strength" but rejected "[her] Chinese ways" when she started school (89, 253). It was in the mirror of a beauty parlor, right before Waverly's second marriage, that mother and daughter chanced to "look at each other," both awed by the moment of mutual recognition. "These two faces," Lindo Jong concludes, "[are] so much the same! The same happiness, the same sadness, the same good fortune, the same faults" (256).

Using the mixed language of blood and kinship, superstition and tradition, these chapters attractively express the pedagogical authority of the mother and transform the daughterly articulation of maternal silence into a powerful maternal determination of daughterly identity (Hirsch 1989: 15–16).[5] But strikingly, the maternal lessons are all derived from a pre-immigration and pre-American era. As faithful daughters of China, the mothers may mature and age in America, but their minds and memories are forever mummified in their ancestral land. Unlike *The Woman Warrior*, which engages in an uneasy negotiation between a mother and daughter who share a U.S. history, *The Joy Luck Club* is the narrative of a one-way passage of irrefutable generational destiny. It is predictable that the artificial conflict between generations will find its natural resolution in the genetic fusion of geocultural gaps and historical discrepancies.

In the final chapter, Amy Tan indeed reverses the novel's opening image of the swan stretching its neck toward America by sending Jing-mei, its narrator, back to China. Although the body of *The Joy Luck Club* repeatedly emphasizes Jing-mei's ignorance about her mother's past, an entirely different scenario unfolds some two hundred pages later. The repressed maternal murmur surfaces to reclaim Jing-mei's body and soul: "The minute our train leaves the Hong Kong border and enters Shenzhen, China, I feel different. I can feel the skin on my forehead tingling, my blood rushing through a new course, my bones aching with a familiar old pain. . . . I am becoming Chinese" (267). What might be her mother's longing for her birthplace is now Jing-mei's natural emotional inheritance, and where this psychological transfer occurs is also of great importance. Jing-mei's becoming Chinese happens within minutes of departing Hong Kong for mainland China. Faithful to the geopolitical borders of the sovereign and colonial China, and more so to the conceptual and symbolic boundaries of East and West, Tan does not consider the then British colony of Hong Kong to be the true China. The miracle island of capitalistic and technological savvy is a principally Western conservatory of Chinese impurity, while the People's Republic is the real good earth of ancient tradition and magical wisdom. It is in the authentic China that Jing-mei is finally home: "'Some day you will see,' said my mother. 'It [Chinese-ness] is in your blood, waiting to be let go.' And when she said this, I saw myself transforming like a werewolf, a mutant tag of DNA suddenly triggered, replicating itself insidiously into a *syndrome*, a cluster of telltale Chinese behaviors" (267).

By the time Jing-mei reaches Shanghai and embraces her newfound half-sisters, her mother's prophecy has come true. "And now I also see what part of me is Chinese," she enthuses, sounding like her mother (267). And later, "It is my family. It is in our blood. After all these years, it can finally be let go" (288). As the Polaroid picture of the three sisters develops, as their image sharpens and deepens, Jing-mei sums up the feeling for all: "Although we don't speak, I know we all see it. Together we look like our mother. Her same eyes, her same mouth, open in surprise to see, at last, her long-cherished wish" (288). With identical visage, identical feelings, and identical attachment to the land of origin, the mother-daughter discord eventually evaporates without a trace of historical justification. China is not only the origin of Suyuan's immigration; it is also, by Amy Tan's reckoning, both the genetic locus of Jing-mei's affective ease and the narrative climax of her symbolic repatriation. The return of the Asian American native to her Asian geopolitical origin is complete.[6]

This chromosomal cohesion of generations, though hinting at the repression of ethnicity, naturalizes both the voluntary removal of Asian Americans from the United States and the essential purity of its European American construction. The genetic integration of the mother and daughter promulgates the filiality of the family and the descent base of the nation, leaving troubling implications for both feminist and multiculturalist reconstructions. Since a plot based on genes is a plot of irreversible lineage, the native-born Asian American women cannot but inherit the inclinations of their immigrant progenitors. Since a plot based on genes is also about ancestral origin, it demands a geocultural allegiance unaffected by personal experience, political history, or place of residence. And since Asian American women are differentiated by both their genetic heritage and their geocultural immutability, the struggle of many sisters against a single father on the familial stage, to echo Michie, is not viable, as the Asian American place in the family of U.S. women itself becomes questionable. Although Asian American women exemplify the kind of mother-daughter tension all women share, Tan appears to say, they actually prefer a separate womanhood. The kind of Asian-American-turned-obedient-Asian-female subjectivity in the course of *The Joy Luck Club* thus proves felicitous in dissolving the contradiction between the universal and the particular. A transracial American gender solidarity is finally accomplished upon the withdrawal of Asian American women and their displacement onto an Other nation.

Such voluntary national leave-taking is, not paradoxically, Amy Tan's simultaneous partaking of historical Anglo-American nationalism and orientalism wherein the legitimacy of Asian American membership is always suspect. Her genealogical construction of kinship is also attuned to the 1980s discourse of family values, a neoconservative legacy that the center too has come to embrace (Stacey 1994: 55). In her reading of Eric Hobsbawm, Angelika Bammer has tried to convince us that in the era of the "'post'..., the nation ... is no longer the guarantor of social coherence or cultural authority, [as] ethnicity steps into the breach to provide a new identificatory locus." The "family, in the more literal (domestic) or community/clan sense," should, in her view, become the nation's alternative (94). Amy Tan's affirmation of the private nature of Asian Americans as both filial and parochial is synchronous with this premature definition of a nation's obsolescence. By accentuating the natural and perpetual forms of allegiance and feelings of affinity, *The Joy Luck Club* miraculously merges the neoconservative rhetoric of "tribalism" (M. Baker 1981) with poststructural and multicultural celebrations of diasporic subjectivity that overlook the interconnection of race and nation. Moreover, it has revived the Asian American literary desire to return to Asia.

II

Amy Tan's appeal to the Asian maternal mystique is echoed in spirit by Frank Chin's proposal of a pan-Asian consciousness in *The Big Aiiieeeee!* (Chin et al. 1991). In his opening essay, Chin poses two overarching questions for the anthology:

> What if all the whites were to vanish from the American hemisphere, right now? No more whites to push us around, or to be afraid of, or to try to impress, or to prove ourselves to. What do we Asian Americans, Chinese Americans, Japanese Americans, Indo-Chinese, and Korean Americans have to hold us together? What is Asian America? (2)

The questions mark a radical change in Chin's programmatic emphasis. Whereas *Aiiieeeee!*'s edge comes from a determined repudiation of what Asian Americans are not, *The Big Aiiieeeee!* tries to substantiate what they are. If the 1970s Chin repudiates the orientalist conflation of Asian American geocultural belonging by vehemently arguing for a nation- and nativity-bound sensibility, the 1990s Chin seems to disregard both the nation-state as an instrument of white supremacy and the generational discrepancy of Asian Americans. In posing the rhetorical question of what holds Asian Americans together, Chin brings the Asian diaspora together under a shared cultural rubric, paving a common ground between diverse groups through the recognition of their essential similarities. The question of what holds them together also anticipates Chin's proposed communal adhesive, the "heroic tradition" of Asian folklore, which, in his view, always binds the soul of the race. Reversing an earlier position that Asian culture and history do not inform his experience (Chin 1972b), Chin returns to Asia with a vengeance.

But Asia is already a congested symbolic universe. Not only is there a whole orientalist tradition; there are also more recent Asian American representations that garner enormous attention. If Maxine Hong Kingston's magical realistic performance of Asian folklore opens the door, Amy Tan's further popularization almost makes it a distinctive Asian American form.[7] To explain his "heroic tradition," Chin again has to say what it is not. Not surprisingly, *The Big Aiiieeeee!* is conceived in bellicose terms—it is a battle of "the real" against "the fake," of authentic texts against counterfeit works. The "real" combats the "fake" on two fronts: the white orientalist tradition on the one hand, and its yellow "ventriloqui[sts]" on the other (Chin et al. 1991: xi).[8] Unlike *Aiiieeeee!*, whose most formidable foe was white racism, *The Big Aiiieeeee!*'s confrontational edge is thrust upon Asian American converts published by major presses to perpetuate the orientalist vision (8). The "real" of the Asian folklore and the "we" of Chin's proposed Asian American solidarity are thus not equivalents; the war of "the real" against "the fake," rather, is a struggle both for the control of Asian popular culture texts as an artistic agency and Asia as an Asian American symbolic reserve on the multicultural American marketplace.[9]

Chin's entry into the established terrain of the Asian imaginary comes from his contestation of Kingston and Tan's appeal to oral tradition. Rejecting their inventive myth-making justified by poststructuralist notions of orality and discontinuity, Chin argues that "myths are, by nature, immutable and unchanging, because they are deeply ingrained in the cultural memory" (ibid.: 29). The heroic tradition is to Chin traceable, continual, and written, from its sources in texts of antiquity to popular dynastic novels, further onto Chinese American phrase books, tong bylaws, and his authorized contemporary literary endeavors. Departing from *Aiiieeeee!*'s initial claim that Chinese and Japanese Americans, "American born or raised, who got their China and Japan from the radio, off the silver screen, from television, out of comic books, from the pushers of white American culture"(Chin et al. [1974] 1983: vii), *The Big Aiiieeeee!* asserts the existence of a "most fully grown Chinese subconscious." Through its own means of distribution, Chin maintains, "the Chinese people—in the Chinese marketplaces, toys, comic books, popular household curio shop and restaurant art and design—have already set the canon, kept it, taught it, and used it" (Chin et al. 1991: 33–34). Chin argues that *Three Kingdoms*, *Water Margin*, and *The Monkey* are not only familiar tales of the Chinese, surviving "the Cultural Revolution and the theocracy of Indonesia," but find their reincarnations in the Japanese evolution of *Momotaro* and *Chusingura*. In short, the heroic tradition is the fountainhead of a Pan-Asian universal that constitutes its own unbroken pipeline across the Pacific Rim (33, 34, 36).

Although Frank Chin's program of Asian cultural cohesion rests on the assumption that whites are absent from the United States, his inquiry into what holds Asians together indicates the undeniable existence of a white dominant cultural pressure. The proposal of a unique and universal Asian subconscious is clearly Chin's take on Jung's formulation of civilization and Herder's program of romantic nationalism, but his attempt to maintain a distinctive Asian cultural space is also appropriately "negritudinal."[10] Not only does the program of the Asian "real" share with the "Negritude movement" the objective of fashioning a new mode of thought against European colonialism, it also employs a strategy of reversal and performs its game of opposites so that the colonized can assume control of their own definition and destiny.

"The differences between Western and Asian civilization are real, sharply defined, profound," Chin argues, yet "easily stated: Western civilization is founded on religion" while "Asian civilization—Confuciandom—is founded on history" (Chin et al. 1991: 34). Chin's assertion is almost a point-by-point answer to Hegel's *Philosophy of History*, which divines the binary division of an East without "conscience," "individual morality," and a West "whose fear of the Lord is the beginning of wisdom" and "philosophical knowledge" (10). Though Chin has chosen not to delve into the reasons why a religious civilization is less desirable than a historical one, as he did in an earlier version of the essay, he has nonetheless highlighted the model of "the perfect Confucian individual" as "a self-sufficient soldier" (4).[11]

Employing an innovative etymological reading of the Chinese first-person pronoun that for him establishes the Asian "character" both in shape and substance, Chin points out:[12]

> Unlike the personal pronoun *I* in the languages of the West, the Chinese *I*, me, and we do not descend from the mysterious syllables *Yahweh* and do not mean "praise God." The Chinese *I* is not an act of submission to a higher authority but an assertion of the Confucian ethic of private revenge. . . . The ancient form of the character looks like a coat of arms. Like every coat of arms, the Chinese *I* means "I am the law." This is the first person pronoun of the language of "life is war, and we are all born soldiers." (Ibid.: 38)

The contrast between a religious and a historical civilization is only apparent in the kinds of personality that each produces, according to Chin, and the unique linguistic signs are only evidence of the inherently submissive character of the former and the self-sufficient character of the latter. These essential differences, he contends, are also embodied in the specific literary forms and expressed in the distinctive means of transmission that the respective civilizations adopt. While the religious individual of the West "trains himself to better express faith . . . to overcome reality with dreams, and to defy the effects of knowledge with belief," the "individual in the Asian moral universe trains himself to fight" (35):

> The Western believer sums up his life in the form that expresses the religious content of the civilization, the autobiography, a combination of confession and testimony that follows the rise, fall, and redemption of the heroes of religious literature and its literary form, tragedy. . . .
> The [Asian] fighter expresses his wisdom and essence in a set. One learns tai chi, kung fu, and martial arts by memorizing a set of poses, stances, and movement in a specific order and rhythm. . . . In the advanced stages of recital, one begins to free-associate with the moves and poses of the set. . . . The way Chinese learn martial arts is the way Chinese learn everything: memorization, recitation, and internalization. (35–36)

Chin's martial conception of the Asian subject, from the telltale signs of the ideographic character to the idiosyncratic way of learning, flips the coin of orientalism. Refuting the perpetual passivity and compulsory collectivity of the Asian, Chin installs a prototype Asian of individualist Confucian "ethic of private revenge" and "popular revenge against the corrupt state," who appears more aggressive and heroic than the Caucasian (35). The reversal has at least two sweeping effects. First, in light of the resurrected Asian tradition, Chin sees the U.S. Declaration of Independence against the tyranny of British monarchy as no more than "Thomas Jefferson's paraphrasing of the Confucian mandate of heaven" (40).[13] Chin thus "re-Orients" the genealogy of American democracy and reverses the origin and imitation, master and disciple relation in the national gradation of rights. Second, by valorizing a learning style of Asian exclusivity, Chin recodes the received value of Eastern and Western cultural assets and replaces the dominant cultural icons with new Asian heroes in hope that Asian Americans will be empowered to explain their origin and continuity and to identify themselves with the United States seamlessly (35, 39).

Frank Chin's negritudinal affirmation of an absolute Asian humanity thus bears the mark of what Sartre calls, in characterizing Aimé Césaire and Léopold Senghor's negation of colonialism, the "anti-racist racism," and what V. Y. Mudimbe calls the "panacea of otherness" (Mudimbe 1988: 85). "A Jew, a white among white men, can deny that he is a Jew, can declare himself a man among men," Sartre writes, while "the Negro cannot deny that he is Negro nor claim for himself this abstract uncolored humanity." Given the peculiarity of his condition, the Negro will have to "vindicate his negritude," Sartre resumes, as though responding to DuBois's call to end the double consciousness of African Americans, "in a revolutionary movement [that] places himself, then and there, upon the terrain of Reflection, whether he wishes to rediscover in himself certain objective traits growing out of African civilization, or hopes to find the black Essence in the well of his soul" (quoted in Mudimbe 1988: 84). This negritudinal essence is for Fanon an empowering negativity against colonialism, which entails economic and political dependence and subjective self-victimization of the dominated. It also provides intellectual and emotional opposition to the ideology of white superiority. For Senghor, negritude is the warmth of being, living, and participating in a natural, precolonial African spiritual harmony as well as the self-fulfillment of depersonalized Africans in the postcolonial recovery (see Mudimbe 1988: 92–93).

The criticism of negritude as a philosophy and social movement is an appropriate context in which to discuss Chin's kindred maneuvers in *The Big Aiiieeeee!* Not only do Chin's Asian Americans share with colonial Africans a history of domination and dehumanization, but Chin, like Senghor before him, could also appear to entertain "perspective proper to certain racist theoreticians" (94). Senghor's "Negro emotion confronting hellenistic reason; intuitive Negro reasoning through participation facing European analytical thinking through utilization" have in Chin's hands turned into Asian heroic individualism versus European Christian submission, Asian recitation to free association counterposed against Western creative thinking. Such binary polarities can easily be accused of promoting, in Mudimbe's words, "a detestable model for a division of vocations between Africa and Europe," to which we can now add between "Asia and America" (94).[14] But the poststructuralist critique of essentialism, of which Chin's negritudinal practice is an undoubted specimen, can often miss the point. "Those progressive white intellectuals who are particularly critical of 'essentialist' notions of identity," writes bell hooks, "have not focused their critiques on white identity and the way essentialism informs representations of whiteness."[15] And those progressive ethnic intellectuals who are eager not to reproduce the paradigm of oppression can often miss the picture that in the terrain of theoretical contemplation "it is always the non-white who is guilty of essentialism" (hooks 1992: 30). The observation of these two essentialisms is not to exempt either from critique but to hold both to an equal standard. The abstraction to the universal of the Anglo-Saxon particular, the securing of white dominance by the concealment of its specific racial signifier, must be addressed as the framing condition to which ethnic nationalism—or what I prefer to call the "alter-essentialism of the minor"—responds.

Before moving toward a more historically anchored critique, we can approach Chin's negritudinal maneuvers via Kwame Anthony Appiah's helpful distinctions among "racisms." For Appiah, racisms not only presuppose a racial essence but use it to different ends—it is at the level of executing the interpretations of such essence that the incongruities between what he calls "extrinsic racism" and "intrinsic racism" emerge:

> Extrinsic racists make moral distinctions between members of different races because they believe that the racial essence entails certain morally relevant qualities. The basis for extrinsic racists' discrimination between people is their belief that members of different races differ in respects that *warrant* the different treatment. . . .
>
> Intrinsic racists . . . differentiate morally between members of different races because they believe that each race has a different moral status, quite independent of the moral characteristics entailed by its racial essence. Just as, for example, many people assume that the fact that they are biologically related to another person gives a moral interest in that person, so an intrinsic racist holds that the bare fact of being the same race is a reason for preferring one person to another. (Appiah 1990b: 5–6)

Although Appiah leaves no illusion that both racisms suffer from a "cognitive incapacity" and a "distorted rationality" (8), he notes that "those who have used race as the basis for oppression and hatred appealed to *extrinsic* racist ideas" (e.g., Nazi racism and South African racism under apartheid), while "the discourse of racial solidarity" (e.g., the Black nationalism of the 1960s, Pan-Africanism, and Zionism) "is usually expressed through the language of *intrinsic* racism" that does not "contemplate using race as a basis for inflicting harm" (10–11). Chin's alter-essentialism of a unique Asian psyche and epistemology clearly belongs to the intrinsic variety, which both accepts the racialism orientalism presupposes and reacts to the racism it has inflicted institutionally.[16] This form of antiracist racism in answer to what binds Asian Americans and constitutes their solidarity is theoretically enabling, given that its practice is "strategic," to borrow Spivak's term, and its nature "synthetic," to echo Sartre. As long as it situates itself on the historic continuum of dominant racism and is considered both an antithesis to the original thesis of European racism and a stage in the ultimate transcendence of racisms, it remains provisionally useful.[17]

III

Chin's alter-essentialism counters the Anglo-American formation of the United States with an Asian difference, but his appeal to ontological purity only rhetorically inverts the terms without necessarily decoupling the artificial integrity of race and nation. Despite its promise of psychosocial warmth of feeling, the employment of "heroic tradition" tends to substitute folkloric patterns for historical measures. To illustrate the "immutable" civilizational consciousness, for example, Chin turns to the bylaws of the "Lung Kong Tin Yee Association of U.S.A.," which explicitly evoke the fraternity oath in *The Romance of the Three Kingdoms* (Chin et al. 1991: 30–33). Rather than treating the association's use of fictional genealogy as a strategic means of forming collectivity and intervening in the dominant white culture, Chin has turned it into an expression of "the Chinese subconscious" (33). The genealogy of the original immigrant families and the memory of the collective unconscious liberally mingle, as divergent historical responses are totalized in a timeless "Confucian mandate" of "kingdoms rising and falling" (35). In this residually feudal and perpetually cyclic version, history ceases to be a force of erratic transformation and uneven contestations—it becomes the glorious acts of kings and admirals, of noble ancestry and impeccable filiality. Although the Chinian "common" responds to both the post-1965 Asian professional immigration and the consolidation of a native Asian American constituency under transnational capital and domestic policy change, it harks back to the period before 1965. The successions of Cantonese Chinese American immigrants and their descendants, along with some issei and nisei, are deliberately "pilgrimized" in ways that are sanctified by the Puritan origins of America, to unify an Asian American past and reproduce an Asian American present.

Such an absolutist and genealogical conception of Asian American culture begins to "register," as Paul Gilroy has remarked on the variant modes of pan-Africanism, "incomprehending disappointment with the actual cultural choices and the patterns of the mass." A form of "intellectual vanguardism" emerges to compel the community toward the "real" track and the "authentic" origin, the recovery of both an evasive essential nature and its "overintegrated culture" (Gilroy 1993: 31–32). The privileging of an invariant Asian universal thus risks standardizing the different patterns of Asian American immigration, settlement, assimilation, and resistance, subordinating the multiple determinants of gender, generation, region, nationality, language, dialect, and class under racial consciousness, and finally precluding any hybrid cultural alternatives. It can also elide cultural difference into a form of "otherness" that may readily coincide with the neoracist shift toward the naturalization of tribalism. The call for the spiritual essence of a people, moreover, places undue pressure on Asian Americans to tap their inner resources so whatever difficulties they encounter can be resolved individually, at the level of consciousness rather than through group social intervention.

Although Frank Chin wants to appropriate Asian tradition for the construction of an enabling Asian American identity, his evocation of the Asian subliminal is quite similar to Amy Tan's appeal to the chromosomal trope of cultural reproduction. Sworn enemies can be strange bedfellows, it seems, as Chin's racialization of Asian American character and Tan's spatialization of Asian American geocultural belonging both concur with the orientalist divide of the East and West. In their attempts to cultivate a distinctive Asian American folk form, both have steered away from the messiness of historical ebb and flow and succumbed to the dominant culturalist interpretation of individual character that the ethnic nationalists in the 1970s rejected. While Amy Tan understands, Frank Chin appears oblivious to the fact that Asian folklores and myths are deemed acceptable simply because of their temporal association with the past and their spatial connotation of distant, foreign terrains.[18] Together, Tan's metaphor of generational destiny as descending stairs and Chin's figure of the unbroken civilizational pipeline into the Asian American identity constitute a significant literary revival of Asia-centrism, contemporaneous with both the neo-Confucian revision of capitalism and the Western discursive revamping of the Pacific Rim.[19] But a form of descent determinism seems to mar both their endeavors.

Not only is their appeal to blood heritage and ancestral subconscious regressively feudal and antidemocratic; more important, it mystifies the very process of cultural reproduction and brings Asian American subjectivity to a historical standstill. Both Chin and Tan's Asia-centric maneuvers turn a blind eye to the transformations in Asia since the mid-nineteenth century, during which indigenous cultures had to grapple with the upheavals of Western colonialism, Communist revolution, capitalist modernity, and wars.[20] Both seem also willfully indifferent to the fluctuation of Asian meaning in the dissemination of the dominant American culture. Chin's ritualistically reconstructed Asian tradition risks profound incomprehension not only by recent immigrants of non-Cantonese origin but also by those who grew up with native traditions that were different from those of their parents and ancestors.[21] Tradition's relevance to the native-born generations close to Chin's own, who either actively or involuntarily refused contamination by things Asian, may be even more dubious. Consequently, the "popular" cultural forms that Chin himself has studied as an adult and hopes to revive for the present generation of Asian American children and college students will appear "esoteric" to them as well. One contemporary college student captures the sentiment succinctly with the title, "Daddy, I Don't Know What You're Talking" (Cho 1993).

Frank Chin and Amy Tan's orientation of Asian American literature toward ancestral traditions finally demands an examination of the material mediations of culture, of how symbolic Asia is registered and through what channels its significance is reproduced. To address these issues of ethnic cultural reproduction is to move beyond the models of hermit heritage and genetic regeneration implicit in both authors' works. It requires a return to the uneven relations of ethnicity and nation in which Asian American identity emerges, and it demands a fresh look at the ways that symbolic Asia compounds the issues of social geography and human subjectivity.

Eccentric Homes:
Topography, Pedagogy,
and Memory

T he romantic embodiment of Asia in genes and consciousness is revised in a host of works that willingly or unwittingly tie the production of the cultural symbolic and communal identity to the determination of place and history. David Mura's *Turning Japanese: Memoirs of a Sansei* (1991), Frank Chin's *Donald Duk* (1991), and Fae Myenne Ng's *Bone* (1993) are all concerned with the draw of a cultural Asia at a time when the Pacific Rim's place in the global economy is rising. But whether about transpacific travel to Japan, the ambivalent shuttling in and out of San Francisco's Chinatown, or even the mythologization of the ethnic enclave, these narratives invariably engage the feelings of home and belonging not only in the present but also throughout the long processes through which subjective identifications with the geocultural space are formed. Questions of Asian American affiliation and allegiance, these texts suggest, have much to do with how a cultural arbitrary asserts its authority over the individual and how it imprisons the subject's desire.[1] By turning to the dialectic tension between family and school, ethnic community and mainstream society, homeland and land of ancestry, where the struggle among cultural arbitraries is waged, Ng, Chin, and Mura not only show the intricate links between subjective and social spaces but participate as well in the heated debate over multicultural education in the United States.

I

Frank Chin's *Donald Duk* is as much about the transformation of its adolescent protagonist as it is about the irresistible transformative influence of Chinatown. The title character is a twelve-year-old boy, a resident of Chinatown and student in a private school, who seems to be endowed with all the blessings of a young life yet hates everything about himself—his name, his look, and his Chinese background. During the fifteen days of the Chinese New Year celebration, the span of the novel, Chin puts Donald through a cultural baptism that only Chinatown can offer. From Dad King Duk, he learns to shed his vulnerable "softie" walk and to practice Chinese folk tale psychology. With Uncle Duk, he repents for his selfish indulgence of flying his model plane alone and learns about the family enterprise. Cantonese opera teaches him restraint and discipline, while his incessant dreaming about folk heroes and railroad pioneers takes him on a mythological pilgrimage that eventually brings him out from the nadir of self-contempt to the zenith of self-confidence. With this inspiring tale, Chin clearly puts a creative spin on *The Big Aiiieeeee!*'s critical assumptions about "the Asian subconscious." He also tries to establish narratively an essential equivalence between the nature of an Asian American place and the nature of the Asian American people. In doing so, *Donald Duk* begins to at once transform the fictional topography of Chinatown, a generic convention of which Chin himself is very much a part, and to highlight the role of education in the reproduction of local and national identifications.

Like *The Big Aiiieeeee!*'s reversal of *Aiiieeeee!*'s rejection of cultural Asia, *Donald Duk*'s glorification of a thriving Chinatown contrasts starkly with the Chinatown of decay that inaugurated Chin's artistic career. In "Food for All His Dead," a 1962 publication that is in many ways a precursor to both *The Year of the Dragon* and *Donald Duk*, the protagonist, Johnny, has this to say about himself and his birthplace:

> Maybe I'm not Chinese, pa! Maybe I'm just a Chinese accident. . . . Pa, most of the people I don't like are Chinese. They even *laugh* with accents, Christ! . . . You know, nobody shoulda let me grow up and go to any school outside of Chinatown. . . . Here, in Chinatown, I'm undoubtedly the most

enlightened, the smartest fortune cookie ever baked to golden brown, but out there. . . . Here, I'm fine—and bored stiff. Out there—Oh, hell, what'm talking about" (see Hsu and Palubinskas 1976: 53, 58–59).

Johnny's exasperation is echoed almost verbatim by the protagonist of *The Woman Warrior*:

> It's your fault I talk weird. The only reason I flunked kindergarten was because you [Maxine's mother] couldn't teach me English, and you gave me zero IQ. I've brought my IQ up, though. . . . Do you know what the Teacher Ghosts say about me? They tell me I'm smart, and I can win scholarships. I can get into colleges. . . . I can make a living and take care of myself. (Kingston 1976: 234)

The resonant backtalking of Johnny and Maxine is not just Asian American adolescent rebellion against the parents but the teens' rejection both of the geoculture they represent and the physical space of home and community that they have been born into. The Chinatown of confinement and claustrophobia that Chin and Kingston capture already departs from its more affirmative representations in Jade Snow Wong's *Fifth Chinese Daughter* (1945) and Louis Chu's *Eat a Bowl of Tea* (1961). While obviously resigned to Chinatown's segregation and seclusion, Wong and Chu were confident of its power of cultural arbitration and eager to have its authenticity and authority recognized. But the postwar, postexclusion opening of social space, especially the desegregation of school for Asian American children, ironically dampens their confidence.

Pierre Bourdieu and Jean-Claude Passeron (1977) have instructed us on the mediating role of "pedagogical action" in reproducing economic inequities and class divisions. As a form of "symbolic violence" imposing "a cultural arbitrary by an arbitrary power," pedagogical action may be exerted by a "family-group" (family education) or "a system of agents explicitly mandated by an institution" ("institutionalized education") (5). Schools, as part of a larger symbolic institution and the site of enduring pedagogical work, function to discriminate between different family pedagogical actions by simultaneously validating the culture of the ruling classes while discrediting the cultures of other groups (28). Whereas children whose families share the dominant cultural capital (the school-sanctioned linguistic competences, manner of communication, and forms of knowledge) stand to benefit from its reproduction, those whose families have a tenuous relationship with it are at a disadvantage and made to recognize "the illegitimacy of their own cultural arbitrary" (40–41). Although the school does not directly and explicitly execute the interests of the dominant class, they argue, it tacitly and subtly reinforces them by both distributing the normality of the dominant culture and reproducing the existing social hierarchies.

Although Bourdieu and Passeron are principally interested in the role of education in the reproduction of class inequities in France, their observations are pertinent to our understanding of pedagogical action in the division of major and minor cultures and how it affects geocultural mobility. With the advantage of unprecedented access to the means of national cultural production, namely the public school, the post–World War II generation to which Johnny and Maxine belong can envision life outside their native ghetto. However, a public school system that teaches the virtues of a meritocracy, and a family upbringing that cannot deliver rewards even inside its own ghetto economy, cause discrepancies in the identitarian chain of self, family, and ethnic community.[2] Without understanding their privileged place in history, Johnny and Maxine abandon their allegiance to Chinatown and its culture of rationalizing self-sufficiency, which both Wong and Chu cultivated as a means of resistance and survival. Generational revolt is now expressed as a particular form of geocultural antagonism, an orientalist split between Asian tradition and American progress. Chinatown is described in terms of social death, Asian parents are depicted as unfeelingly oppressive and laughably ineffectual, and Asian American youngsters are celebrated for escaping from the prison of ethnicity. This prototype of Chinatown and Asian American adolescents is precisely what *Donald Duk* intends to rewrite. Very much to Frank Chin's credit, he now conceives the resurrection of an Asian American existential space as a necessary reclamation of its pedagogical authority. The production of place and personality is necessarily political and material in nature; it is also an effect and a function of social reproduction in general.

II

Donald Duk's unapologetic plot of conversion demands that the protagonist form a new relationship to the site of his tutelage and a new definition of his teacher. At least in these two respects, the novel marks a critical change of reference for its author. Chin clearly gives up his earlier thesis that because Chinatown is inimical to the adolescent's intellectual development, rebellion against parents is as necessary to his self-assertion as escape from the ghetto is to his independence of spirit. In its stead is the new Chinian persuasion that the resourcefulness of the adult figures and the richness of the Chinese culture should make any kid doubt the wisdom of deserting Chinatown. If the problems of Johnny and Maxine are in part attributable to their dismissal of their parents' advice in favor of their teacher's, Chin is bent on recuperating the pedagogical authority of the paternal, maternal, and avuncular figures his earlier teen characters vehemently disregarded.

Dad's lesson of the "mandate of heaven, *tien ming*,' thus overpowers the explanation of Mr. Meanright, the history teacher, that it "is why Chinese are cutesy chickendicks" (F. Chin 1991: 11).[3] And Uncle Duk's railroad book brings to light the image of the "great-great-grandfather" and his coworkers with their "sledgehammers and pickaxes" in hand that is absent from Donald's textbook (24). "I know how that private school you go to has pulled the guts out of you and turned you into some kind of engineer of hate for everything Chinese," remarked Uncle Duk, and he is determined to send his nephew on a trip of self-discovery (23).

By delegating pedagogical authority to Donald's parents and adult relatives instead of Mr. Meanright, Chin transfers the agency of knowledge legitimation from the school to the family, from the objective, the public, and the universal (colorless) to the subjective, the private, and the specific (colored). With this, he registers an important recognition of familial pedagogical action on the psychosocial formation of the Asian American subject. The ethnic family is the ideal site, Chin seems to suggest, for a durable "process of inculcation" to bring about "a *habitus*, the product of internalization of the principles of a cultural arbitrary capable of perpetuating itself after pedagogical action has ceased" (31). The realization of the incompatibility between the ethnic familial cultural arbitrary and the school-sanctioned one, and the realization of the school's power to delegitimate and discontinue the family's before the formation of an individual disposition, clearly motivate Chin's privileging of the parental pedagogical authority in *Donald Duk*.

Chin's transfer of the pedagogical authority is his attempt to prolong the earliest phase of a child's family upbringing and to produce conditions ideal for the conservation of inherited Asian traditions so that both the side effects of dominant pedagogical work and the historical course of Asian American assimilation can be reversed. In this manner, the narrative proposal addresses the child's internalization of dominant cultural values, the parents' complicity therein, and the resultant mutual disenchantment that has been a source of intergenerational alienation between Asian Americans since the rescission of exclusion and school segregation. Chin's intent is to change what is happening to present generations of Asian Americans and to radically reorient the life scripts of generations yet to come.

But the discursive conversion of the characters is at the same time a process of authorial self-education. The writers' conjuring of ancestral "ghosts," in other words, is as much to benefit their fictional creations as it is to compensate for their own earlier ethnic exorcisms. "Before we can leave our parents," Kingston writes in *The Woman Warrior*, "they stuff our heads like the suitcases which they jam-pack with home-made underwear." Yet, "to make my waking life American-normal," the narrator says, "I pushed the deformed into my dreams, which are in Chinese, the language of impossible stories" (Kingston 1976: 102). "Gathering the essential works of the universal Chinese and Japanese childhood *would have been* easier," write *The Big Aiiieeeee!* editors, "had we paid attention to the Cantonese operas and Kabuki we were taught, as youngsters, to exclude from our serious perception and memory.... It *would have been* easier had we not erased the stories the old folks, the busboys, the immigrants told to describe the shrines, the posters, and the knickknack porcelain and clay figures of animals, babies, and warriors" (xv; emphasis mine). That which was naturally transmitted and could be organically acquired was self-censored by the adolescent who, years later, returns to school/Chinatown, to begin the arduous but heroic journey of mental decolonization. It is a journey to turn "would" into "will," subjunctive into indicative, all in the spirit of King Duk's mandate, "History is war.... You got to keep history yourself or lose it forever" (123).

The unevenness of power between the warring parties of history, however, cannot be altered with a simple pronouncement of pedagogical authority's reversal, since the authority of a cultural arbitrary always derives its persuasiveness from its supposed value in an economic or symbolic market. Chin's grasp of this logic of exchange leads him, not by chance but with purpose, to a full-scale recoding of ethnic cultural capital. But to succeed in making the dominated ethnic culture equal in value to the dominant one, the site of Donald Duk's tutelage must be proven capable of cultural pay-off.

III

"Everyone loves looking down Chinatown main streets from the top of a Chinatown roof," says *Donald Duk's* narrator, inviting the reader to enjoy the bird's-eye view:

> Every day till Chinese New Year the crowds will get larger down there. At night they all seem to be bobbing at the bottom of a huge long pool of ice water. All their brightness, all their noise, all the rumble of their feet and the thumping of the automobile engines bounce up the faces of the three-story buildings on both sides of the street. Chinatown life lay against Donald Duk's cheek like a purring cat. He feels the purring in his teeth. He feels the purring in his toes. The giggling and the mumbling, snickering cars plod slowly one way only down Grant toward Broadway, and the milling crowd flows all the time like algae in a marsh through Chinatown steadily as a river. (15)

With the flow of traffic and the vibration of movement, Chin's Chinatown is the symbol of exuberant energy that sustains both the material and the spiritual life of the Chinese American community. From the "clatter of crab legs" at the market to the shoppers in their "best clothes" (30, 38), from the "well-tuned orchestra" of Dad's cooking to the "drums and gongs" of Cantonese opera (64, 153), Chinatown is garnished with a fairy-tale quality. As the place is punctuated with ritualistic celebrations, so do its people stand for traditional "Chinese" occupational and cultural practice: in addition to Dad the restaurateur, the opera singer uncle, the tai chi master, and the herbal doctor all suggest the integrity of the culture as well as the autonomy of Chinatown. Between Grant and Broadway, Stockton and Bush, amid the "water margins" of mainstream America, Chin would have us believe, lies the stronghold of a vigorous civilization, the replica of that fabled marshland of the outlaws in Chinese antiquity, not just alive but regenerative.[4]

The desire to unburden himself from the effects of a colonial education and the need for an enduring ethnic site of cultural reproduction led Chin to reconstruct Chinatown as an autonomous Asian American common place that stands indifferent to the external world and to its time. The narrative temporality of *Donald Duk* is both ritualistic and mythical. The fifteen days of Chinese New Year celebration "typifies" the happy life of Chinatown year round, as Chin becomes comfortable with the holiday conception of culture and community life.[5] The anger at the tourist's colonization of Chinatown's existential space, so characteristic of his earlier works, gives way to a narrative format of "heritage festival." Donald's school pal Arnold, a white boy with a genuine interest in Chinese culture, is invited for a fifteen-day sleepover so that he can educate the uncouth about Chinese customs: from *lay see* (luck money) to *ho see fot choy*, an oyster and vegetable casserole; from *bai sun* (ancestor worship) to the discovery of Soong Gong, the outlaw leader nicknamed "The Timely Rain" (34, 45, 65, 119). The rhythms of the New Year celebrations are then synchronized with Donald's dreams, in which railroad construction and visits from folklore heroes merge.[6]

In this way, the history of Cantonese Chinese American immigration is mythologized with popular cultural texts of Chinese antiquity to authorize a certain form of social experience and authenticate a certain location of culture as the Asian American norm. Although the narrator of *Donald Duk* recognizes the Southeast Asian making over of present-day Chinatown, he is not willing to forsake its Cantonese origin or to acknowledge its Cantonese departure (34, 42). The new immigrants from Vietnam, Laos, Cambodia, and Thailand are granted ethnic Chinese identity and regarded as such a force of cultural infusion that "Chinatown is jumping again" (41–42). When restaurant owners provide free rice for the poor, Chinatown becomes a symbol of an altruistic and just society where the descendants of nineteenth-century railroaders and the boat people of the twentieth century can live together in full cultural harmony and material prosperity.

As the agenda of the Asian subconscious replaces historical differences, Chin also narratively revises the white presence in Chinatown. If Ross in *The Year of the Dragon* is a hunter of oriental exotica, Arnold Azalea in *Donald Duk* is a welcome student of the rich ethnic pageantry. If Ross is the resented anthropological observer of Chinatown, Arnold seems a contemporary barbarian, a Marco Polo in the imperial Chinese court, to be impressed with unheard-of Chinese superiority in arts and technology, though in this case the arts are folklore and cooking.[7] Donald Duk and Arnold Azalea's search for Asian American contributions in U.S. history departs from Chin's earlier opposition to "people [who] are pushing 'interaction with the dominant group' as a criteria for children's books on yellows and badmouthing books that show Asian Americans socializing exclusively with their own" (1976: 29). It also idealizes an unmistakable yellow-white pairing that replaces the yellow-yellow and black-yellow male bonding in Chin's earlier corpus.

While the narrative arrangement represents Chin's confidence in the use-value of Asian culture beyond the citadel of Chinatown, it also provides a qualified vision of multiracial America. "Arnold can play Chinese, he can eat Chinese and go gah-gah over Chinese," remarks the novel's omniscient narrator at one time, "but no matter what, he is white. He can leave Chinatown. He can leave the Chinese. He can go home to hear the spaces between the trees and never come back" (47). In noting that Arnold and Donald indeed have very different relationships to Chinatown, the passage betrays a rare moment of sobriety amid an authorial enthusiasm for the Asian symbolic. As a white kid, Arnold can benefit from the wealth of Asian culture, but he can also choose to be indifferent. After all, he does not really need it to shuttle between spaces. As a yellow kid, however, Donald will have to exemplify Chineseness. Instead of questioning the whiteness that entitles Arnold his border-crossing privileges, Chin fixes Donald's yellowness to his birthplace. The passage thus presumes an integrity of race and social space and perhaps the desirability of its stability upon which the novel pivots. Since the issue of race is no longer a struggle for even social spaces but for the ability of different cultures to compete in a free market, the superiority of an enduring common Asian heritage will stand not only unaffected by the historical process but also capable of marshalling it.[8] Chin's faith in the amplitude of Chinese civilization finally leads him to a conceptualization of Chinatown almost identical to Jade Snow Wong's: her eschewal of the nation-state and confidence in self-reliant Asian culture is now Chin's as well.

One can argue in support of Chin's invention of Chinatown as a measure against the corrosive effects of the dominant pedagogical work, which denies, in the phrase of Cornel West, "the intelligence, ability, beauty, and character of people of colour" (1993: 214). One should also credit his endeavor to arrest the impact of the dominant symbolic violence and to nurture an Asian American habitus. However, in making Chinatown the sole symbolic structure of Asian American living, Chin confirms the preexisting boundaries of ethnic enclaves and mainstream societies. Since any topographical exercise makes visible social formations at large, the designation of Chinatown proper for proper Asian Americans helps cultivate a mentality that unwittingly rationalizes keeping one's place. Despite its pedagogical inspiration and civilizational vision, one has every reason to hesitate about transforming such a discursive Asian American "non-topos" into an actual social space.

IV

Fae Ng's *Bone* crosses Frank Chin's path with deliberate difference, rewriting his San Francisco Chinatown and returning to the haunting issue of topography and memory. The novel is an interwoven story of two generations of a Chinatown family, but the narrative register sides neither with the edifying influences of the adult nor with the emancipatory gestures of the adolescent, while always shifting between the two adult generations, suggesting the reluctant fusion of some drab fate with the individual's intent to escape it. In contrast to Chin's celebratory Chinatown space is Ng's claustrophobic terrain: the death of Ona, the middle daughter, with her suicidal dive from the housing project; the departure of Nina, the youngest, who lands a job as a flight attendant, materially and metaphorically transcending her familial woes; the detainment of Mah and Leon, struggling with a marriage of complicated love and ready resentment; and the dilemma of Leila, the eldest and the narrative conscience of *Bone*, who has to carve out her own living while wishing she could make her parents' life better. Although the story is told from a first-person perspective, the interlocking yet distinctive destinies of Ng's characters defy a singular Chinatown topography and deny the possibility of its totalizing history.

A walk in a Chinatown street is to see "drift-abouts, Spitters. Sitters. Flea men in the Square" (13).[9] A visit to the home of the immigrant students is to learn that "both parents work. Swing shift. Graveyard. Seamstress. Dishwasher. Janitor. Waiter. One job bleeds into another" (16). The "cramped apartments, . . . rolled-up blankets, . . . cardboard boxes everywhere" are depressing reminders of "bare lives" to Leila, the daughter of immigrant parents of the 1940s, that "nothing's changed about making a life or raising kids" in 1990s Chinatown (17). There is no evidence of Chinian folkloric consciousness to pull the people up from the ghetto. Neither is there any panoramic shot of Chinatown's bubbling motion from the rooftop. Conscious of the ethnographic looking glass that often distances and objectifies the observed, Ng directs her reader not to the tourists' "slow view . . . from inside those dark Greyhound buses" but to the sobering reality of persistent poverty, untouched either by the progress of time or the exercise of will to power (144–45).

For Ng, Chinatown is not a mythologized space punctuated with happy rituals but a place of hardship, a reminder of endless worries and the perpetual rhythms of work. When Leila and Nina eat out, Chinatown is to be avoided at all cost. "The food's good" there, both agree, but "at Chinatown places, you can only talk about the bare issues. In American restaurants, the atmosphere helps me forget" (26). Even the Chinese New Year ceremonies that center Chin's holiday conception of culture are for Fae Ng signs of loss and pain: "Wong Moo taught us [when we were kids] an old village chant, a counting rhyme that matched ten living things to the first ten days of the New Year . . . [so that] all life was celebrated. . . . Now, I counted up to today. The day of Thieves. Someone stole Ona. Ona hadn't wanted to go" (121).

Resisting the temptation of the spectacle and abandoning the simplicity of ethnic enlightenment, Fae Ng plunges into the unshaped and undigested Chinatown life that screams for the solidity of reason and the necessity of expressive form. The result is a well-wrought narrative that is unflinchingly realistic and intensely moving. Leon's constant shipping out on a merchant vessel and the perpetual motion of Mah's sewing machine form the basic rhythm of Chinatown family life; husband and wife often worlds apart, maintaining a marriage with "a long view, which was endurance, and a long heart, which was hope" that somehow their children's future will be brighter (176). The integrity of the family is a precarious preservation of faith and perseverance against physical absence and spatial separation, all driven by the necessity of economic survival. Neither Amy Tan's notion of genetic ties nor Frank Chin's concept of cultural pipeline can make sense of Fae Ng's faith in the affiliative nature of human relationships—"it is time that makes a family," Leila recalls Leon saying, "not just blood" (3). However, when time is always "overtime" for economic subsistence, when "life was work and death the dream," the narrator of *Bone* cannot but wonder in what space the marriage of Leon and Mah exists, and what emotional sustenance they can possibly draw from it (181).[10]

Ona's inexplicable death only furthers Leon and Mah's doubt about the meaning of their marriage, collapses their faith in the next generation's capacity to transcend misery, and triggers the unrelenting guilt trip and blame game that constitute the core of *Bone*'s circular narrative. By refusing to ascertain Ona's motive, Ng honors the character's personal choice and at the same time locates her suicide in a chain of tragic loss and numbing sorrow that are inextricably familial, circumstantial, and historical.[11] For Leon, Ona's death is karmic punishment for his failure to send Grandpa Leong's bone back to China. For Mah, it is punishment for her brief affair with Tommie. For the reader, however, the causes of their misfortune are never singularly definable yet always relatable to official histories and their lingering consequences. "In this country," Leon remarks, "paper is more precious than blood" (9). A paper son himself, Leon's life story is a necessity of invention, part of an interventional oral tradition against the written documents of exclusion laws. He recited the records of the Leong family, impersonated the fourth son of a Sacramento farm worker, passed the interrogation on Angel Island, but never reached the promise of America. Mah's marriage to Leon, on the other hand, is a conjugal convenience to secure the latter's green card. The impersonal exclusion laws have such an effect on the very personal choices and destinies of Asian American relationships that, although they circumvented the laws, Leon and Mah are confined, both emotionally and socially, by the power of official paper. Fifty years after entering the country illegally, Leon is caught in the social security office: "the laws that excluded him," the narrator tells us, "now held him captive" (57). Leon had no proof of his years of service. Leila's search of his gold mountain suitcase, her sorting of the letters "stacked by year and rubberbanded into decades," reveal far more: "A rejection from the army: unfit. A job rejection: unskilled. An apartment: unavailable":

> My shoulders tightened and I thought about having a scotch. Leon had made up stories for us; so that we could laugh, so that we could understand the rejections.
> The army wanted him but the war ended. He had job skills and experience: welding, construction and electrical work, but no English.
> The apartment was the right size but the wrong neighborhood.
> Now, seeing the written reasons in a formal letter, the stories came back, without the humor, without hope. On paper, Leon was not a hero. (57–58)

The daughter's recognition of her father's social exclusion gives dignity to the indignities he has suffered and authenticates his experience as an inauthentic national. Not only is his personal plight linked with larger historical forces over which he has little control, but his social disadvantage and deprivation are also what his daughters are born into. Although all Leon's children have the benefit of attending public school, the presumed institutional equalizer of social inequities, they cannot but inherit the negative determinations of their parents' history.[12] The individual's actualization of herself must therefore entail a negotiation of histories that she did not choose and that are not her own.

Ng's use of history is remarkably different from Kingston's in *China Men* and Chin's in *Donald Duk*. While her predecessors employ epic to illuminate Asian American heroic accomplishments so that the progenitors can claim noble ancestry and rightful belonging, Ng is uncertain about the power of either affirmative historical reclamation or of absolute historical determination. The problem Fae Ng faces is one that minority and colonial subjects have to deal with all the time—that is, whether to reconstruct their history in a favorable light that elevates them in the eyes of others, or in a way that portrays them as victims. Rather than emulating Chin, who first wrote the latter version and then the former one, Ng provides readers with a sense of history as an ongoing mediation that is not marked by ritual celebrations or by dates on calendars.

Because of its author's ambivalence toward history, *Bone* is able to straddle the two extremes, thus sustaining the tension of meaningful dialogue. Leila comments at one point: "Family exists only because somebody has a story, and knowing that story connects us to history. To us, the deformed man is oddly compelling, the forgotten man is a good story, and a beautiful woman suffers" (36). With these recapitulations of the Leon family's life plots, Fae Ng envisions her characters' history as one that at once binds and burdens, that is worthy of committing to memory on the one hand and advantageous to leave behind on the other. The imperative of familial cohesion demands its repetition: "I [Leila] am the stepdaughter of a paper son and I've inherited this whole suitcase of lies. All of it is mine. All I have is those memories, and I want to remember them all" (61). At the same time, the individual instinct for survival begs that it be let go: "The blame. The pressing fear. I wanted a ritual that forgave. I wanted a ritual to forget" (54). It is in this incommensurable space of memory and oblivion that Fae Ng locates her Chinatown, a place that is neither the determinist's hell nor the romanticist's heaven, but a place "backdaire" that the Leon family calls home (194).

In keeping with the recurrent conversation of remembering and forgetting, Ng calls into question both the purist's pursuit of an integral and intact ethnic history and the assimilationist's rejection of the past, while making apparent a point rarely championed in minority literature, that to be obliged to forget is itself a way of imagining the possibilities.[13] Maybe memory works best when it forgets, when it rids itself of hostility and allows one to become. Leila's farewell to Chinatown is therefore not simply a poststructuralist escape to a world that transcends history and materiality, but a necessary leave-taking, another migration, another exile, compelled by circumstance and by choice:

The heart never travels.

I believe in holding still. I believe that the secrets we hold in our hearts are our anchors, that even the unspoken between us is a measure of our every promise to the living and the dead. And all our promises, like all our hopes, move us through life with the power of an ocean liner pushing through the sea. (193)[14]

V

At one point in *Bone*, Leila goes to the suburb of Redwood City with Mason, her mechanic fiancé, and their friends Diana and Zeke, to deliver a Mercedes he has fixed for his Aunt Lily. At her ranch house, next to "lollipop-colored lawn furniture" at the side of the pool, the gang of "hood" Chinese met their suburban counterpart, Mason's cousin Dale (44). As Mason handed over the keys to Dale, all the latter asked was "What do I owe you?" (43). Leila was prepared to accept Dale for who he was: a product of "an all-white school on the peninsula," a fourth-generation Chinese American who spoke no Chinese and sounded white, but she could not empathize with his attitude (43). "Money was out of the question," Leila realized when she saw Mason's "fuck-this-guy look. If money was a question, Dale should've taken it to a shop. Why'd he ask Mason? Dale had no clue. He didn't even know that Mason was doing him a family favor" (44). Mason agrees: "For a computer wiz, the guy's sure stupid." "No manners," says his friend Zeke. "No home education," echoes his friend Diana (45).

Leila and Mason's excursion to the suburb introduces the other sites of Asian American living that Chin omits from his topographic exercise. It is Fae Ng's way of interrogating Chin's artificial correspondence of race and the subconscious. While Chin's ethnocentric agenda necessitates his construction of an insular Chinatown with a unitary heritage and unitary memory, Ng intends to subvert the illusion of unity by engaging the diversity of the Asian American community. For the author of *Bone*, Asian Americans are not content hermits in autonomous ethnic zones; neither do they all live in the inner city. The encounter of the Chinatown folk and their non-Chinatown kinsmen is her way of showing not just the geographic dispersal of Asian Americans but also what such residential variance suggests about social positions and individual dispositions. Dale's mistake, Ng makes us aware, lies in his inability to conduct himself in a mode familiar to Mason. By offering to pay for Mason's labor, Dale immediately translates a family courtesy into a debt. In doing so, he cheapens the value of blood ties and also indicates his unwillingness to perform a similar favor based on kinship. In this, Dale unconsciously embodies both the naturalness of commodity exchange characteristic of "possessive individualism" and a form of dominant cultural arrogance that deeply offends Mason. Besides highlighting the Asian American class differences that Chin seems at pains to conceal, Ng wants to attribute the differences between Mason and Dale as much to social geography as to education. Mason's comment that Dale is stupid despite being a computer expert is interestingly modified by Diana's judgment about the latter's lack of "home education," the ethnic familial pedagogical work that precedes the inculcation of the dominant symbolic capital (45). Dale's ignorance about how to deal appropriately with his relatives is, in other words, the result of his physical absence from the site of socialization where Mason and Leila learned about necessary dependency and mutual assistance. The predominantly white school he later attended only completed the process of disconfirming the value of familial closeness and kinship bonding that his cousin embodies.

With Mason and Dale's conflict, Fae Ng draws our attention to the spatial dispersal of the Asian American population in our time and its social implications for the reproduction of Asian American culture and practice. The failure of communication between the cousins helps to illuminate both the tenuousness of blood that Amy Tan makes so prominent in *The Joy Luck Club* and the precariousness of cultural continuity that Frank Chin has refused to admit in *Donald Duk*. Unlike Tan and Chin, Ng does not want to rush into the comfort of inherent natures and coherent traditions that will eliminate the need to register class difference within a racially defined collectivity and displace the consideration of place in a socially uneven Asian American space. By highlighting Mason and Dale's different sensibilities, Ng reveals the gap between the urban and suburban in the inculcation of ethnic practice and shows the contradictory national spaces occupied by the same racial group. She thus enables the reader to appreciate the discrepancies in the Asian American habitus, the Bourdieuan amalgam of practices that links habit with inhabitancy (1977: 83), and to propose its mediation. In this, Chin's preoccupation with appropriate pedagogical sites is Ng's as well: their turn toward Chinatown seems a compelled artistic response to the crisis of an Asian American common place. Given the geosocial diffusion of the population, both authors seem to ask, where are we to find and how are we to imagine a social space capable of reaffirming and reproducing the ever-changing form of Asian American knowledge?

VI

David Mura's *Turning Japanese: Memoirs of a Sansei* (1991) provides its own unique answer to Chin and Ng's concern. For this third-generation Japanese American poet, the negotiation between subjective space and geocultural belonging takes place not in the intersections of ethnic ghetto and mainstream America but between a life "landlocked" to a Midwestern Jewish suburb, and a life reexamined while traveling as a resident writer in Japan, the ancestral homeland he learned about from war movies, cheap baseballs, and Godzilla (8–9). Having grown up in a Euro-American culture and with an acquired disaffection for Japan, the author shares Chin's preoccupation with the dominant pedagogical action and his desire to assuage its impacts. Mura's writing about his passage in and out of the experiential terrains of Asia and America resembles Ng's novel of generational mediation and geocultural translation. *Turning Japanese* is a book of profound individual psychosocial transformation, achieved through transnational travel. It is also an important conceptualization of diasporic subjectivity that throws Asia and America off center and off balance, while opening both to new standards.

The memoir posits the problem of individual identity as the problem of locating home early on. "The Japanese," Mura writes, "are highly conscious of their *kuni* [home]":

> The man who emigrated—my grandfather—carried within him the memory of home, the former world, the place where he was once "real." It tore at him, that memory, and yet kept him anchored: he knew where his home was, knew he had lost it. The son of that man—my father—believed he could make the new place his home. The task was probably impossible, but it kept him occupied. The son of that man—myself—realizes what? That the new home—in my case, a Jewish suburb—is no home; is in fact, for me an absurdity, a sham, and that the old home is lost in unreality. (Mura 1991: 32–33)[15]

If the grandfather is the sojourner assured of his lost abode who succeeds in returning to Japan, and the father the anxious ethnic who, despite the internment, is determined to make America "home," the son is the one who "suffer[s] from a lack of center, a fixed point to chart the stream" (32). The passage delineates the generational alternatives of repatriation, assimilation, and alienation, calling particular attention to Mura's own feelings of displacement. By disregarding Skokie as his home, the author rejects the choices of his progenitors and conceives his own problem as the failure of the nation to properly incorporate its colored native son. Against a Japan that he has no affiliation with and an America that refuses to acknowledge him, Mura felt that he "was constantly sinking into the foam of formlessness—What is my history, the stories of my family, the myths of my people?" (32).

An answer seems to come after a fourteen-hour plane ride. As he tumbled out into the terminal at Narita, Japan, Mura felt "exhausted and exhilarated," "frightened," and "astonished that all the faces at the customs looked like mine" (11). From this first impression, the writer began to question the trajectory of European imperialist travel, in which movement away from the *axis mundi* is always believed to correspond not only to supranatural distance but to increasing differences of places and people from the heart of culture (Helms 1988: 4). His identification with the local immediately unsettles the premises that undergird traditional anthropology, among them the West as the site of intellectual origin and the rest as sites of exploration, the unmarked Western self as the investigating subject and the native of primitive societies as the object of knowledge.

As a "heroic explorer, aesthetic interpreter," and a resident writer in Japan, Mura becomes an exception to the dominant meaning of "traveler," which, as James Clifford suggests, is always tangled with the history of "European, literary, male, bourgeois, scientific, heroic, recreational, meanings and practices" (1992: 106). As an occidental traveler/writer to the Orient of his ancestry, Mura both reverses the trajectory of issei labor in monopoly capital and registers symbolically the changing relation between nations in a multicentered universe of transnational culture and capital. The thrill of identification with the Japanese crowd at the terminal, besides foregrounding the condition of postcoloniality and the rise of the native elite, also foreshadows the predicament of Mura's "field work," so to speak, when the anthropological observer and the object of his observation look alike:

> Thousands of faces that look like mine . . . like my aunts, my mother, my brother, my cousin, my sister. . . . And I love it all, the sea of faces, the uncanny resemblances, the hints of foreign genes in the cheekbones . . . and yet the singular stamp of the Japanese in each face, and I feel a wave of happiness coming over me, a calm and combustive joy, a stamping of the feet in my soul, a smile and a voice that says, You are unnoticeable here, you have melded in, you can stand not uttering a word and be one of this crowd. (42)

The overwhelming comfort that comes with racial anonymity and acceptance might rush a less experienced writer into a premature embrace of absolute origins and pure roots, but Mura does not yield to this temptation. Though deeply affected by the sensation of inclusion, he refuses to pronounce Japan as the lost *kuni* regained, but approaches it instead as a site of defamiliarization, in order to question the received relations of race and place, national space, and individual consciousness across the Pacific Rim.

The generous accommodation of his body and visage in Japan thus throws into stark relief his periodic "eczema," a facial rash that has inflicted pain and embarrassment upon him since childhood. The irresistible desire to scratch, "this seeming desire to scrape my skin," the adult Mura concludes, "might somehow have been connected with what the world around us was telling me, silently, about race" (122). Although his arrival in Japan relieved his racial "stress" and instantly cured his socio-somatic dis-ease

(121), Mura makes evident that his achieved visual affinity and affective ease are significantly qualified by an imperative verbal silence; without the willing suspension of his American English, his psychosocial merging with the Japanese cannot be possible. By treating the autobiographic subject as a racial identical and cultural alien in Japan and a racial Other and cultural American in the United States, the book begins to fundamentally challenge the natural equivalence of race and culture in the formation of a national subject and provides a powerful prism through which to investigate Asian American subjectivity. It also measurably reconstitutes autobiographical and anthropological writing as a study both of "relations of dwelling" and of "relations of travel," making *Turning Japanese* a "multiply centered work of ethnographic cultural critique" (Clifford 1992: 99, 102–3).

VII

The relations of dwelling are indeed altered by relations of travel, as Mura recounts the changes in his marital relationship with Susie, a descendant of the *Mayflower* who was his college sweetheart and later became his wife. One day on a streetcorner in Japan, Mura writes, Susie suddenly requested a kiss. Declining to oblige on the spot, he recalled "how often in the past she had resisted public physical gestures" and relished the fact that "the tables had been turned" (23). The scene is Mura's way of connecting the private and the public, and his way of conceiving the affective as inevitably political. That Mura is usually the one who needs assurances of affection from Susie in the United States is revealing both of his ambivalent national membership and her authentic American citizenship. Likewise, Susie's involuntary acquisition in Japan of her own insecurity correlates the reversal of the couple's social/sexual practice with their changed national status, not legally but symbolically. Moving on from the initial shock of being in the visual majority, Mura begins to reflect on home and (be)longing in the intricate web of sex, romance, race, and nation space.

"For years, in the States," Mura recalls, "each beautiful white woman had seemed a mark of my exclusion. . . . As an Asian male, I was placed in a category of neutered sexuality, where beauty, power, and admiration were out of the question, where normalcy and acceptance were forbidden" (148, 149). The racial denial of national access is linked with the deprivation of power in sexual terms, as Mura meditates with confessional candor on the connection between his "sense of inferiority and rage" about "race and color" and his desperate assertions of misogynistic mastery (341, 68). Here, as in *Tripmaster Monkey* and *Jasmine*, the Asian and Caucasian relationship symbolizes at a more general level an affair of the Asian American subject with the nation, and Mura's erratic erotics with Susie are both a compensation of unrequited love for and a struggle of acceptance by the United States.

But the "heady encounter with the Japanese" produces such a "splintering confusion of [a] new sense of identity" that it tilts the apparent equilibrium of his romance and makes Mura feel as if he were "drifting from the certainties of [his] American life" (115). Although the vow between himself and Susie is never practically broken, Mura's interludes with two women, Gisela, a German painter, and Yuri, a Japanese poet, indicate the eccentric force Japan has on him. More than revealing the shifting measure of beauty and attraction, these episodes reflect Mura's thinking about the larger issues of conviction and doubt, faith and betrayal, not only in marriage but in national allegiance as well.

Mura met Gisela at a Butoh class. She smiled at him. He smiled back (130). Later, when Mura "banged on the metal door" of her apartment, we are told:

> It opened like an envelope. She was smiling, her face lit by the bulb on the balcony. She was beautiful as I remembered. . . . Her face seemed unattached to her body, hidden again beneath a dark, loose-flowing dress, like a woman in mourning. I entered, holding a folder of my poems awkwardly at my side like wilted flowers. . . . I told myself Gisela had asked to see my work. (143)

The meeting with Yuri started at a street corner and proceeded to a tempura restaurant:

> Across the boulevard, a Japanese woman strode straight towards me. . . . Her hair permed, her face small, oval . . . her lipstick bright coral. . . . Yuri had looked me straight in the eye and thrust out her hand in greeting. Her eyes and smile carried a wry, suspicious air. . . . Certain minority women in America have this toughness, this unwillingness to waste time with bullshit. Sometimes it's strength, sometimes bitterness, sometimes both. With Yuri I couldn't tell. (151–52)

While both are characterized as pleasant encounters, the kinesthetic imagery tells how the two meetings differed. The receptiveness of Gisela and the timidity of Mura shroud their encounter in an unmistakable romantic air, complete with "loose-flowing dress" and "wilted flowers." Yuri's speedy pace and no-nonsense smile and Mura's defensive reading of her gait and gesture, dispel any suspicion of intimacy. If Gisela's softness and femininity mark a difference that invites Mura's entry, Yuri's "masculine" strength speaks of a similarity between them that only compels his respect. Interestingly, Mura identifies Yuri, a Japanese woman who has lived in the United States, with the women of color there, who always register in his mind a worldly wariness and toughness, a style of efficiency and emotional economy that repel romantic playfulness and pleasure. Gisela, a Prussian German, on the contrary, is cast in the mode of European leisure and cultural superiority. While both women are Mura's intellectual equals, with similar tastes and interests in the arts and books, they are assigned different class status. Echoing the Jamesian international theme, Mura seems to admit his cultural yahooism next to Gisela's European sophistication despite their location in Japan, which occupies a prominent place in a multicentered global culture. (144–45). Yuri, on the other hand, represents a denial of Mura's high cultural transcendence, a gravity that pulls him back to earth, to his Japanese American experience, and the need to recognize it.

It is perhaps ironic that the subject of sexuality remains veiled in Mura's intercourse with Gisela but explicit with Yuri.[16] Mining the same territory of Asian American sexuality from different gender positions, Yuri and Mura use their verse to delve into the common pain of intraracial gender misconception, rage, and revulsion. Their conversation achieved "an easy camaraderie" and the "presence of a community" that were perhaps not possible between Mura and Gisela (153). Yet, as much as he sentimentalizes their visage "amid the flow of crowds" as "just another Japanese couple," and as much as he finds "Japanese women attractive," Mura nevertheless concludes that "I felt more like Yuri was sister, part of my family" (148, 155). His relationship with Gisela, however, is distinguished by "the intimacy of foreigners. . . . The sense of minds clicking into each other, the give and recognition of intelligence" (162). It is this conspiratorial delight that finally sets his Gisela affair apart from his spiritual fellowship with Yuri. Bewildered, Mura wondered "why I knew Yuri and I were going to be friends and nothing more. No complications, nothing like the way I felt with Gisela" (155).

While he does not seem willing to analytically engage his bewilderment here, the way Mura initially introduces his sex life through race and nation provides the key of understanding. Though a Japanese citizen, Yuri is not a messenger of Japan's mythic past or of its technological present. By emphasizing her work on the sansei and her affinity with ethnic American women, Mura generously includes this diasporic subject as part of multicultural U.S. politics and considers Yuri a family member, a sister in the racial community of political affiliation and opposition. Gisela's European aristocratic ease, on the contrary, implies the civilizational confidence of the West that still evades the Asian American Mura. If romance is a mode of psychological resistance to history, it must by necessity defy the mundane dailiness of social limits, however momentarily. Whereas contacts with Yuri suggest exchanges of disempowerment, Gisela represents for Mura both a transcendence of his material burdens and an enjoyment of power and pleasure. The potently sexual relation with Gisela and the unambiguously asexual liaison with Yuri thus reveals the tenacious hold of Western domination on the Asian American and the overall white monopoly of American national charisma. One only needs to note how differently two ice skating champions, the German Katarina Witt and the American Kristi Yamaguchi, are portrayed in U.S. advertising to realize Mura's profound complicity with the dominant coding of race and nationality.[17]

In light of this view, Yuri's inclusion as a sister, and Susie's final triumph as a marital partner over Gisela, the potential lover, may be seen as the author's choice between Asian American ethnicity and white American nationality. The asexual and sexual modes of liaison with the women indicate the opposite ways in which different communities are conceived. The acceptance of Yuri into the racial community of the Japanese American as a newfound sister, heavy with suggestions of kinship and blood ties, illuminates the essential political process of ethnic affiliation. The Asian American collectivity is fundamentally a solidarity, Mura appears to say, of political will and social organization. The affirmation of the marital vow with Susie through Mura's rejection of Gisela, on the other hand, suggests national wedlock via conjugal union. Though clearly limited by the experience of the author and the confines of the autobiography, the book's treatment of an Asian American subject's relationship with the nation remains both faithful to the nation's dominant definition as white and to the Asian American tradition of symbolizing individual and national integration with a white mate. Although miscegenation provides a healthy alternative to racial hybridization of the nation, ethnicity as a form of racial difference is not considered even a fictional viability capable of its own reproduction. In this scenario, the acquisition of Asian American national identity is not so much a voluntary contract with the nation as it is a sorry dependence on white spousal accommodation. Such a narration of the nation may devalue the appeal of Asian Americans for each other in familial and communal alliances, while unwittingly submitting the future of Asian American collectivity to what Leslie Fiedler has called, in the Jewish American context, "the silent Holocaust" (1991: vii).

VIII

Mura's loyalty to Susie is a symbolic pledge of allegiance to the United States after weighing his Japanese and German options. The achievment of a national commitment via interracial union, however, is balanced by the realization that an absolute white American identification is for Asian Americans both impossible and undesirable. Japan has convinced Mura that he could not possess and should not aspire to possess a European

American cultural assurance. Rather, he "had a much different, more way-ward and contradictory, story to tell" (76). Echoing the sentiment of Derek Walcott, a black West Indian poet, Mura imagines meeting T. S. Eliot and John Donne, and concludes that both "would have considered [Mura] ei-ther a curiosity or a savage; in any case, an unlikely candidate for a poet of the English language" (77).

Mura's imaginary encounter with Eliot and Donne revises Du Bois's famous rendezvous in *The Souls of Black Folk* using the icons of Western civilization:

> I sit with Shakespeare and he winces not. Across the color line I move arm in arm with Balzac and Dumas, where smiling men and welcoming women glide in gilded halls. From out of the caves of evening that swing between strong-limbed earth and the tracery of stars, I summon Aristotle and Aurelius and what soul I will, and they come all graciously with no scorn nor condescen-sion. So wed with Truth, I dwell above the veil. (Du Bois [1903] 1979: 76)

Rejecting Du Bois's romantic picture of liberal humanism and civilizational egalitarianism, Mura suspects that the chances of transcending race and lifting the veil are in his own historical time still remote. "My admiration for their [Eliot's and Donne's] work," he therefore argues, "would always be tinged with detachment, even anger, and a political awareness of my place in the world. Those who think this detachment and anger mean I want to dispose of Eliot or Donne distort my position out of fear and an unconscious desire to keep the tradition white and intact" (77). Unlike Du Bois, who prematurely announced the arrival of an equal cultural relation-ship between blacks and whites, Mura seems to suggest that the conversa-tion is yet to begin, and that to begin it in earnest one must dispel the illu-sion of an inherent white liberal hospitality to minority cultures. Demon-strating his familiarity with Western cultural legacy while rebelling against its refusal to incorporate ethnicity, Mura confirms the necessity, on the one hand, of a dialectical engagement between Eastern and Western cultures, and on the other hand, of transforming American canon's color and con-tour. "The trick, then," he writes, "was to learn to write out of my sense of duality, or rather, plurality . . . to listen to voices that my father, or T. S. Eliot or Robert Lowell, did not dream of. Voices of my family, of Japan, of my own wayward and unassimilated past" (77).

To execute this, Mura describes the scene at the American Club in Tokyo, a scene that recalls the Club Oriental scene in *No-No Boy*. Kenji, a dying G.I. and the narrative conscience of the torn Japanese American psy-che, likens Club Oriental to "home. . . . only more precious, because there are . . . not many places a Jap can go and feel so completely at ease" (133). Yet, while the club provides a haven from the racism of white society, its Chinese owner also curses the black customers, driving a disgusted Kenji out, wondering, "Was there no answer to the bigotry and meanness and smallness and ugliness of people?" (134).

> Maybe the answer is that there is no in. Maybe the whole damned country is pushing and shoving and screaming to get into someplace that doesn't exist, because they don't know that the outside could be the inside if only they would stop all this pushing and shoving and screaming. (160)

Though suspicious of his utopian impulse, Mura takes up Okada's enabling double vision of critique and empathy by resituating the in/out contradiction of Asian Americans in Tokyo's American Club.

Eating "scrambled eggs, eggs Benedict, slices of lamb, ham, bacon" are American families displaced by transnational capital yet resistant to the transformative influences of migration and travel. "The language . . . English, the atmosphere American, the viewpoint colonial," the American Club is an island within an island, recreating a false familiarity and superiority that only exacerbates Mura's alienation: A casual compliment from his countrywoman on his accentless English intensifies his identification with "the coat checker and the waiters" and accentuates his discomfort at being among the "white faces" of "privilege" who are wearing blinders (200–201). But the disaffection of the American abroad, of which he is but a different specimen, is less an expression of ethnocentric revolt than an eccentric critique of rampant jingoism across national boundaries. In the spirit of Kenji, who detests prejudice of any shape and color, Mura considers the American Club only an analogue to Japan, the country whose obsessive self-preoccupation rarely extends beyond its borders. This self-preoccupation, this racial superiority and nationalistic myopia, are directly responsible for the historical "atrocities that the Japanese have perpetrated in Asia," Mura concludes, and for the perpetuation of a public insensitivity to racism, sexism, and class oppression as well (201–2). With his deliberate juxtaposition of American and Japanese nationalistic practices against the transnational settings of critical examination, Mura achieves a healthy distance from both the culture of his birthplace and that of his ancestral home. It is his distance from the centers, the dialogue of the local and the global, and the departure from the unadulterated East and West that allow him to begin a cautious identification of himself: "In the world of the tradition, I was unimagined" (77). And to imagine himself, the memoir culminates in a succession of images that visualize the abstract issues of history and identity. The visit to his grandparents' shrine and his daughter kicking in Susie's womb constitute Mura's vision of both the past and the future, providing a partial resolution to the conflicts the autobiography broaches: between tradition and modernity, displacement and belonging.

As if consciously responding to Tan's chromosomal cultural continuity and Chin's authentic civilizational consciousness, Mura turns his narrative of ancestral homage on its head with the trip to his grandparents' village. But even before he reaches his destination, we are informed of the misplaced urns, the lost relatives, and the names of his grandparents that he cannot read (354). Transplanted roots, newfound cultural affiliations, and deromanticization of origin are followed by a further deconstruction of "origin" itself. Mura comments specifically on Ise Shrine, not only because it is a stopover on his way to his grandparent's *kuni* but also because the great Japanese poet Basho immortalized the place in print. Mura is shocked to learn that the wooden shrine is actually rebuilt every twenty years "using the exact same design and traditional methods of carpentry" (354). The "centuries-old tradition" of "tearing down and rebuilding" thus exemplifies the process of "formalization and ritualization" at the heart of what Eric Hobsbawm and Terence Ranger have termed "the invention of tradition" (1992: 4). Mura appears on the one hand to shatter the myth of tradition's permanence and accordingly the naturalness of his own inheritance, while on the other hand he affirms the need of its demolition and reconstruction. The question is thus less one of sources than of the techniques of renewal.

As Mura paid his respects and said his prayers at the temple of his grandparents' birthplace, he realized once again that although the grounds were a place of worship for his ancestors the buildings would not be familiar to them: "Everything is new; the connections are lost" (358–59). But just as he takes leave, "a lighted soft drink machine, with red dots which seem to connect little streams of light and a display case where you could see cans of Coke, Fanta, Kirin Orange," arrests his eyes:

> It is what I remember most vividly about the place, what I see most clearly in my mind's eye. And it is there that I think I glimpse the ghosts of my grandparents. . . . They are lit on one side, the side where my grandfather is standing and waving, by the soft fluorescent light of the machine. The other side, where my grandmother stands soberly, quietly, not waving, is the dankness of the evening, the darker shadows of the temple pines. As I turn a corner, I am, according to Japanese custom, still waving, till they are out of sight. (359)

This sighting of the ancestral ghosts in the fluorescent light of the soda machine is perhaps Mura at his most illuminating. The image is of tradition both lost and found. Instead of employing the symbolic properties of the shrine to invoke some sacred past and unfamiliar history, Mura chooses the familiar secular icon of a soda machine to translate his message about the necessary adaptations of tradition in ever-changing conditions.

As a material object of transnational consumer culture, the soda machine symbolizes the laws of supply and demand, of physical need and artificial fulfillment. That this symbol of material commerce should also be the medium of spiritual commerce upon which his grandparents' visage is summoned and ancestral connections are made shows Mura's insistence on the integrity of tradition and modernity, particularly their meaningful exchange of currency. If the ubiquity of the soda machine at the Japanese site of worship suggests the indispensable coexistence of Western invention and Eastern tradition, the soda machine as an American commonplace will serve for Mura upon his return to the United States as a transnational sign of tradition's repetition and ritualization. In an incongruous and inauthentic juxtaposition of modernity and tradition, the past and present are finally linked. When the image of Asia (Mura's grandparents) is reflected on the display of America (Coca-Cola), the contour of U.S. culture is already undergoing a welcome and welcoming reinscription. It is in rewriting the national tradition of cultural inclusion that Mura can begin to contemplate his status as a searcher for "a world culture" and anticipate the birth of his daughter, who will have his Japanese genes as well as the English and Hungarian Jewish genes of his wife (370, 372–73). While Mura would like to think that his daughter will be "part of a movement taking place everywhere throughout the globe," that is, a movement of mixed-race children as the miscegenational promise of peace in a transnational future, he does not allow himself to think of his daughter as the magic solution to his own historical alienation in the United States. That split between America and Japan, "this fusion of two histories" that has troubled his entire life, "will reside in her, in a different, more visible way," Mura concludes, and his daughter will have to overcome the split and negotiate the fusion on her own terms (372).

Mura recapitulates his lesson in travel by saying, "Japan allowed me to see myself, America, and the world from a perspective that was not white American. I do not feel as bound now by my national identity, do not feel that being an American somehow separates me from the rest of the world" (368). This change from a single-minded American, though a racialized alterity, eager for national incorporation, to a multicentered cosmopolitan U.S. citizen cognizant of his rights and commitments, represents the birth of a diasporic sensibility. Mura does not leap into the bohemian bliss of transnationality by dodging the relevance of nation for Asian Americans; nor does he advocate a bourgeois transcendence of the obligations of citizenship. Instead, he achieves a consciousness of relatedness between individuals and nations, between concrete places and imagined communities, and a coarticulation of the unresolved dialogues between the East and the West, ethnicity and nationhood, rootedness and at-homeness. *Turning Japanese* is an eccentric autobiography that transforms as it informs.

Representation Reconsidered

This part looks at how Asian American writers negotiate the normative pressures of the nation at the level of the visible. Representation is first treated as a question of cultural intelligibility: how Asian Americans look, why they look the way they do, and what those looks reveal about social differentiation and national distinction. Through the "transvestic" acts in David Henry Hwang's *M. Butterfly* and the "transpirational" coding of the Asian in David Wong Louie's *Pangs of Love*, Chapter 7 reconsiders identity as self-determined performance and relates the threat of Asian "derealization" to the abstraction of American citizenship. The artistic difficulties of embodying Asian American subjectivity come to evidence the persistent power of abjection in an era of formal equality for all.

Chapter 7 poses anew the query whether Asian Americans can simultaneously claim their cultural specificity and maintain their legitimate national membership. Chapter 8 investigates the question of representation as an inevitable social contract for Asian American writers and critics. The book's concern with intra-ethnic debates over an appropriate Asian American subjectivity receives full theoretical consideration as the issue of identity is linked with the issue of agency. Here, we review the cumbersome social relations involved in the literary imagining of the nation, canvass the possibilities of "free agency" and "mere agency," and attempt to reinvigorate efforts at Asian American representation.

7

The Look, the Act, the Transvestic, and the Transpirational Asian

R ecall the scene in *Tripmaster Monkey* when Nanci Lee recounts her trouble at auditions: "They say, 'You don't *look* oriental.' . . . And the director says, 'Can't you act more oriental? Act oriental'" (Kingston 1989b: 24; emphasis in original). While Nanci's genetic makeup is unquestionably Asian, she has failed to observe the normative correspondence between the look and the act that the director expects of Asians in the United States. Her difficulties with the director demonstrate that Asian American representation does not mean simply staking a claim to the nation or the ancestral homeland; it also means gaining control of ethnic cultural intelligibility. Race is both appearance and performance, or rather an appearance-generated performance. Since appropriate behaviors are demanded of certain morphological compositions, this normative equivalence between race and performance contradicts the state's commitment to formal equality and overtakes its role of social regulation at the level of everyday feelings and interactions.

The political economy of the look and act, and the hope of transcending it artistically, constitute the core of David Henry Hwang's and David Wong Louie's works in this chapter. Hwang's *M. Butterfly* (1989) and Louie's *Pangs of Love* (1991) deal subtly with the symbolic suggestion of (the) "Asia(n)" not only as a geopolitical referent but also as a racial and cultural signifier. Hwang and Louie's authorial bypassing of "Asian" representational restrictions, their masquerading strategies to enable its public presence, reveal the troubled relation of national essence and social space not only upon Asian American representation but on the fundamental promise of American democratic consent.

I

In May 1986, the *New York Times* reported on an espionage trial in France involving a former French diplomat and a Chinese opera singer. A Mr. Bouriscot was accused of passing information to a Mr. Shi, who had been his "mistress" for twenty years. This "'impossible' story of a Frenchman duped by a Chinese man masquerading as a woman," both confounded and titillated Western readers, but it seemed "perfectly explicable" to David Henry Hwang: "Given the degree of misunderstanding between men and women and also between East and West, it seemed inevitable that a mistake of this magnitude would one day take place" (98).[1] For Hwang, mistaken sexual identity is merely a natural outcome of racist and sexist epistemologies and a political economy saturated with imperialist and colonialist fantasies. Familiar with the pervasive orientalist system of Asian representation in Western arts, the playwright decided to dramatize and "deconstruct" the actual incident (94).[2] After glowing press reviews from the *New York Times* (Frank Rich), the *New Yorker* (Edith Oliver), and *U.S. News & World Report* (Marian Horn), *M. Butterfly* won the 1988 Tony award for best play and continued to overwhelm audiences around the world, leading *Time* to pronounce Hwang "the first U.S. playwright to become an international phenomenon in a generation, since the heyday of Edward Albee" (Henry 1989: 63–64).[3]

Not surprisingly, *M. Butterfly* has also received avid scholarly attention. Giving it a reception nearly identical to the one that greeted *The Woman Warrior*, the academic left generally applauded Hwang's radical impulse in poststructuralist and postcolonial discourses. The ethnic contingency, some of whom occupied a more or less similar academic platform, vigorously faulted the play for inaccurate Asian American representations. Focusing on the play's challenge to entrenched assumptions, Marjorie Garber wrote that *M. Butterfly*'s transvestism presents "an irresolvable conflict that destabilizes comfortable binarity", and represented for her "the third space of possibility, the cultural Symbolic, the place of signification" (1992: 17, 239). Echoing Garber while taking on anthropological theories of the self, Dorinne Kondo was fascinated by how "Hwang conceals, reveals, and then calls into question so-called 'true' identity," and how "*M. Butterfly* opens out 'the self' to 'the world,' softening or even dissolving those boundaries, where 'identity' becomes spatialized as a series of shifting nodal points constructed in and through fields of power and meaning" (1990: 6, 7). Against these celebrations of border-crossing and meaning-making are *The Big Aiiieeeee!* editors' opposition to *M. Butterfly*: "It is an article of white liberal American faith today that Chinese men, at their best, are effeminate closet queens. . . . No wonder, David Henry Hwang's derivative *M. Butterfly* won the Tony for best new play of 1988. The good Chinese man, at his best, is the fulfillment of white male homosexual fantasy, literally kissing white ass" (Chin et al. 1991: xiii). Less strident in tone but equally insistent in his focus on the significance of the play's main Asian character, James Moy laments that Song Liling is a "disfigure[ment]," and his cross-dressing "not an articulation of Asian desire" but an affirmation of "a nefarious complicity with Anglo-American desire in its representation of otherness" (1990: 54).

Despite their differences, both critical camps are concerned with *M. Butterfly*'s masquerade and its implications for issues of identity. The admirers are sympathetic to the playwright's interpretive suggestion that Gallimard and Song's misguided romance is a metaphor for the failed communication between East and West, women and men, the colonized and the colonizer. Applying deconstructive insights to their own analyses, they are quick to expose the faults of Western binary thinking and ready to propose masquerade as subversion and the sanguine solution to racism, sexism, and imperialism. This line of argument is not as convincing, however, if we recognize that Song is not a material woman. Since the audience is aware of Song's gender, his relationship with Gallimard is not a true substitution for the man-woman relationship.[4] Such an approximated male-female relationship, if successful in exposing gender inequality, does so in the absence of an actual woman. Although Song plays the part of a woman and may figuratively stand for a woman, he is a material man and thus ultimately incapable of replacing a woman. The women in the audience may see Song as a phantom of themselves, subjected to similar structural suppression, but they are unlikely to regard him as one of their own. The identification of Song as a woman is possible at an intellectual but not a psychological level.

Similarly, the fact that Song is Chinese and Gallimard is French again approximates an East-West relationship that expunges the United States as a concrete geopolitical space. The energy of anti-imperialism emanating ostensibly from this disclosure of orientalist economy thus resides significantly outside the American national context, which is, after all, the primary site of production for the play and for its criticism. Hwang's proclaimed deconstruction of binarity is thus enacted with a set of approximated, or shall we say, dissimulated oppositions, so that his dialectic of women versus men, East versus West, does not have to engage their more local manifestations. While readings of *M. Butterfly* in terms of gender metaphysics and international politics can be valid, and are indeed validated by the playwright's own cues, they may stop short of unmasking what the play at once conceals and reveals: racism within the borders of the United States. In this sense, the play's detractors, with their almost exclusive focus on the figure of Song, have hijacked *M. Butterfly* from its poststructuralist readings and force-landed it on the American ground of racial hierarchies.[5] Their simultaneous rejection and acceptance of Song—while he is not us, he is nevertheless a metonymic representation of us—point to the inevitability of mainstream cultural recognition, the need of its engagement in the lived social actuality of Asian America, and finally the hidden link between Song's strategic masquerade and Hwang's own double agency, both of which are symptomatic responses to the residual integrity of race and national competence in the United States.

Only in the context of American racial dynamics can Song Liling's much quoted yet little explicated statement be fully grasped: "I am an Oriental. And being an Oriental, I could never be completely a man" (83). Most telling is Hwang's word choice for Song's self-description, "Oriental." No self-respecting Chinese will ever call himself or herself "an Oriental" unless otherwise indoctrinated in the discourse of Western imperialism and orientalism, and no Chinese man is likely to question his male authority within the Chinese national context. Even after the Western conquest of China and during its semicolonial status from the Opium Wars to its civil war, there had been no tradition of Chinese men masquerading as women for white men; the operatic tradition of actors assuming the role of actresses is an altogether artistic matter.[6] If we take China's anti-imperialist history and its history of male domination into consideration, Song's masquerade is indeed out of his "Chinese" character. The confession of Song thus seems to derive from an entirely different context, not the simple opposition between East and West, women and men, but a context that approximates David Henry Hwang's own living and writing.

"As an Asian, I identify with Song. As a man, I identify with Gallimard," said the playwright (quoted in Gerard 1988: 89). Not only is Hwang's remark almost identical to Song's, but he is literally caught in an identity split: "Asian" and "man" become a new pair of irreconcilables that the playwright has to puzzle out. In this sense, Hwang takes a position parallel to that of his male Asian critics, although his treatment of Asian American gay subjectivity is not as readily seduced by the heterosexist model of masculinity in the dominant culture. Here, the telling sign is again Hwang's diction, this time the conspicuous "Asian." The referent "Asian" is a contemporary American substitute for "Oriental," a usage indicative of a significant shift of power stateside. Hwang's choice of term places him firmly in the 1960s ethnic nationalist discourses that gave rise both to the self-designation "Asian American" ("Asian" for short) and to the playwright's own artistic career. That only a few Asian Asians call themselves Asian and that a sizable number of Asian Americans in the United States still automatically refer to themselves by their specific racial and national origins—Korean, Vietnamese, Filipino, Indian, and so forth—makes Hwang's lexicon distinctively ethnic nationalist. The "Asian" reference thus evidences a political awareness in the bulk of Hwang's earlier works that address particular Asian American experiences and subjects in a U.S. national context.[7] Given this backdrop, Song's theatrical use of "Oriental" is only a disguise for Hwang's habitual use of "Asian," a minority linguistic put-on tactically aimed at mainstreaming. Like Kingston's Mu Lan, who cross-dresses to enter the masculine field of combat, Hwang alters his verbal attire only to infiltrate the white-male-dominated stage of Broadway. If *M. Butterfly* constitutes a political as well as philosophical critique, it does so in and through masquerade, the mutuality between Song and Hwang merely beginning to suggest masquerade's multiple meanings.

II

The most important writing on this subject is perhaps Joan Riviere's "Womanliness as a Masquerade," which has been retrieved through the feminist critique of psychoanalysis and given currency in discussions about identity, representation, and sexual difference. "Womanliness could be assumed and worn as a mask," Riviere asserts,

> both to hide the possession of masculinity and to avert the reprisals expected if she was found to possess it—much as a thief will turn out his pockets and ask to be searched to prove that he has not the stolen goods. The reader may now ask how I define womanliness or where I draw the line between genuine womanliness and the "masquerade." My suggestion is not, however, that there is any such difference; whether radical or superficial, they are the same thing. (Riviere 1986: 38)

Riviere's observation significantly blurs the distinction between being and doing, but for feminist critics, her immediate usefulness is in attributing the capacity for masquerade almost exclusively to women. "It is not that a man cannot use his body in this way but that he doesn't have to," Mary

Ann Doane argues; "the woman seems to be *more* bi-sexual than the man. Male transvesticism is an occasion for laughter; female transvesticism only another occasion for desire" (1982: 81, 82). Masquerade is a necessity for a woman "to take part in a man's world," agrees Mary Russo (1986: 224). While both acknowledge the artificiality of womanliness and masquerade, Doane and Russo's retaining of the distinction between "man" and "woman," though explicable as a historical gesture that reflects white patriarchal culture and its feminist resistance, ultimately limits Riviere's insights and eliminates the consideration of race, class, and sexuality in the configuration of different gender identities.[8]

Masquerade cannot be explained as an expression of gender essence, as what women do to make evident their essential selves. The recurrent transvestism in Maxine Hong Kingston's oeuvre shows, as do studies of imperialist and racist dominations in general, that womanliness and masquerade are not determined by biological sex. Recall that in the opening vignette of *China Men* Tang Ao, the male Chinese immigrant, is forced to perform the rite of feminization through which he actually *becomes* a woman (Li 1990: 487–88). This process of becoming a woman not only reflects Riviere's statement that "womanliness could be assumed and worn as a mask" but also draws our attention to the function of masquerade to "avert the reprisals expected." Kingston's Tang Ao and Riviere's professional woman become "women" not through their own volition but under regulatory pressure. When Riviere suggests that there is little difference between "masquerade" and "genuine womanliness," and when Kingston has the queen compliment Tang on his femininity, they are urging us to reconsider two apparently antithetical theories of (gender) identity, substance-based (womanliness, manliness, etc.) and performance-oriented (masquerade, or to use Judith Butler's definition of gender, "the repeated stylization of the body," 1990: 33), without losing sight, however, of the coercive circumstances that determine their dialectic. Resuming the Kingstonian and Rivierean rumination, Hwang astutely attends to the social pressures on Song Liling's being and doing, treating his masquerade as a means of inversion with dual possibilities, at once subverting substantive identity and reinforcing gender dichotomy. *M. Butterfly* shows that masquerade is not innately radical or conservative. Its effects always depend on where and for whom it is enacted and with whose rules and interests in mind.

The play's insight about masquerade and identity begins with Hwang's conceptualization of them as sets of relations. We have the pairing of Rene and Renee, Gallimard and the Danish exchange student, for example, who appear as male and female antitheses only to have its meaning revised. Renee's forwardness forces Gallimard's admission that it is indeed "possible for a woman to be *too* uninhibited. Too willing, so as to seem almost too . . .

masculine" (54). Hwang defies the property-defined gendering of identity
and places Gallimard repeatedly in positions where his masculinity is far
from assured. Gallimard's lack of aggression toward the "great babes" in
that "Marseille condo" and his masturbation over "girlie magazines" point
to his inadequacy both by Western codes of manhood and within Western
social settings (7–10). A "wimp" in Europe could be a whip in Asia, however, when imperial power relations and resources transform even the least
able of its male subjects into knights in shining armor/amour (9). "We, who
are not handsome, nor brave, nor powerful," Gallimard says, confessing his
orientalist desire, "somehow believe, like Pinkerton, that we deserve a Butterfly" (10). When Song Liling masquerades as the butterfly of the Orient,
delicate and docile before his eyes, Gallimard's wild dream of the "perfect
woman" came true and he *became* a man. "I felt for the first time that rush
of power," Gallimard ejaculates, "the absolute power of a man" (32).

Gallimard's reclamation of his manhood on the other side of the globe is
itself instructive. Hwang makes clear that his protagonist's masculine identity is consolidated with Song's femininity and alterity, a beguiling combination that makes the former whole. With the pair's simultaneous transformation, Song into a perfect woman and Gallimard into a "real man,"
Hwang unveils the acquired nature of Gallimard's manhood and the mask
of Song's womanliness. There is no natural and unchanging correspondence between sexual makeup and gender constitution, Hwang is saying;
neither is there any link between specific sets of attributes and certain
geopolitical spheres. In his dramatic deconstruction, Hwang succeeds both
in dissociating substance or essence from identity and in proffering a liberating possibility particularly for the Other within a binary construction to
assert itself, thus redefining identity and its signified social relationship.
This foreshadows the play's climactic change, when Song reveals his male
anatomy, a signal frequently taken to mean the fulfillment of a structural
inversion and the subversive potential of masquerade. In such an affirmation of masquerade's disruptive power, however, identity seems to become
an equivalent of garments, to be worn and discarded at ease; the social dimensions and the power relations that occasion masquerade in the first
place are lost.

With these thoughts in mind, we can closely inspect Song's sartorial
transformation in the play. At the beginning of act 3, Song has already
washed away his makeup. Removing his wig and kimono, he is seen under
full stage lights in a well-cut suit, moving upstage. Both performatively and
theatrically, his transformation into a man is rendered and experienced as a
moment of explosive and self-possessive power. While we are led to con-
strue it as positive, what this unmasking displaces is perhaps less affirmative. The restoration of masculine signs implies a hidden misogyny that ul-

timately rejects womanliness/masquerade, and the Armani suit encodes maleness in Western terms.[9] Beyond the discarding of the kimono as a devaluation of femininity broadly conceived, Song's borrowing of the suit seems to be an unprotesting acceptance of the authority of the West, prompting us to ask whether his act of transformation has actually altered the hierarchy of value between men and women, between West and East, and the corresponding relationships dependent on it.

One way to consider this question is to pursue the next stage of his striptease, when against Gallimard's repeated entreaties not to, Song drops his briefs (86–89). Calling Gallimard "my little one," Song indulges himself in the French diplomat's cowing and collapse, the physical revelation of his "manhood" matched with remarkable verbal postures of domination. Song's becoming a man is paralleled with Gallimard's becoming a woman. Assuming the Butterfly role of Puccini's opera and dressing himself in a kimono, Gallimard winds up the play with his own seppuku—victim and victimizer, it appears, simply switch places. Both repeating and revising the paradigmatic gender relation, this final dramatic change ensures two possible readings. First, it indicates that the hierarchical relations embedded in male/female and West/East can be invaded and interfered with—a sign of optimism. The second, however, seems less encouraging. Song's transgression of the rigid binary structures is replaced with a new hierarchy that does not necessarily change the nature of oppression. The premise of both interpretations hinges on the assumption that Song and Gallimard have indeed changed places, not just as man and woman, East and West, but as subject and object as well. While such a premise is supported by the characters' change of costume, whether they have also reversed roles and redefined their identities is still debatable.

Here, the introduction of another set of concrete responses to the play seems helpful. In an early review of *M. Butterfly*'s Broadway production, Robert Brustein spearheaded critical renunciations of Song Liling's "unusual cunning," which, in his view, surpassed even the "standards of inscrutable Oriental shrewdness" (1988: 28). Likewise, Kent Neely considered Song's masquerade "perverted, because s/he uses deceit and cunning to build another and imperious hierarchy to that of Gallimard" (1991: 170). Both seem threatened by the intimations of Song's masquerade but manage to suppress its subversive suggestion by dismissing it. Song becomes in their eyes a version of the *femme fatale*, a dragon lady—or lady in drag— who attempts to evade white patriarchal law and order through disguise. By calling his act perversion, Brustein and Neely effectively relegated Song to the realm of the Other, turning him into a contemporary symbol of Pearl Harbor, resonant with Asian economic menace.

In a candidly liberal and self-critical analysis, Janet Haedicke provides us, however, with a contrary example of white female indifference to Song's climactic transformation. "Safely ensconced" in her "feminist identity, a defiant female position of object-oppressed," she writes, "I had hardly noticed his [Song's] nakedness, a testimonial, unfortunately, not to a non-erotic gaze but to my own objectifying one" (1992: 27). The unmasking of "true masculinity," upon which so much of the play's meaning depends, has failed miserably to shock or to evoke any visceral reaction. Despite his nudity and Hwang's gesture of defamiliarization, Song the Asian man remains invisible; he becomes that which is unconsciously averted, the perfect abject. Whether punished or ignored, Song's masquerade is muted, or remains unregistered. Masquerade as a means of displacement, it seems, will have to confront the discursive history of the image, or its potential for resistance will most likely be lost or reabsorbed. The actual mainstream theatrical reception of *M. Butterfly* has shown the unrelenting power of orientalist reassertion, while the much celebrated reversal is only a "minority" wish fulfillment.[10]

III

Another way of looking at the issues of masquerade and reversal is through the prism of the play's dramatic structure, the artistic mediator of social relationships that directly affects audience perception. When Frank Rich of the *New York Times* wrote that one must be "grateful that a play of such ambition has made it to Broadway," he seemed to comment both on the famed middlebrow conservatism of the theater and on the play's surprising breakthrough (1988: C13). What he missed, however, is the double nature of Hwang's script and stage direction, the radical message and the way it is cloaked. The playwright shows a superb understanding and command of the Broadway medium as he carefully and consistently contradicts his representation. A declared deconstruction of orientalist metaphysics, *M. Butterfly* opens with a scene in a parlor, where an unnamed trio gossips heatedly about how Gallimard could not have known. Anonymous stand-ins for the audience, the two men and one woman rehash the original media coverage of the real incident and prompt a likewise aesthetic experience of the play along the lines of "clandestine love and mistaken sexual identity," seriously undercutting if not trivializing the proclaimed higher purposes of cultural critique.[11] Although Song has occasional outbursts of abrasive language, like the one that accuses the West of "international rape mentality" (82), such verbal delivery is again, in the words of one reviewer, obscured in "the color, the light, the gongs and songs of Eastern and Western music, the theatrical gamesmanship masquerading as a profound play of ideas"

(Kroll 1988: 75). Hwang's adoptions of Peter Shafferesque flashbacks and Kingstonian mythical mirage, director John Dexter's creation of "a purely theatrical imaginative space" (Rich 1988: C13), Eiko Ishioka's "impressive transvestite costumes" and "classy symbolic scenery," Lucia Hwang's "deft score," and "Jamie H. J. Guan's martial arts intermezzo" (Sauvage 1988: 22), all made possible through producer Stuart Ostrow's expenditure of $1.5 million (Street 1989: 42), turned *M. Butterfly* into the most lavishly staged spectacle of the season. The combined media conjured up an exotic Orient that could have undermined any esoteric thematic statement.[12] When there is a semiotic discrepancy between the visual and the verbal, the triumph of consumable spectacle over contentious didacticism seems all but inevitable.

The stage diversion of authorial meaning speaks of the normative constraints of Broadway and the collaborative nature of dramatic production. The playwright cannot have full control over his artistic content. However, he is doubtless in charge of his composition and characterization, even though these elements of play writing are also under constant pressure of generic and productive dictates. To further illustrate Hwang's contradictory double engagement, we must take up the play's descriptive focus and return to its final scenes. Since the manifest sadism accompanying Song's male transfiguration has already been noted, Gallimard's donning of Cho Cho San's oriental garb now deserves our attention.

Calling Song "a cad, a bounder," we recall, the French diplomat confesses near his dramatic denouement that he is no more than a "warp[ed] love[r]," enamored with the "vision of the Orient" (92). He says, "It is a vision that has become my life, [and] to you," as he addresses the audience, "I will prove that my love was not in vain" (91):

> Death with honor is better than life . . . with dishonor. (*He sets himself center stage, in a seppuku position.*) The love of a Butterfly can withstand many things—unfaithfulness, loss, even abandonment. But how can it face the one sin that implies all others? The devastating knowledge that underneath it all, the object of her love was nothing more, nothing less than . . . a man. (*He sets the tip of the knife against his body.*) It is 19—. And I have found her at last. In a prison on the outskirts of Paris. My name is Rene Gallimard—also known as Madame Butterfly. (92–93)

Gallimard thrusts the knife into his own body in the full blare of the "Love Duet," collapsing into the arms of the dancers who then reverently lay him on the floor. The image holds, before a dim spotlight moves on Song, "who stands as a man," puffing cigarette smoke into the air and uttering in derision, "Butterfly? Butterfly?" (93). As smoke rises and the lights fade, the curtain falls to signal the end of the play.

With this stunning coup de grace, Hwang has heroically revised the fated doom of the Asian character, an entire theatrical and cinematic tradition since *Madama Butterfly* of what one critic has aptly termed "the death of Asia on the American field of representation" (Moy 1993: 82). Gallimard's crumbling self-destruction and Song's upright stance may evidence some Hegelian truth about the master's elemental dependency on the slave for his own preservation. Through his deliberate self-exposure, Song's masquerade represents the revolt of a hysteric/woman, or a slave/servant, who willfully "misses her identit[ies]" and refuses to "play the game" altogether (Heath 1986: 51). This failed masquerade or aborted play of the subject/object relationship on the part of the subjugated shatters the master's illusion of his sovereign autonomy and suggests the former's indisputable power of disruption. Gallimard's obstinate embrace of "fantasy" over reality must be understood against this upset relationship, with the conspicuous absence of Song's complicity in the game of domination. Gallimard's subsequent dressing in women's clothes, therefore, does not display any real love for womanliness, but rather expresses a desire to replace the loss of the fetish and recuperate the pleasure of power. As Carole-Anne Tyler's Freudian reading of a gay man camping indicates, "the fetishist both worships and castrates the fetish object, romanticizes it and reviles it for its differences" (C. Tyler 1991: 42). When Gallimard cross-dresses and plunges the dagger into himself, he unites both the fetishist and the fetish in one self, achieving as it were, an impossible masturbatory control of his "vision."

While the concluding scenes of *M. Butterfly* may reasonably lend themselves to this intellectualized and radical reading, it is again undercut by Hwang's script. The subversive impact of Song's de-masquerade, it seems, must be absorbed by another act of concealment or risk impropriety. In these last moments of the play, the theatrical resources are so unevenly expended on Gallimard, both visually and verbally, that there is little room for the audience not to concentrate on the drenching details of his demise. As a result, Gallimard dies a dignified death. Though perhaps an ex-imperialist, a racist, and a sexist, he expires as a befuddled lover, a committed romantic, a fool in the eyes of some but an idealist in the eyes of many.

With his suicide, Gallimard's downfall is no longer construed as punishment for his mindless domination but as the consequence of someone else's abuse of his innocence and illusion. Gallimard in death becomes a symbol of human fallibility and gullibility, dramatically transforming himself into a de facto tragic hero, perhaps along the lines of Lear and Othello, evoking feelings of pathos from the audience. Song Liling, the truly exploited player in other people's games (both Gallimard's and the Chinese communists'), on the other hand, becomes an abstract embodiment of Gallimard's forsaken vices, gloatingly sadistic and smugly domineering, a worse version of Gallimard because of his knowing calculation and paper-thin character.

While Gallimard is a full-blown protagonist, fleshed out in complex human terms, Song, the Asian character, is underdeveloped and underinvested, desperately in need of sympathetic depth. A rare Asian survivor of the American stage, he is inescapably chained to a succession of one-dimensional signifiers—the victim, the victimizer, and the villain. After all, *M. Butterfly* is Gallimard's play, and its plot is enacted through *his* memory, from his jail cell to his childhood, his diplomatic career to his marriage and affair, his trial and back to his cell. Even during the critical exposure of his partner's "manhood," Gallimard's response is the intended focal point for the audience rather than Song Liling's penis. A phantom of the opera, Song is destined to sustain and service Gallimard's development, always reflecting but never reciprocating the white man's deepest fantasies. In the end, the orientalist drama of West/subject and East/object interplay goes on, awaiting another curtain call.[13]

While *M. Butterfly* may reverse gender and race roles, it never quite inverts the dominant gender/race relations it intends to disavow. However, Song Liling's insubordination apparently proved so disturbing that David Henry Hwang felt compelled to assure his audience that the play is neither "anti-American" nor "a diatribe against the stereotyping of the East by the West, of women by men." It is instead "a plea to all sides to cut through our respective layers of cultural and sexual misperception, to deal with one another truthfully for our mutual good, from the common and equal ground we share as human beings" (100). The sincerity and the utopian impulse of Hwang is beyond doubt, but the statement could be yet another instance of masquerade. The plea to "all sides" to "cut through misconception" so reduces gender and racial inequality to matters of individual perception that it obscures the very social structures that produce discrimination. Similar to the professional woman of Riviere's study who feels compelled to exaggerate her femininity to make up for her "theft" of "male" intellectual accomplishments, Hwang has to compensate for his critique of the West/man both through an extra-textual appeal to universal humanity and by explaining away his "imposture" to Broadway. The notion of racial/social boundary has been so inbred, the desire for its transgression, and the trepidation about consequent reprisal so internalized, that any offensive action is necessarily doubled with defensive reaction, de-masquerade coupled with re-masquerade. As Song Liling claims, "being an Oriental, I could never be completely a man," so does David Henry Hwang echo, "As an Asian, I identify with Song. As a man, I identify with Gallimard." One ever feels his twoness—an American, an Asian; two souls, two thoughts, two unreconciled strivings; two warring ideals in one Asian American body, whose compelled and chosen masquerade have kept it from being torn asunder.[14]

IV

As Hwang did in *M. Butterfly*, David Wong Louie consciously attempts racial concealment in his fiction. "After receiving his first stack of rejection slips in the mid-1970s," writes Janice Simpson of *Time*, "David Wong Louie made a painful change in the stories he sent out: he stripped them of all traces of ethnic identity." "What I'd do," Louie later confirmed, "is write in the first person about somebody like myself, but I wouldn't identify him as Chinese-American" (Simpson 1991: 66). Learning that "ethnic subjects" should not call attention to their physical features but should assume the look of "universal subjects" abruptly terminates the writer's age of innocence and initiates him into the world of publishing with its invisible commandments. Not surprisingly, the knowledge also became his entree to magazine publications and led finally to *Pangs of Love*, his collection of short stories, which was hailed for its "notable refusal to confine itself to those so-called ethnic themes" (Krist 1991: 13) and commended as "the furthest thing from a genre ethnic writer" (Eder 1991: 3).[15]

Although the table of contents of *Pangs of Love* shows Louie's desire to frame its Asian (subject) matter, inaugurated with "Birthday" and brought to a coda with "Inheritance," the publishing sequence of the eleven pieces reveals a trajectory of self-conscious "ethnic cleansing" and excavation:

1. "One Man's Hysteria—Real or Imagined—in the Twentieth Century" (*Kansas Quarterly*, 1981)
2. "Bottles of Beaujolais" (*Iowa Review*, 1982–83)
3. "Disturbing the Universe" (*Colorado State Review*, 1983)
4. "Love on the Rocks" (*Quarry West*, 1983)
5. "The Movers" (*Mid-American Review*, 1985)
6. "Warming Trends" (*Kansas Quarterly*, 1986)
7. "Birthday" (*The Agni Review*, 1987)
8. "Displacement" (*Ploughshares*, 1988)
9. "Social Sciences" (*An Illuminated History of the Future*, 1989)
10. "Inheritance" (1991)
11. "Pangs of Love" (1991)

Not until the fourth story in the sequence do Louie's characters begin to bear Asian names, but the clearly identified Asian American protagonist of the stories does not really appear in his own voice or first-person perspective till "Birthday."[16] The last two stories, which significantly shape the Asian contour of the collection, were previously unpublished and can with reasonable certainty be construed as Louie's conscious coloring of his work after signing a contract to publish with Knopf.

If Song's transvestic disguise and disclosure figure measurably in Hwang's strategic access to public culture, the sequence of ethnic repression and return in *Pangs of Love* shows Louie's vintage "transpirational" maneuvers against Asian American derealization. "Transpire," according to the Oxford English Dictionary, has the following main meanings:

> 1. To emit or cause to pass in the state of vapor through the walls or surface of the body; *esp.* to give off or discharge (waste matter, etc.) from the body through the skin. 2. Of a volatile substance: To pass out as vapor through pores; to escape by evaporation. 3. "To escape from secrecy to notice"; to become known esp. by obscure channels, or in spite of secrecy being intended.

To transpire is therefore to simultaneously evaporate and emit. If the Asian is under hegemonic pressure to pass out as gas and escape into thin air, this passage cannot be equated with the elimination of manifest racial matters. Instead, the figure of transpiration makes evident the secretive process of Asian American abjection in the U.S. body politic. Though the shapeless overflow of the Asian demonstrates the dominant discursive control of its contour, its interstitial issuance and vaporization, not incidentally, also free the Asian from the usual constraints and enable his authorized circulation.

Paradoxically, the trope of "transpiration" confirms Toni Morrison's thesis in *Playing in the Dark*: "Until very recently, and regardless of the race of the author, the readers of virtually all of American fiction have been positioned as white." It also bears on Morrison's central concern: "when does racial 'unconsciousness' or awareness of race enrich interpretive language, and when does it impoverish it?" and "what does positing one's writerly self, in the wholly racialized society that is the United States, as unraced and all others are as raced entail?" (Morrison 1992: xii). The figure of transpiration illuminates Louie's experiential grasp of what the presumed whiteness of American literary imagination entails for his own creative look and act. It also illustrates, beyond its suggestiveness in the publication chronology itself, his formal mediation of the persistent American contradiction of racial endowments and national competence. For our purposes, we shall examine the first and fifth stories on the list in order to engage Louie's transpirational textual performance of race on the requisites of Asian American identity and American consent.

V

"One Man's Hysteria—Real or Imagined—in the Twentieth Century" is the story that inaugurates Louie's publishing career, after his reluctant decision to narratively fade out race. Its plot is simple: against the backdrop of some hallucinatory nuclear fallout, the writer/protagonist proposes the reading of poetry as the world's salvation. Its style is metafictional: barely into the third page, the person who was understood to be the narrator Stephen's wife, "Laura," is suddenly revealed to be his life companion, "Nancy." Peering over his shoulder, Laura/Nancy interjects, "You can't use their [their neighbors'] real names in a story . . . it's not ethical" (138).[17] Thus revealing his strategy, Louie both surprises and prepares his audience for a self-reflexive intrigue that will shuttle them between Stephen's "imagined" plot and his "real" life, creating along the way scenes of multiple orgasm to the accompaniment of Prufrockian mermaids and the birth of a fictive son, Todd, who, Stephen believes, is destined to change the postapocalyptic world.

Louie's "frame breaking," while purposefully mixing the ontological fact of the text with that of the real world, does not adhere to the well-known postmodern emphasis on "the reading rather than the writing of fiction" (Hite 1991: 702–3). The violation of readerly trust, while clearly instilling hermeneutic suspicion in the audience, is not meant to question the representative truth of the writer per se but to call attention to a writerly genesis of reality. The world of fiction, Louie wants to assure his audience, is the world of authorial creation. By prompting the audience to the source and origin of readerly pleasure, Louie could then effect the materialization of an Asian image that is nowhere seen in the text proper but can be inferred through his authorship. In light of this suggestion, the story's apparent dialogue of annihilation by mushroom clouds and survival via poetry recitation is not just the expression of anxiety for a man of the nuclear age. The topics, rather, seem opaque translations of editorial maiming of the minority writer and his determination to sustain artistic life. While the shell power of rejection slips makes necessary a defensive narrative shelter against foreseeable future bombardment, having built the shelter by erasing his race, David Wong Louie is plagued with worries about extinction. One man's imagined hysteria about nuclear destruction seems just another man's authorial anxiety about his own physical survival.[18] The textual elimination of racial markers calls for an extratextual compensation through metafictional transpiration.

No wonder then, amid the evocations of Herbert, Hopkins, Shelley, and Campion, that there is a concurrent disguised revolt against them, irrespective of the fact that these masters of English poetry provide effective white cover for the colored aspiring writer. In Stephen's own classification of the world's people as creators, consumers, and retainers, the major poets of the creator category rank humbly below the contemporary retainers (140). Louis asks: "Who else among the survivors—those who manage to be liquid in fire, steel to flying glass, granite against shock, alchemists all; those who miss the express (vaporization) but catch the local (irradiation)—who will have coherent speech except the retainers?" (141–42). The nuclear assault of the population and the retainer's Houdini-like escape are rich with connotations. Who else is best suited to outlive editorial ethnic cleansing, Louie could be saying, than the transpirational Asian, whose conditioned evaporation is also his irresistible consolidation? In such a postapocalyptic world, Louie resumes, "the retainers will emerge and recite in sibylic rote the world's last true words," suggesting that after the purgatories of white publishing, the true Asian will have the last say (142).

In spite of this optimistic tone of survival, the narrator takes no chances. "While the world teeters ever closer to Armageddon," he muses, "my most urgent need is to propagate my species. I want a child to bear my name into the future, its bleakness notwithstanding" (149). He even attempts to commission Nancy/Laura to "commit to memory an antebellum elegy, a poem in which [his] name appears at least once in the text, not necessarily spelled out but hidden perhaps in the manner of how Shakespeare is buried, as it is rumored, in the Forty-sixth Psalm" (149). Against the threat of aversion and abjection (a yard sale where Stephen is deliberately ignored serves as a suggestion), the narrator wants to balance his design of Shakespearean self-burial with his desire for its instant excavation. The yearning for nominal survival and bodily preservation is so intense that the propagation of his species and the permanence of his print become interchangeable measures of marking his existence. Louie adeptly intertwines the perils of authorship with the anxiety of patrilineage to suggest at once the difficulties of Asian American heritage in the nation and expose the impossible demands of a white American universality.[19]

Still, for fear that the transpiration of his racial unpresentability will elude the most intelligent reader, Louie/Stephen calls attention to the portrait of the artist by writing into being Todd, his invented son. "Come look," Todd nudges his dad, pointing to a red Gauguin. "Red isn't always blood," he responds to his fictitious son, "just like black isn't always hair," hinting at a correspondence between hair color and racial identity. Then, Louie/Stephen ventures a reflection on the relation between the use of color and the use of words: "Gauguin took liberties. He dared to presume. And in the same spirit I wonder now what color Todd's blood is. Does it even have color? Is there blood between us, me and this creation of mine?" Like Gauguin, who took artistic license, Louie/Stephen also dares to turn the descendants of yellow peril into Nabokovian pale fire. Todd has not failed to notice. "Your hair is black too," the boy says, remarking on the family resemblance that transpires a possible trace of race. One wonders if it is Todd, the new alchemist/retainer who has survived Armageddon to tell the tale or if it is the metafictional magician himself who has conjured up an Asian image despite efforts to remove it (157).

Besides being a story of strategic entry into the white world of publication, "One Man's Hysteria" is a tale of transpiration that foregrounds the contradictory significance of race and color in the formation of the nation. Louie's linking of Todd and Stephen's lineage, although apparently affirming race as an essential representational signifier, also disputes the naturalness of national inheritance. Since the father-son relation between Stephen and Todd is not of blood line but of imagined family/community, Louie stops using race as the chain of biological transmission and challenges the logic of national descent. The fact that a literary and not at all literal son could resemble his father and represent his identity is Louie's way of reconceiving the family as an artificial procreative entity. The family as an affiliative rather than a filiative community becomes his metaphoric vehicle for reaffirming the consensual ideal and constructed nature of American citizenship and reconfiguring the nation as an "empty signifier" (to borrow from Ernesto Laclau) that is capable of being multiply signified (Laclau 1992: 90). "One Man's Hysteria" not only exposes the normative correspondence of race and cultural practice and its negative impact on Asian American representation; it also dares to imagine possibilities for realizing America's creational myth of democracy.

VI

The dilemma of Asian American cultural intelligibility in the nation is dealt with very differently in "The Movers." Instead of putting an Asian face on an apparently Caucasian protagonist, Louie presents us with a first-person narrator who is ostensibly white and whose unbecoming conduct prompts queries about his real racial identity. At the outset, the nameless male protagonist of the story is jilted by his lover Suzy. Abandoned in the empty house they rented, with no phone and no electricity, he waits alone for the Salvation Army to arrive with the furniture he has ordered. While in this powerless state, he is interrupted by George, a previous resident, and his girlfriend, Phillis, two adolescents apparently in heat. After they forced their way in, the thirty-something narrator retreats to "Suzy's corner" to avoid being discovered while the intruders march upstairs to his and Suzy's bedroom, declaring unashamedly in resounding colonialist rhetoric, "Nobody lives here. This is open territory, like outer space" (124, 123).

The perpetrators' penetration of the house is a powerful symbol of rape and castration, but more disturbing still is how the narrator tolerates the violation of his private space, his personal property, and his parameters of self. Louie intrigues his audience with a number of incongruities that contradict and confuse our sense of social normality: the reversal of authority between teens and adults, the narrator's abdication of his legal rights, and the trespassers' appropriation of territory, all of which constitute an essential enigma waiting to be unraveled.

The unraveling takes place with the arrival of Phillis's father, which suggests yet another attempted entry. "I didn't mean to barge in," Grey introduces himself in his "full, confident" voice. Assuming the narrator to be George's father, he asks the whereabouts of Phillis. "Your daughter's safe with my boy," but as soon as "my boy" crosses his lips, the narrator informs us, he is himself astonished by his own "daring" (125). Fearing that his "voice lacked the easy authority of a parent," he immediately "took a precautionary step back into the dark house where age could be discerned by a careful touch of my skin" (125–26). Although we are told that his voice would betray his age, it is his "skin" that he endeavors to conceal. The disclosure of skin as the object of secrecy belies Louie's transpirational genius, which now makes clear the reason why the narrator accepts his personal violation without protest, and why he insists on masking himself in borrowed identity.

"Skin, as the key signifier of cultural and racial difference," argues Homi Bhabha, "is the most visible of the fetishes, recognized as 'common knowledge' in a range of cultural, political and historical discourses, and plays a public part in the racial drama that is enacted every day in colonial societies" (1994: 78). The narrator's abnormal responses to his invaders are like those of the colonial who has already internalized the limitations of his social space because of an all too self-conscious recognition of his skin. His precautionary step back into the dark house is to prevent Grey from seeing his skin, for "skin, as a signifier of discrimination, must be produced or possessed as visible" (79). In the absence of the visible, the most discriminating "common knowledge" that both regulates racial hierarchy and governs social etiquette will automatically fail to activate, transpired as it were.

It is no surprise that with the enveloping gloom of the house, the narrator succeeds in his "man-to-man talk" with Grey (126). However, the moment he is out in the open, as he is when the movers arrive, his identity becomes questionable:

"What's your relationship to Miss Tree? You Mr. Tree?"
I told them [the movers] no.
"Her brother?"
"No."
"I know you're not her father. . . . [A]re you Miss Tree's sweetheart?" (131)

While refusing to deliver his furniture, the movers delight in taunting the nameless narrator. Once his epidermal condition is exposed, the entire inventory of racial meanings is activated, leaving him the true object of dispossession. "All I knew was," the narrator is forced to confess, "if Suzy were here, this guy would be apologizing for their tardiness: he'd be almost too polite" (128). As in the previous scene, with its unusual distribution of authority between adult and adolescents, the revelation that Suzy is better equipped to handle the macho culture of truckers and movers than the male protagonist himself appears another inversion of social hierarchy that begs to be deciphered beyond gender.

It finally dawns on the reader that the reason the narrator is not able to claim his furniture is because his name does not appear on the invoice. Despite the fact that he has paid for it, the signature of "Suzy Tree" practically writes off his ownership and voids his entitlement. His right to property is contingent upon his love relationship with Miss Tree. However, even in that capacity, it remains a relationship based not on a written contract, a legally enforceable document such as a marriage certificate, but on a verbal agreement. Although Suzy Tree has opted to renege on their relationship, the narrator is hopelessly bound by its restrictive power without the accompanying rewards. In desperation, he threatens to call the police, and when that fails to produce the intended effect on the movers, he retreats into the house as if to make good on his threat while knowing full well that he does not have a phone:

> There are no directions in the dark. All one has is memory and I had no memories of that house. I took recklessly long strides away from the vestibule, as if I were trying to outstep the darkness, as one steps over puddles. I waved my arms like a drowning man, groping for something solid. (132)

Unlike the teens who trespass with the confidence of an owner, every step echoing the knowledge of native geography and the right of possession, the narrator has "no memories of that house," an imperative consciousness of self and an appropriate personal claim on national space. The cumulative imagery of his persistent alienation and abjection within the house, to which he has every legal right, finally hits the reader with unmistakable metaphoric impact: the narrator begins to stand for the most recently nationalized Asian whose guarantee of formal rights in the United States is undermined by the dominant cultural denial of his or her sense of entitlement. Like the narrator, the Asian American is made a stranger in the master's mansion, "groping" blindly for direction and "drowning" while grasping for something solid (132).

The narrator's coerced deracination and inflicted illegitimacy come to explain what appeared previously to be the totally inexplicable—that is, his spying on the teenagers and his protection of their whereabouts. Although George's presumptuous occupation of the house and his "masterful lovemaking" make a mockery of the narrator's anticipated romantic consummation, the narrator seems to take some masochistic pleasure in the violation of his space. Barred from playing his own game, he turns himself into a spectator seeking substitute fulfillment. Placing himself in the body of George, he pictures the "white knees" of Phillis/Suzy, "bare and strangely luminous, two moons in the gray light of the room, reaching for the ceiling—or more ambitiously, straining for the heavens—as they cradled the boy," or shall we say, the narrator's projected self (125). His vicarious participation in the act seems the only obvious way to close his wounds, and his transpiration into the white body the only vehicle for his yellow desire. By having his protagonist/narrator deter Grey at the vestibule, like a faithful servant jealously guarding the privacy of his master, Louie ruthlessly satirizes the pathology of the "model minority" and warns against the universal abstraction of American citizenship.

Finally, Phillis's counterfeit signature for Suzy saves the narrator his unwanted load of furniture, proving once again the power of writing and naming that he inherently lacks. As Phillis fades into the night, he pines for a visual identification of, or rather with, George (134). "I might see all we had in common—the slant of our eyes, the breadth of our noses, the cut of our hair," he contemplates, "and, should Suzy appear, our mutual love for the same woman" (135). Like Tam of *The Chickencoop Chinaman*, who "grew blind looking hard through the holes of his [the lone ranger's] funny papermask for slanty eyes" (F. Chin 1981: 31), Louie's protagonist wishes to imprint a stereotypical Asian look on George, or more likely, borrow his Caucasian appearance to improve his own image. While the narrator may be guilty of an idealized exchange of women in the service of male desire, the inequity of romantic outcome between the two male lovers for the "same" woman, personified nationhood and homeland as it were, shows both the absence of commonality between them and the epidermal schema of race as an inescapable social effect in the United States.

If "One Man's Hysteria" is a transpirational tale that optimistically debunks an Asian American inability to assume a normative national culture, "The Movers" is one that cautions against the uncritical abandonment of race-specific national embodiment. Through a consistent chain of contrasts between the narrator and other characters in the story—his lack of confidence and George's unaffected sense of command, his timidity and Suzy's no-nonsense approach, his ineffectual bluff and Phillis's power of signing, and even the two polar opposite "I"s in the social arena, the exposed self caught in the paralysis of inaction and the hidden self asserting authority in invisibility—Louie clearly marks his Asian American protagonist as an inadequate and inauthentic white subject. Rather than naturalizing whiteness as essence, however, his skillful linking of the visual and the social, of the superficial signs of race and their substantial social implications, shows it to be nothing but a skin-generated privilege. Whiteness guarantees white people a sense of social and cultural entitlement in the United States. Those who do not look white, however, must suffer an imposed and an internalized national illegitimacy. The protagonist of "The Movers" is abnormally "white" and perhaps stereotypically "Asian," not because of his racial innateness but because his improper look has inevitably resulted in his inadequate and inappropriate representation within the nation. Though perhaps just skin deep, the way we look profoundly affects the way we are treated, and the way we act out our "appropriate" sense of self in the (re)public.

While Louie's transpirational narrative strategy and Hwang's transvestic theater are capable of bringing Asian American characters to the threshold of visibility, these figures of artistic performance reveal far more about the threat of Asian American derealization in the representational democracy of the United States. Hwang's split identification with Song and Gallimard as an Asian and a man, and Louie's vicarious subjectivation through apparently white protagonists make clear that Asian Americans not only lack the legitimate appearance of the nation's normative subjects, but in its absence they must also sacrifice their bodily intactness in order to participate in public culture. Similar to the proletariat in Marx, who is forced to expropriate both "the product of his labor and his sense of his own productive activity" for the capitalist's accumulation of wealth and power (Williams 1985: 35), Asian Americans are impossibly positioned to retrieve their contribution to and participate in the cultures of the United States.[20] If the visible forms of hyperethnicity risk displacing Asian American subjects onto Asia, the requisite invisibility of Asian American democratic participation only betrays the contradiction of American consent. In the abstraction of American citizenship, Asian Americans seem destined to remain "model minority" abjects.

Ethnic Agency
and the Challenge
of Representation

T he call for Asian American visibility summons the spectral questions of cultural representation: 1. What is deemed appropriate for view? and 2. Who is responsible for bringing it to the public? These problems have been extensively analyzed as problems of American consent, as ethnic struggles both to gain access to public cultural resources and to make the nation fulfill its democratic promise, but they have not yet received full theoretical treatment as specific problems of Asian American agency. In this chapter, we consider the difficulties of ethnic representation as sets of challenging fiduciary relationships involving the agent and the principal, the minority writer and the subjects of his or her writing. We do so using Hanna Fenichel Pitkin's philosophical treatise of *The Concept of Representation*. Although her elegant book never takes up the author/audience relationship, Pitkin's meticulous analysis of representation's interrelated aspects—the formalistic, the descriptive and symbolic ("standing for"), and the agential ("acting for")—will help us conceive Asian American cultural articulation into the nation also as the layered creation of an intra-ethnic representational contract.

For Pitkin, representation can be construed in terms of a formal arrangement that either initiates it or expressly terminates it. There are two basic formal arrangements: in one, "authorization" grants, through election, a representative the right to act that she or he did not have before (Pitkin 1967: 38–39); in the other, "accountability" holds the representative responsible for his or her actions by voting either to extend or end consent (55–56). Though the formalistic views of representation make explicit its political nature and its place in participatory democracy, it appears to be limited to applications in electoral politics. Since no writer of any racial constituency is ever elected to write, communal authorization and individual accountability would seem to be moot issues. However, one may argue that this distinction does not necessarily void the political implications of representation in the aesthetic realm. In the selective publishing process, an editorial community authorizes or chooses writing agents, and "all authority," as Pitkin observes, "is representative" (53). Representation, in this latter sense, is the inevitable appropriation of dispersed and disembodied authority. Unpublished writers are nonrepresentative or a-representative because they have not yet had access to the public, but published writers cannot but be representative because they have become "authors," and with this status comes the authority over those to whom they refer, however fictitious, and for whomever they act, however indirectly.

Two additional factors stand to complicate the situation. First, the "interpretive community" that initially authorizes the Asian American writer is usually not the ethnic constituency to which the writer belongs. Second, authorization may not always occur before action and can be achieved through attribution after the fact. "Anyone who performs a function for the group may seem to be its representative," reasons Pitkin, "for his actions are attributed to it and are binding on it." She continues: "Representatives defined in this manner need not be elected to office. The manner of their selection is [also] irrelevant so long as they become organs of the group" (1967: 41). The premise of collectivity is at the core of the so-called *Organschaft* theory: rather than being the agent of an individual, the representative is seen as the organ of a group (39). Since the organ of a group is always larger than the individual member who enters it, the member cannot realistically disavow this given and the relationship it entails. In this view, the Asian American author becomes a representative for the ethnic community despite either his or her will or the conditions of his or her prior authorization. Without either election or appointment, the Asian

American writer automatically becomes a representative by virtue of membership in an ethnic group.

There are two conceivable objections to this theory. The first is that the unchecked author may be seen as capable of appropriating communal interest for individual gain. The second holds the communal claim of the individual author as arbitrary, both unreasonably binding and unduly restrictive on the writing agent. The debate over the value of a particular "ethnic" text centers inescapably on these two conflicting views of representation, often at the same time (see esp. Chapter 2). One appealing alternative to this conflict is for Asian American writers to detach themselves from the representative burdens exacted by their received community, from which their fellow writers of white descent are practically free. That I am writing for myself or that I am imagining a world apart from the solidarity of actual community are thus familiar ethnic self-defenses. If the ethnic writer has an obligation at all, it is to the invisible authorizing community and the subjective needs of the majority consumers of culture rather than to the ethnic community the writer belongs to (see Hongo 1993: xxx–xxxv).

Such responses are induced by a reception of minority texts that views the meaning of the text, the experience of the author, and the status of the ethnic constituency as unproblematic equivalences, but the rejection of social identity's relevance, however misconstrued, ignores its representational inevitability. What is overlooked in the argumentative retreat to individual aesthetic autonomy is the potential influence of attribution on authorization itself. Although the Asian American constituency is usually not directly involved in authorizing the publication of its writing agents, this does not mean that it exerts no influence on the authorizing process. The post-1960s invention of "Asian America" as a means of collectively addressing the state, for example, has put a hitherto unarticulated racial formation on the political map, which makes both possible and available (the) "Asian America(n)" as a discursive category and a social identity for classification, distribution, recognition, and attribution. Not only does the consolidation of an oppositional identity influence structural reorderings within the nation-state, leading to the widening of Asian American access to employment, education, and dominant cultural capital in general, the pronounced public existence of the community allows their racial composition to be figured into whether a text gets published and whether it gets taught, thus enabling yet another round of cultural dissemination. Racial self-determination, or ethnic attribution in the historical chain of definitional struggle, in other words, significantly contributes to mainstream accommodation as well as authorization.

The formalistic views of representation have shown us the troubling relationship between the representative and the represented. That the Asian American writer is in general authorized by a constituency other than his or her own ethnic group but will ultimately be considered a part of it is a condition for double allegiance and double agency, conflicting loyalties and fantasies about being able to discard them. The Asian American author could be held responsible both to the dominant cultural community that provides the outlet for his or her work and to the ethnic community that claims it for the group. But the issue of authorial accountability cannot be adequately addressed until we recognize representation's "standing for" functions, or its symbolic powers.

When representation serves as symbolization, Pitkin posits, "a political representative is to be understood on the model of a flag representing the nation, or an emblem representing a cult" (1967: 92). This symbolic effect is particularly pertinent to minority literature in a majority context when an ethnic author and an ethnic text are considered almost without exception to stand for their community. Although the lack of exposure is the main source of this symbolic association and the enhancement of its metonymical power, symbolic representation tends to eliminate the historical distance between the agent and the constituency, the minority group and the dominant culture. As a believer in or practitioner of this mode of representation, the Asian American writer may either project immediate or local experiences as communal or profess a commitment to the community so as to authorize and authenticate an otherwise individual expression or assessment of reality. Whether an unknowing idealist or a conscious manipulator, the minority writer who appropriates this symbolic covenant is endowed with too much power over its constituency to effectively articulate its interests. When used in scholarly preservation or pedagogical dissemination, symbolic representation becomes, on the one hand, an empowering argument for minority inclusion within the traditional canon; on the other hand, it can blur the necessary distinction between textuality and social reality, cultural production and political process.[1] An understanding of the now canonical author or text is likely to be equated with an understanding of the community at large, while the presence of a minority writer in an anthology is mistaken to be symbolic of the broader democratic access enjoyed by the writer's ethnic group.

An imperfect existential condition, symbolic representation is most akin to descriptive representation in that both make present and stand for that which is missing. Unlike symbolic representation, however, descriptive representation is not content with any form of metonymic effect. Instead, it demands the "virtue of a correspondence, a resemblance or reflection" and it so exhausts the metaphor of "map and mirror, of miniature and sample" that the relationship between the representative and the represented is reduced to a matter of "likeness" (Pitkin 1967: 61, 80). In political terms, it has meant that the importance is laid less on what the legislature does than on how it is composed and whether the representatives possess "some large measure of identity of characteristics with group qualities." Representation is considered a "consensus of characteristics between politically unequal parties of which one is representative and the other the constituent" (61, 78). The emphasis on correspondence serves the proportionist argument that the presence within the legislature of spokespeople of all groups suffices for representation. What matters is being seen and being heard, and the chosen representatives become nothing but conveyers of information about the constituency (63, 82).

While one can easily see how this descriptive view works in congressional redistricting to ensure minority representation, for instance, one should also recognize its effect on the reception of ethnic literature as well. Resemblance and reflection are such quintessential elements in psychosocial identification and subjective interpellation that their role in an individual's political and aesthetic experiences should not be dismissed as trivial. This is particularly true when the abstract universal of the nation is concretely manifested as white, and when any racial minority's appearance in and access to the (re)public is limited from the start. However, an insistence on facsimile can produce untenable positions. We may cut through the controversy over *Miss Saigon* to ask simply if the casting of the lead Eurasian pimp in the musical by an actor of pure Asian descent necessarily fulfills the requirement of corresponding characteristics. In this scenario, the satisfaction of a physiological match only seems to further concerns whether the role itself warrants an "accurate" or "truthful" rendition of Asian American moral conduct or merely recycles an earlier stereotype. Representation, it seems, should be less a matter of saving face than of whether we are content with face value, and how we are to negotiate looking and acting, appearance and performance.

Pursuing the dilemma from a different angle, we may question whether writers of Asian ancestry are necessarily better representatives of an Asian American ethos and whether writers of non-Asian origin are necessarily incapable of representing Asian Americans. Another controversial example was Robert Olen Butler's Pulitzer Prize–winning *A Good Scent from a Strange Mountain* (1993), a collection of first-person short stories about Vietnamese immigrants in Louisiana. The *Times Literary Supplement* billed it as a "great feat of imagination—the successful imitation of the voice of a people," against what it termed "the current American climate" in which "writing is often seen as a textual envoy for a particular experience and identity" (McNeil 1993: 19). The Vietnamese American author and critic Monique T. D. Truong condemned the book as "a blatant textual act of yellow facing." Historicizing Butler's book in the context of recent anthropological transcription of Vietnamese oral history and the phenomenon of native-white coauthorship in the production of Vietnamese autobiography, Truong read *A Good Scent* as "a finalizing step in the removal and replacement of the authorial agency of the Vietnamese American literary voice."[2]

The center of contention is not so much the question of authenticity—though it inevitably shades into it—but the question of attribution, access, and the affective.[3] It is about whether writers of Asian origin are competent to define themselves, whether Asian Americans can hear the resonances and validate their appearances through one of their own, or whether they should continue their dependency upon whites to write about them, either out of respectful compassion or for the purpose of cultural hijacking. Under these circumstances, descriptive "standing for" has crucially retained the affective both to secure "insider" creativity and prevent "outsider" appropriation; however, it offers no guarantee of either accurate or desirable representations. The yardstick of descriptive representation may help delegitimate white writers about Asian American subject matter and point out the failure of Asian American writers to be faithful to their own histories and myths, but the significant disregard of writing as discursive mediation of reality ultimately makes the descriptive theory highly vulnerable; for it is unable either to account for the infinite multiplicity of the community itself and the finite nature of representation, or to address what features are to be reproduced and who will determine their relevance. Recognizing the pertinence of an author's social identity in the reading experience should not preclude the admission that textual representation is after all mediated by literary structures of expression—and with mediation also looms the question of representation's agential function.

Treating representation as "acting for" where activity for others is involved, Pitkin is particularly keen on characterizing the "tie between a representative and those for whom [s/]he acts" (1967: 114–15). Refusing to confine representative agency to the political arena, she introduces a host of terms that both summarize the representative's role and specify the nature of the representative and represented relationship—actor and agent; trustee and guardian; substitute, deputy, and attorney; and delegate and ambassador—each of which, in her view, constitutes "a fiduciary relationship, involving trust and obligation on both sides" (128–35). The difficult maintenance of the variations of the same relationship, Pitkin argues, lies very much in the semantic ambiguity of the word "agent," which, on the one hand, seems to "imply freedom to act, strength, initiative" while on the other, "can mean someone acting *for* someone else . . . not autonomously but in some way dependent on his principal" (122). This duality between "free" and "mere" agency is what underscores the conflict within the process of "acting for" and its terrain of struggle for equivalence between the representative and the represented.

Despite her fairly comprehensive categorical analyses, Pitkin does not address the author and audience nexus of our main interest. However, she does make provisions about representative agency that enable a reasonable anchoring of the minority writer and constituency relationship within the range of representative analogies she has drawn. First, she contends that representation can be an activity without entailing authorization (116), and second, she asserts that representation is fundamentally a "vicarious performance of tasks that cannot be personally exercised" (134–35). Both equip us with the necessary instruments to better perceive and navigate the points of tension between writerly agency and readerly interest.

According to Pitkin, the test of representation is not whether the representative is elected or appointed but how well he or she acts to further the objectives of those he or she looks after or is concerned with (116). Although she implicitly invokes the criteria of both effect and intention to ascertain the agency of representation, it is her main point that representation does not require formal arrangements. We can have representation "without formalities—without the exercise of another's rights or the ascription of normative consequences, without an 'official' representer" (142). In this, Pitkin seems to anticipate Michael Shapiro, who claims that representations are "practices through which things take on meaning and value" (1988: xi). Pitkin and Shapiro seem to concur that representations, whether intended or not, are activities through which objects or subjects take on both meaning and the relationships inherent in all forms of signification. Applying this insight to Asian American textual representation, we may reasonably argue that a writer's reference to the social entity called "Asian America" automatically qualifies him or her as its representative, a representative without formality but one constituted in activity. Coupled with our earlier discussions of representation as a mode of authority contingent upon its presence within the public sphere, as a correspondence of features associated with the affective, and the representative as necessarily a member of a larger organ or social constituency, the suggestion that representation is a covenant-forming activity urges one to regard the reception of Asian American texts as cultural events, which, in all their practicality, link the Asian American writer to his or her (un)willing community, binding them both, so to speak, in a marriage of representational (in)convenience.

Such (in)convenience is the product of the modern society, whose increasing complexity demands that a "citizen" fully exercise the rights and obligations of that role by being "in all places all at once." This requisite condition of modernity that one must but cannot be simultaneously present in many places is crucial for at least two reasons. First, it illuminates the importance of individual and group cultural presence in a representative democracy. Pitkin seems to suggest that the health of a modern citizenry depends on its members' full participation in the nation-state, both politically and culturally. Second, such demands of full citizenship intensify the need for help. Representation, in both the political and aesthetic senses of the word, becomes this help by making present what is actually not and by presenting the interests of the missing party. Pitkin states: "Any specialization of function involves the idea of representation"; and we may similarly regard the making of literature as a form of professional service that a writer/specialist performs for others (Pitkin 1967: 135). What makes Asian American and other minority writers unique in this situation is that although their performance of specialization does not involve any specific agent or client contract or formal arrangement, they are locked in by the suggestion of an equivalent relationship and bound by the association with an assigned collectivity. This is probably what Deleuze and Guattari have in mind when they conclude that the "cramped space" [of "minor literature"] "forces each individual intrigue to connect immediately to politics." However, rather than attributing ethnic "collective enunciation" to its lack of "talent" as they do, we should view this condition of constriction as exemplary of the representational unevenness within the nation (Deleuze and Guattari 1986: 17). That is, while European Americans can be represented as individuals who simultaneously stand for an American "universality," Americans of color can hardly transcend their ethnic collectivity to claim sovereignty of the self.[4]

The foregoing analysis provides a tentative description of the Asian American author and audience relationship as one of compulsory representation, a vicarious performance without consent. Although this is not a pretty or pleasant picture either for the ethnic writer or the ethnic constituency, it is a realistic admission of their "minor" and "ethnic" position and an honest step toward turning their constitutive confinement into empowerment in the nation. The understanding of literary production as a specialization of social function will, in this instance, facilitate the balance of representational needs. On the one hand, it helps the Asian American reader both to respect the knowledge and skill of the writer and to appreciate the formal conventions of language and the institutional structures of publication within which the writer works. At the same time, it encourages the writer not to ignore his or her inevitable social function or fundamental relatedness with the world outside the text—that is, the people who read and to whom the writer refers.

Instead of praising "free agency," in which the writer is said to be independent from the given racial constituency, or affirming "mere agency," in which the writer is condemned to the passive role of a communal mouthpiece (that is, to writing for only one reading community), we need a view that is capable of conceiving agency as mutually constitutive of both the author and the audience, since we are all too aware that "[a]t the extremes," whether it is tilted in favor of the agent or the principal, "representation disappears" (Pitkin 1967: 211). The definitions of representation by Pitkin as "vicarious performance" and by Shapiro as "practices through which things take on meaning" hint at this potentially liberating conceptualization. A slightly different elaboration of the same issue is found in the work of Judith Butler, who posits in the context of gender construction: "If gender is a construction, must there be an 'I' or a 'we' who enacts or performs that construction? How can there be an activity, a constructing, without presupposing an agent who precedes and performs that activity?" (1993: 7). Attempting to break through the barrier of deconstructivist dismissal and determinist control of agency—or variant forms of "free" and "mere agency" in our terms of discussion—Butler hones a rather cogent argument:

> If gender is constructed, it is not necessarily constructed by an "I" or a "we" who stands before that construction in any spatial or temporal sense of "before." Indeed, it is unclear that there can be an "I" or a "we" who has not been submitted, subjected to gender, where gendering is, among other things, the differentiating relations by which speaking subjects come into being. Subjected to gender, but subjectivated by gender, the "I" neither precedes nor follows the process of this gendering, but emerges only within and as the matrix of gender relations themselves. (Ibid.)

The applicability of this observation to the construction of an Asian American identity or to the process of bringing it into being becomes readily apparent if we substitute race for gender, and racialization for gendering. The value of Butler's formulation rests not so much on her illumination of the performative aspects of identity as it does on her insistent inquiry into the very material conditions of identity's emergence and operation.

Just as the performative articulation of identity involves the matrix of social relations to and by which the "I" and the "we" are both subjected and subjectivated, representation as "substantive acting" (to switch back to Pitkin) involves the same nexus of relation and agency mediated in the intricacies of language acts. There is no way to avoid representation without taking the beaten path of ahistoricism or solipsistic individualism. The argument for representation in the context of Asian American literary production, reception, and its reproduction in academic culture finally reveals itself as expressive of a desire to retain and/or restore an endangered author and audience, critic and community relationship so that the element of agency may be preserved to rearticulate existing social arrangements. This, perhaps, is the challenge of Asian American representation, a challenge that one of our best writers, Maxine Hong Kingston, has already answered: "I am nothing but who I am in relation to other people" (1991: 23).

Conclusion

Asian American Identity in
Difference and Diaspora

In the preceding chapters, I have treated Asian American literary imagining of the nation as a strategic struggle against the dominant definition of national competence and its uneven redistribution of democratic entitlement. "Claiming America" affirms the United States as an Asian American geopolitical space so that Asian Americans can secure the rights and obligations of citizenship in the nation-state. "Whither Asia" attempts to recognize Asian American family values in order to propose diasporic sensibilities and cultural alternatives. And the "Transvestic and Transpirational Asian" explains how those minority groups endeavor to enter the (re)public by eluding the negative racial register they embody. While these textual strategies are productive negotiations of Asian American social conditions and affective affiliations, the difficulties and dilemmas involved in these representational acts—"claiming America"'s potential lapse into nativism, "whither Asia"'s probable displacement onto ancestral culture, and "the transvestic and transpirational Asian"'s liable material disembodiment—betray the fundamental contradiction of contemporary American citizenship and the effects of alienation and abjection that Asian American literature can neither satisfactorily resolve nor erase.

In this final chapter, I correlate the creative imagination of Asian America with its critical representations and capture the literary contestation of and collaboration on the articulation of Asian American identity from a theoretical point of view. For the sake of classificatory and conceptualizing convenience, I divide contemporary Asian American criticism into three rough phases: "the ethnic nationalist phase" of the 1960s and early 1970s occasioned by the civil rights movement, the new immigration, and the emergence of a significant Asian American middle class; "the feminist phase," starting with its signature piece, *The Woman Warrior*, in 1976 and going through the 1980s, during which Asian American texts proliferated and received increasing academic legitimation; and the phase of "heteroglossia" (Bakhtin), present and ongoing, that coincides with the influence of market multiculturalism and the steady professionalization of Asian American critics. A synopsis of the first two phases paves the way for an engagement with "difference" and "diaspora" in poststructuralist modes of discourse, "postidentitarian" and "postnational" among them, which seriously questions "race" and "nation" as essential components of the Asian American construct.

If the emergence of Asian American literature has been tied to the rise of the Asian American middle class, the poststructuralist ghost writing of Asian American discourse cannot be independent from the increasing professionalization of our intellectuals. Besides its usefulness against orientalist divisions, the application of Western high theory to Asian American studies seems nothing less than an act of self-legitimation for both the subject of study and the subject of speech within the ivory tower. Like the writers to whom they devote their careers, Asian American academic critics are turning their alienation and abjection within the nation into its compulsory claims, but the effect of appropriating poststructuralist theory to articulate an anxiety rooted in structural unevenness is not without its irony.

I

The ethnic nationalist manifestations of Asian American literature in the 1970s at once responded to the history of the exclusionist mapping of the nation and resonated with contemporary movements of antiracism and anti-imperialism within the United States and with movements of decolonization elsewhere. The "No-No Boy" declaration of Asian American literary independence from white America and ancestral Asia enabled an unprecedented archaeological project of ethnic recovery as well as a simultaneous creative invention of culture on native American ground. *Aiiieeeee!*'s negative ethnocentrism, which both rejected American culture's Anglo-Saxon superiority and focused on Asian American subjecthood, provides an example of how the category of race could be strategically employed to form empowering collectivities. However, the desire for Asian American racial coalition is not without its problems. Given the history of Asian exclusion and the feminization of the Oriental within the United States,

Aiiieeeee!'s claim to truth and authority also took on a notable masculine tone. The "noise of resistance" became both a gesture of necessary over-compensation and an uncritical repetition of dominant cultural values on universality and masculinity. When the generational sensibility of post–World War II, post-exclusion, native-born Asian American intellec-tuals—predominantly male, perpetually emasculated, and persistently re-bellious—took center stage as the leading voice of counterhegemony, the racial unity of Asian Americans themselves was taken for granted and the question of identity was settled prior to internal dialogue and debate.

For all its sound and fury, the nationalist writing of the period remained largely unpublished in mainstream venues, and its reading was conducted in basement classrooms and dingy ethnic enclaves. These material limita-tions significantly qualified the purported power and the promised reach of a vocal literary program based on identity politics. The idea of an Asian American identity did not quite register in public imagination and national literary awareness until the publication of Kingston's rather private and personal memoir. *The Woman Warrior* was able to achieve perfect pitch on its formal excellence while striking a resonant chord with the rise of liter-ary feminism as both a legitimate and a legitimating critical practice. For the first time in history, an Asian American book was embraced as a work of art in the dominant national culture, and its achieved transcendence of racial boundaries on the shared category of gender produced a heteroge-neous readership beyond ethnicity. Not only has the novel chiseled an in-dispensable foothold in mainstream publishing for Asian American litera-ture, but the very fact of its dominant institutional validation has ensured the respectability of Asian American literary criticism.

Given the unprecedented positive visibility accorded to the text and its gendered nature, it is both materially feasible and logical that Asian Amer-ican literary criticism at this point turned feminist. Feminist frameworks made room for the ethnic woman that the ethnic nationalists had crowded out, and they also provided an enabling language with which patriarchy could be fundamentally interrogated, the female voice and tradition recu-perated, and the specificity of Asian American criticism legitimated. The feminist critique significantly challenged the blind chauvinism of the ear-lier phase and prompted a meaningful doubling of identity, not just in the obvious sense of allowing a multivalenced construction of ethnic subjectiv-ity to emerge, but also in the sense of opening up the racially exclusive ter-rain of nationalistic resistance to both Asians and non-Asians,whose inter-ests and investments were, however, primarily literary.

This doubling of the constituency was an occasion for internal splits and the formation of new alliances. On the one hand, the appropriation of texts by Asian American women within the academy secured wider distribution for the literature. Given the historically racialized and hierarchical nature of cultural institutions, white critics' attention to an Asian American text at once gave it importance and allowed Asian American critics to enter the field of criticism through the back door. The flow of traffic between territories, however, was never even, and the etiquette governing passage into the academy demanded appropriate passports. The transition to the feminist phase of Asian American literary development must therefore also be correctly understood as a crucial coeval transition to the emerging phase of Asian American literary professionalization. Asian American writers can now seriously contemplate the possibility of earning a living by selling books and teaching in the English departments of colleges and universities, and graduate students can now begin to anticipate a career of professing Asian American literature. This is not to say that positions in college teaching had been foreclosed before then, for the number of Asian Americans on science and engineering faculties and in Asian Studies programs in the postwar era would testify to the contrary. What the introduction of Asian American literature has meant is a first-time "Asian encroachment," with its full material embodiment both in text and in person, into the English department, the traditional stronghold of Anglo-American national culture that has a much overrated symbolic significance.

The transgression of the dominant sociocultural space by Asian American academics in the humanities and social sciences may cause more alarm than their colleagues in the practical and theoretical sciences did, for the former are suspected to have the power to threaten the core of the American civilization as we know it, while the latter's technological knowledge is believed to be of service. It is at this stage that the logic of speaking authority based on the authenticity of race and experience begins to grant the properly credentialed Asian American critic permission to ascend the podium and lecture on the texts of "their own."

In addition to complicating racial formation with gender formation, the doubling of identity in this feminist phase further marginalized one unaccepted writing group and nominally included another. The apparent conflicts that ensued between men and women, on such questions as history and authenticity versus art and invention, identity versus multiplicity, and feminism versus heroism (Cheung 1990) was therefore not, I wish to emphasize, simply an ethnic gender war. One only needs to observe that, despite women's numerical superiority, the practice of feminist methodology is not restricted to female scholars alone. Instead, it is a theoretical practice of increasing academic orthodoxy whose influence extends almost equally to women and men in the profession, and whose acquisition and application are to a certain degree tied to the notions of datedness and sophistication invariably embedded within scholarly practice. While the benefits of feminism for women are obvious, Asian American male critics in the academy cannot be indifferent to an emerging discourse that not only is ensured professional authority but also speaks to their own condition of feminization within the nation. What happened in this movement from ethnic nationalist to feminist dominance is the unspoken coalition and consolidation of Asian American academic critics, regardless of gender, with white critics of the academic left and with professional intellectuals of color, all of whom are bound by the institutional and scholarly requisites and pedagogies of literary studies. In light of this trajectory, history should view literary feminism not as a gender-exclusive practice but as an academic practice. Similarly, the battle between nationalists and feminists ought not to be reduced to gender in-fighting. Rather, it should be properly historicized as a competition over the conditions of hegemony between institutionally affiliated writers and critics and the freelancers of the Asian American intelligentsia, with their varied distance from and proximity to the dominant national culture and its apparatuses.

For the most part, feminist critics have been theoretically aware of the need to multiply the construction of identity and generally willing to simultaneously consider the interaction of gender and race. But the nationalist allegation of collusion between Asian women and white men has pressured some feminists into such a defensive posture that they increasingly resort to the preservation of the margin. The urge to pluralize identity has under these circumstances become a promulgation of an additive notion of gender oppression, whether double or triple, in which suffering can be ranked by number and explanation of a female literary tradition can be derived from some Newtonian law of more oppression leading to more reaction. Similar to the nationalist's conspiracy theory, which mistakenly perceives female literary presence as a sign of white suppression of Asian male authors, the feminist's theory of Asian male domination tends to confuse patriarchy in the socioeconomic arena with patriarchy in literary production and distribution. Although there is no known male monopoly in the English language component of the Asian American tradition (unlike in the Afro-American tradition at one point in history, for example), it will have to be conjured up in order for the discourse of critique to proceed. In this regard, both nationalists and feminists alike have been silent on the class privilege they enjoy as men and women of letters. The clamor for voice among the native intelligentsia has perpetuated the muteness of the true subaltern of the Asian American constituency.

The nationalist clearing of discursive ground and centering of a unitary racial subject, and the feminist widening of our literary readership and securing of our texts as deserved objects of professional study, are succeeded by an era of energetic heteroglossia that is able to entertain as never before divergent ideological viewpoints and aesthetic expressions. The consistent output of Asian American creative and critical works in recent years marks at once the growth of writing subjects and the expansion of market avenues. It is also accompanied by the increasing frequency of the term "difference" and its partner "diaspora," in the invocation of "Asian America(n)" as a political and cultural concept. In almost all the recent Asian American anthologies the words are used to explain the works' structure, scope, subjects, and styles, and they are central in critical discourses that radically revise the disciplinary assumptions of Asian American studies.[1]

In fact, the integrity of Asian American studies was under siege the moment it was consolidated. As noted in the Introduction, the emergence of Asian American definition is symptomatic of the United States' transition from monopoly to transnational capitalism. The removal of structural barriers in immigration and employment for Asian Americans has to do with both the ascent of transnational capital and the rise of a postindustrial and postmodern American consumer culture. However, except for the inspiration of third world decolonization, such transnational elements and their influence on Asian American social demography were not recognized in Asian American discourse of the 1970s for two reasons. First, the middle-class intellectuals of the time had an explicitly left-leaning, working-class agenda; the racial formation of Asian America was ostensibly working against its white embourgeoisation. Second, to fulfill its objective for wider social, educational, and economic access, the movement politics wanted both to capitalize on the history of Asian exclusion and its residual effects of alienation, and to refute the abjective "model minority" thesis that Asian Americans had already achieved such access without the nation-state's social rearrangement. By the late 1980s and early 1990s, however, the effects of affirmative action and transnational capital were being felt, as Elaine Kim puts it, in the astronomical increase and diversification of the Asian American population in "origin and ethnicity, language, social class, political situations, educational backgrounds and patterns of settlement" (1993: xi). Drastic residential dispersion, new occupational opportunities, and the revolution in communication and transportation technology dramatically transformed the contour of the Asian American community. But it took at least a decade for these social changes and a recognition of Asian American diversity to register in critical discourse.

The failure of the renewed nationalist strategy in *The Big Aiiieeeee!* both to be truly in tune with the transformed historical reality and to capture the imagination of the people has made the theory of "difference" and "diaspora" a far more attractive explanatory tool. The variety of Asian American literary criticism accumulated in the earlier phases—contextual studies with a tendency toward historicism old and new (e.g., E. Kim's *Asian Amer-*

ican Literature and A. Ling's *Between Worlds*), (inter)textual studies combining formal and thematic exegesis (e.g., Sau-ling Wong's *Reading Asian American Literature*), regional and authorial studies with an archaeological impetus and feminist focus (e.g., Sumida's *And the View from the Shore* and Cheung's *Articulate Silences*)—are now challenged by the surge of "heterogeneity, hybridity, and multiplicty," to borrow the keywords of Lisa Lowe's influential article, which both charts new critical terrain and embraces as its rudimentary philosophical principle resistance to closure and affirmation of discontinuity.[2]

It is not that difference was an altogether fresh concept, as the analysis of the feminist unfixing of racial identity and references to the range of scholarship have amply indicated. What is new at this phase of Asian American literary criticism is the concept's poststructuralist moorings and overdetermination of the way in which the demographic diversity of Asian America is to be interpreted. The critical turn to "post-ist" sensibilities has as much to do with the capacity of postmodernist, poststructuralist, and postcolonialist theories to provide cogent answers to the complexity of postexclusion, post-1965 Asian American social reality as it does with their academic respectability in the post–civil rights era of neoconservative resurgence. As with the transition to the feminist phase, the present move toward heteroglossiac difference must be situated with the "postentry" entrenchment of a limited but real Asian American critical cadre within the academy who wish to retain their institutional foothold. "Difference" begins to profoundly question the role of "race" in identitarian politics, while "diaspora" seriously challenges the ethnic narrative of possessing the "nation." Such revisions of Asian American studies should be engaged both against the movement politics they oppose and within "the postmodern condition" of their institutional production (Harvey 1989; Lyotard 1989).

II

We can start by contrasting two economies of difference, one "structural" and the other "poststructural." As shown in the Introduction, the "Oriental" is a form of difference occasioned, modified, consolidated, and expanded over time by Anglo-Saxon Americanism. The Asian has been structurally and semantically alienated from authentic citizens to occupy the positions of the object and abject. Having recognized the quintessence of race in the organization of the nation-state and the asymmetrical social relationship it regulates, the ethnic nationalists invented the term "Asian America(n)" both to empower a historically negated collectivity and to rearticulate its relationship to the nation. Though their program was never explicitly couched in terms of "difference," the nationalists had a fine grasp of "identity" as a condition of group exclusion. They refused to view the individual instance of deprivation as private, and registered it instead as the exclusionary product of a European American citizenry. Asian American difference was both understood and used as a macro-concept of group identity rather than a micro-concept of individual idiosyncrasy. The conceptualization of difference as a pan-ethnic identity under the umbrella designation of "Asian America(n)" acknowledged the heterogeneous elements within while at the same time rallying formerly discrete ethnicities to collective empowerment. It provided a radically new way of seeing self and others and a liberating view of social reorganization that was able to challenge the dominant formation of the nation.

While the nationalist fashioning of Asian American identity and its movement politics were coding group difference primarily in term of race, race was regarded not as a biological essence but as the visible trigger for social injustice against all Asian groups. This fixation on race, though likely to fix an oppositional identity as stable and univocal, hardly loses sight of the asymmetry of power within the nation. Although ethnic nationalist strategies are likely to ignore the dialogic voices within Asian America and are inadequate for dealing with a plurality of interests, their insights about the hierarchy of social division and the necessity for broad social transformation are perhaps too easily dismissed in contemporary revisionist critique.

The poststructuralist form of Asian American difference, generally speaking, marks a drastic movement away from the notion of racial collectivity toward one of intra-ethnic individuality. Like its ethnic nationalistic forerunner, which emphasizes structural difference to mobilize an oppositional identity, the poststructural formulation of difference is a vehicle Asian American intellectuals use to come to grips with the gap between the present social reality and an earlier paradigm. It attends to the pressing need, on the one hand, of mediating the internal contradictions of Asian American social demography, and on the other, of responding to shifting political climates and dominant discursive pressures. Within intra-ethnic parameters, the conscious recognition of individual diversity appears both a critical alternative and a crucial corrective on the part of the critics to avoid the conflation of representative agent and constituency, which was in part responsible for the nationalist vanguardism of old. The self-awareness of being involuntary racial representatives and the realization that the nature of their work is the business of articulating identity seem to have led Asian American intellectuals to separate their own privilege within the dominant institution from the privation of Asian Americans outside it. The description of the constituency's multiplicity serves at once to uncover the class cleavages within the community and to clarify the confused relationship between intellectuals and the masses that is subsumed under coalition politics. This focus on difference opens up space for a more complex charting of the constituency and a fuller appreciation of plural memberships and conflicting interests of the Asian American individual.

More important, this poststructural individuation of collective racial identity represents an abortive attempt to counter the two complementary strategies of the conservative revolution: "neoracism," to use Etienne Balibar's term, and "neoconservatism," to borrow from Omi and Winant (Balibar and Wallerstein 1991; Omi and Winant 1986). The dominant theme of neoracism, Balibar argues, "is not biological heredity but insurmountability of cultural differences." It respects "tolerance thresholds" and idealizes segregated collectivities (21–23). In this formulation, Asian American difference could become a group difference of an exclusively cultural nature, not only inscrutable to others but transhistorically permanent. Such group cultural difference could be easily appropriated to blunt the radical edge of "multiculturalism" by turning it into a form of tribalism.

However, anxiety about the technologies of neoracism does not necessarily achieve satisfactory resolution in the call for irreducible individual difference. As Omi and Winant remind us, neoconservatism has pivoted upon the exclusive interpretation of racial equality as "a matter of individual rather than group or collective concern" (1986: 129). In this scenario, the poststructural itemization and atomization of difference in the chain of gender, generation, class, and sexual orientation tends both to remove the structural significance of race as the "central axis of social relations" and to become susceptible to the neoconservative agenda of nullifying the programmatic social rearrangements of earlier decades (61). The promotion of such difference, while capable of warding off potential usurpations of internal power and disrupting the imposition of homogeneity, is inclined first to discourage the cultivation of an already fragile sense of Asian American community, and second, to erase the historical differentiations of the national constituency.

Against this background, the poststructural questioning of an ethnic nationalist identity and its intervention against segregation appear hardly a better alternative. Strangely enough, the evocation of difference does not represent a true departure of identitarian thought but rather its privatization. Although the discourse of difference has ransacked the essentialization of identity beyond repair, the prevalent reference to difference as a thing in and by itself, as a floating signifier or a transcendent category of endless enumeration, leads to the reproduction of essentialism in and through categorical isolation and individuation. The poststructuralist recognition of Asian American difference is rarely understood as a concomitant relationship between members, or between members and non-members, but as a contradiction in the autonomous subject itself. As a result, the efforts of negotiation in the social arena are replaced by the needs of individual psychological fulfillment. The historically alienated and abjected Asian American is suddenly believed to be in full possession of the power of meaning-making and self-invention. Identity, rather than being the outcome of normative regulation and contestation, becomes a matter of personal choice, like picking up groceries at the supermarket. "The personal is political" has by now been transformed into either "the political is personal" or "only the personal is political." When difference is finally coded as an idiosyncratic merit or drawback to be either cherished or conquered by the individual, its depoliticization via personal choice is complete: personal biography overrides collective history, the sovereign individual is favored over a critical sense of community, and the past and present forms of historical and social determination are eventually dismissed as extraneous. The parallel between this atomic and ahistorical concept of the self in difference, and the myth of the Asian American "model minority" whose individualist initiative will always triumph, independent of institutional functions, becomes readily evident. Individual difference not only encourages an illusory identification with the conquerors of history but also an active disidentification both with the conquered and the colored makers of that same history. Difference is consequently inconspicuously meshed with the reassertion of an undifferentiated, universal individualism through which the dominant modes of both neoconservative and late-capitalist production are consolidated.

The poststructuralist appeal to discrete difference not only obscures the race relationship that the original term "Asian America(n)" highlights but also obscures the fundamental influence of "capitalist relations of production" on "the whole set of social relations" (Laclau and Mouffe 1985: 160). A discussion of Asian American difference does not make much sense, it seems, until the restoration of the political domain is supplemented with the economic one. Under these circumstances, the realization that "capitalism is the most pluralistic order history has ever known, restlessly transgressing boundaries and pitching diverse life-forms together" is especially pertinent (Eagleton 1994: 4). We may benefit further from the insights of Susan Willis, who has succinctly argued that "the greatest achievement of American democracy is its erasure of fundamental social and economic inequalities and its promotion of a culture where difference is perceived as a variation in style or opinion" (1991: 374).

The Marxist cultural critics help us at once to relate the promotion of Asian American difference to the ceaseless creation of markets and to understand the dynamics between the commodification of difference and the depoliticization of social and economic unevenness in the United States.

The interest of the dominant group in expanding its ethnic market has made it sensitive to changing Asian American demography not as a political constituency but as a community of consumers. The apparent goodwill exhibited by commercial houses in publishing Asian American texts in recent years, and the occasional Asian media presence on network television must be read less as an indicator of cultural equalization than as a new realization of the ancient profit motive that undergirds capitalism. On this note, we recognize that the interest of foreign capitalists in either consolidating their national or regional culture or selling their distinctive traditions to the West also plays a role in the dissemination of Asian and Asian American difference in the postmodern global cultural market. An Asian or Asian American cultural commodity thus meets the demand of the dominant market for fresh products, the desire of the ethnic contingent to see itself as part of mainstream public culture, and the Asian interest in either contending or colluding with the orientalist marketplace. Although these material forces seem to open space for Asian American cultural production and promise that different kinds of capital will vie for control of the Asian image, all is not rosy. Profit may make capital raceless, but the racialized cultural market in the United States will almost always ensure that the subjective interests of the mass audience are unevenly served by the same capital. Relationships among different kinds of capital may determine how social relationships are represented in cultural products, and social relations may affect the way in which capital, both economic and imaginative, is invested.[3]

As a result, the liberating force of capital to mediate between the heterogeneity of Asian American social and existential actuality and the textual world of reified culture will also threaten, as the body of this book shows, to subordinate or sacrifice the satisfaction of specific Asian American psychosocial needs for "general (white) interest" in a practice that Stanley Fish characterizes as "boutique multiculturalism" (1997). This is not to say that a cultural product has only one kind of use value or that a white-oriented product cannot be appropriated for the fulfillment of an Asian American desire. Rather, it cautions against the "United Nations" format of market multiculturalism where Asian American passports of difference are identified as Chinese food, the Japanese tea ceremony, the Filipina dream girl, South Asian spices, and perhaps some Cambodian donuts. When multicultural artifacts and products are turned containable, collectible, and consumable,[4] capitalism's subordination of racialized and gendered labor in the economic realm also becomes invisible. Difference begins to justify the identification of different commodities with different markets and becomes a vehicle for maintaining social distinctions. As it lapses into the ritualistic celebration of infinite self-invention and market choice, the complicity of this poststructuralist concept of difference in turning the study of culture into a form of global fun fair and mystifiying the role of capital cannot be overlooked.

III

Similar to the promotion of difference, the concept of the diaspora questions both the orientalist geography of the antithetical East and West and its ethnic nationalist revision in claiming America. Just as race was made a collective social category in the 1960s, the insistence on the category of the nation not only inscribed the Asian American experience of contribution and exploitation on the broad history of the United States but also helped Asian Americans address the state politically by demanding group rights and resources. However, when the state's removal of overt structural barriers and greater international capital mobility led to greater diversity of the Asian population in the 1980s, scholars in Asian American studies began to rethink their disciplinary paradigms and original missions in the academy.[5] Building on the suspicion of an Asian American paradigmatic indenture to traditional American studies (Hune 1977; S. Chan 1978), these scholars cautioned against subsuming Asian American historical experience within the received narrative of the nation and proposed placing it in the context of international labor and capital migration (Okihiro 1991a: 23; Mazumdar 1991: 29, Hu-DeHart). All seemed to concur on the need to resist the academic absorption of Asian American studies into a single conceptualization of American civilization, but none appeared ready to detach the role of the nation-state and the imbricated function of the Asian within it from their academic disciplines. The concept of the Asian diaspora was introduced to argue against a single national identity with one destiny in favor of a shared history that recognizes different origins and multiple transformations.[6]

More recent versions of the diaspora, however, cast a shadow of doubt on this persistent disciplinary allegiance to the nation and its interest in the Asian American constituency. Similar to the poststructuralist unpacking of racial identity with difference, and contemporaneous with the "postnational" and "postcolonial" discourses in literary studies and the social sciences, they question the adequacy of "Asian America(n)" as a nation-centered racial formation.[7] In an important contribution to this dialogue, Arif Dirlik (1993a) faults the term on two counts. The "'American' side of the term, which identifies a continental notation with a national entity," omits, according to him, recognition of Asian migration to Canada and Latin America. The "Asian" component of the term is "even more problematic" because it "encompasses people of diverse national, cultural, [and] linguistic" backgrounds who share only "common origins somewhere in Asia and a common experience of oppression and discrimination peculiar to Asians at the hands of a hegemonic culture." Combined, Dirlik argues, Asian American "was not so much a descriptive term as a product of a coalition-building political discourse." Since the term is unable to address areas and peoples beyond the boundaries of the United States, and since it suppresses "otherwise vastly different peoples" into a formal homogeneity, Dirlik proposes "Asia-Pacific" as an alternative (305–6).

By calling attention to the movement of peoples in the formation of the Asia-Pacific, Dirlik recognizes Asian immigrants in the materialization of the region and equally "an Asian Pacific element in the construction of the United States as a national entity" (ibid.: 315). However, Dirlik's idea of the "Asia-Pacific" seems to be conceived as the antithesis of "Asian American," thus suggesting a mutual exclusivity that is contrary to his intention of expanding the definitional scope of Asian America.[8] He never substantiates, for example, why a continental denotation of "America" is better than a national one, and better for whom. Nor does he explain why a specific ethnic reference, such as Vietnamese, Laotian, or Samoan, is logically superior to the regional or racial term "Asian." One is equally puzzled why the term "Asian American" should include people beyond the territorial confines of the United States and in what manner the term presupposes a racial homogeneity.[9] Dirlik's near equation of the "Asiatic" in orientalist formation with an "Asian American" collectivity, and his dismissal of "Asian America(n)" as not "descriptive" but merely "discursive" have, inadvertently perhaps, ignored the basic social dimensions that otherwise constitute his informed understanding of the European American and Asian American definitional struggle. However, his inattention to the complex interrelations among region, nation, and race within the term "Asian America(n)," and his oversight of the contradictions within "the Asia-Pacific idea" have resulted in a paradigmatic interruption of the two concepts that appears too hastily drawn.

"To justify a perspective that places their experiences within an Asian-Pacific context," Dirlik both emphasizes and enumerates Asian Americans' "ties" across the Pacific—kinship, social, political, economic, and cultural ties that "bound [them] to their society of origin and to some extent shaped their behavior in the United States" (ibid.: 311–15). While the connections he speaks of are valid, they lack historical differentiation. Not enough attention has been given to how the degrees of bonding between homeland and host country have been influenced by changing modes of capital, by unstable social and political circumstances, and by generational issues. In the absence of these crucial historical distinctions, Asian Americans' ties to Asia seriously retard the development of Asian American subjectivity, encourage the conflation of Asian Americans with Asians, and threaten to undermine the continuing effort to define an Asian American identity within the materiality of U.S. history and geography. When ancestral determinations are believed to override local determinations—the law, taxes, daily life in the United States—the "ties" lose their spatial and temporal significance and become almost permanent (311).

It is worth noting that to confirm the various "ties" he mentions, Dirlik has drawn almost exclusively from pre-1965 data to describe what appears to be primarily a post-1965 reality in which Asian Americans have very different kinds of ties to their ancestral homelands. The ties Dirlik refers to were forged under structures of legal exclusion and segregation that precluded Asian American citizenship, and of the politics of the Cold War that severely hindered, in the case of the Chinese American, communications with the ancestral mainland. In this pre-1965 era, kinship, social, political, economic, and cultural ties were enhanced and reinforced by the inability of Asians to legally form ties with America and reform their allegiances. These ties were at the same time undermined by the lack of normal channels of cultural exchange. The result is the paradoxical existence of Asian Americans bound tangibly to the United States, though without formal recognition, and intangibly to Asia, with which they had little physical contact. While the ties did serve important affective functions for the survival and sustenance of the alienated community, they were weakened by communication barriers and strengthened only through imaginative longings. Such cultural discontinuity, however, has always been naturalized out of existence and replaced with the dominant cultural interpretation of Asian unassimilability in order to justify exclusion.

The emergence of "Asian America" in the post-1965 era thus responded to this hegemonic conception of "Asian" ties and the political need to affirm the buried ties of Asians with America. The "Asian" in "Asian American" is therefore not the same as the "Asian" detached from the national notation of the United States. The "Asian" in "Asian American" has its own historic trajectory that is related to "Asia" as it is conventionally understood, but that has departed in significant ways both from the latter's suggestion of physical geography and from cultural history. The "Asian" in "Asian American" has become more racial in signification and it has tipped, by abandoning the function of a noun and assuming that of an adjective, the geopolitical scale of the diaspora toward an always differentiated American nationality.

The post-1965 reality is also riddled with ironies. The Asian American moment of claiming national allegiance was the moment when the nation-state actually began to experience declining significance. The mid-1960s simultaneously witnessed the deindustrialization of the United States and the industrialization of some parts of Asia. It also saw the breakdown of the state-brokered postwar "Fordism," wherein the labor movement forced employers to partially subsidize the social costs of economic growth, notably by paying higher wages and taxes to support the welfare state. The quest for higher profits prompted U.S. corporations to seek less expensive and more tractable labor, which ultimately led them to shift capital first from the industrialized Northeast and Midwest to the South and the Southwest, then across the border to Mexico, and finally to Asia (Nonini 1993: 164–65). In large part responding to the mounting pressure of transnational capital, the nation-state relaxed its restrictive laws on Asian immigration to facilitate both the transfer of capital from core countries to peripheral societies and to attract both the professional labor and the entrepreneurial class from Asia to America so that the needs of an emerging segmented labor market could be satisfied. It is these changes, coupled with developments in transportation and communications technology and détente and the normalization of relations between the United States and China, that allowed Asian ties of the kind Dirlik lists to become stronger and more practical. It is also these material forces that gave rise to what Bruce Cumings has called "Rimspeak," or the discourse of the Pacific Rim (1993), and the kind of "Asia-Pacific idea" that Dirlik uses in turn to question the validity of an "Asian American" discourse. The central questions remain, however—whether the entity of nation-state upon which the categorical justification "Asian America" rests is becoming obsolete, and whether such a regional formation as the "Asia-Pacific idea" should take its place.

"The Pacific Rim," Cumings rightly notes, "is neither a self-contained region nor a community, but just that: a rim—peripheral and semiperipheral societies oriented toward Tokyo and the U.S. market" (1993: 41). It is "a [transnational] capitalist myth" that both "renews an old tendency of capitalism to rationalize all behavior in the name of economic production," as Woodside has put it, and "contributes to the imaginative dispossession of much postwar Asian nationalism" (1993: 26). The euphemistic "rim" in place of the geographically specific "East Asia" both acknowledges the Japanese origin of the term and centers the Euro-American role in its construction, proffering an egalitarianism that its actual formation, the division of labor and the distribution of power within, contradicts. The "Asia-Pacific" idea, as Dirlik himself has said in a different context, is finally "a EuroAmerican invention" that thrives on political and spatial ambiguity (1992).

As such, it is a regional idea that can effectively exploit transnational economic interests but cannot totally erase transnational inequality. Although collectivities of Western labor are undermined by the transnational alliance of capital with Eastern elite classes and the latter's appropriation of state apparatuses for the exploitation of local labor, the state-transcending myth of the rim is less of "the regional internationalization of even a single ruling class ideology" and more of a "class-based archipelago" (Woodside 1993: 20, Cumings 1993: 34). As Masao Miyoshi reminds us, ours is an age not of "*post*colonialism but of intensified colonialism under [the] unfamiliar guise [of] transnational corporatism." The formation of the regional discourse reveals not so much the declining significance of the nation-state as the increasing significance of class, not so much the dissolution of borders as their recharting, and not so much an all-encompassing inclusiveness as a mystification of economic and political inequality (Miyoshi 1993: 728, 750, 744). Given the complex nexus of nations and corporations, one wonders if the substitution of "Asia-Pacific" for "Asian America" can realistically enable transnational working-class solidarity of the kind that Marx once proposed, or a transracial gender solidarity of feminized labor. The regional formation, or any diasporic formation that dismisses the role of the nation-state as its constitutive geopolitical element, will ultimately prove to be an ineffective means of intervention.

Probably sensing such shortcomings, Dirlik eventually shifts his appeal to the "local" via Stephen Sumida (1991: 324). Unlike Sumida's commitment to an identity based on the colonial and plantation histories of the Hawaiian islands, and on the pidgin as an embodiment of human agency between time and space (xvi), Dirlik's "local" seems placeless. Under the spatial dubiousness of the "Asia-Pacific," the local lacks the geopolitical and racial specificity that the category "Asian America(n)" signifies unequivocally. The insertion of Asian Americans in the formation of the region (the Asia-Pacific) appears to have the effect of removing them from the nation (the United States), resulting in an identity of ambivalent locality and even more ambiguous history. The absence of a dominant national culture in the charting of local cultures and communities, and the absence of a superpower in the formation of the region, however, tend to play into purposeful or premature assertions of postmodern utopianism that a global village of equal membership has already arrived.

IV

The present poststructuralist proposals of difference and diaspora can be regarded as an intensified contradiction of "the professional-managerial class" that Asian American academic critics have come to embody. The interest of this new class, as Barbara and John Ehrenreich remind us, is often "antagonistic" both to "the capitalist" and to "the working class" (Ehrenreich 1979: 21, 17). While not to claim that Asian American intellectuals had a seamless identification with the interests of labor at the emergence of the Asian American movement (see Wei 1993), the very external relation of ethnic nationalists to the institutions of learning enabled both their coalition with the causes of the downtrodden and their initial project to democratize the university and deghettoize the community. Movement politics could be mobilized through a singular conception of the Asian American pan-ethnicity via an equally uniform notion of class constituency—that is, the working class.

When a more diverse and mobile class composition replaced the more uniform and stagnant class formation of old, Asian American critics in the academy were caught not only between labor and capital, whether Asian or American, but also in the leftist historical legacy of Asian American studies itself, whose relation to the institution of their revolution had also been irrecoverably altered. As "salaried mental workers" without their own means of production, Asian Americanists remain antagonistic to both capital and the state, which funded the institutions that they were nominally a part of. Conditioned by "their major function in the social division of labor" as agents in the "reproduction of capitalist culture," on the other hand, their general relation to the Asian American constituency was inescapably paternalistic, despite their good intentions (Ehrenreich 1979: 12, 17).

The class contradiction of Asian American critics is, in other words, both determined and mediated by their own material and ideological ambivalence. Their subsistence and survival within the educational institution, we realize, demand a particular pedagogic and scholarly practice that is intricately linked to the production of knowledge. Although ideologically speaking, Asian American knowledge production in the academy necessarily resists the dominant culture and the political economy of capitalism, it cannot take place without the (re)production of capital and capitalistic social relations; neither can it be indifferent to the academy's system of (e)valuation. While the subject of Asian American studies remains true to its origin, the site and emphasis of its struggle have shifted dramatically. To put it bluntly, we may say that Asian American studies as a political instrument of radical social transformation has been successful only to the extent that it has constituted itself as an academic discipline and has thus ensured a limited intellectual and racial representation within the academy. Rarely acknowledged, however, is the fact that the cultural work of restructuring the ivory tower, of shattering the WASP hegemony and its master tropes of history, of reconstituting individual subjectivity through minority discursive practices and canonical revision—of which Asian American literary studies is doubtless a part—is marked by the left's general retreat from movement politics to textual politics, or the politics of aesthetic representation.

The inability to make true revolutions in a time of increasing class divergence, the deeply felt commitment to the left's utopian vision, and a simultaneous recognition of the scholarly standards of the academy deeply trouble Asian American intellectuals in the academy, who now seem to find comfort in postmodern and poststructural theories. In this context, the theory of difference and diaspora provides a way out of the professional and managerial class contradiction, for it seems able to reconcile the raw political energy of the rhetoric of a bygone movement with the current official reality of acceptable scholarship by basically substituting "discursive" politics for "real" politics. It is in the conflation of the political sites of nation-state and capital at large and the university as their metonymy that we encounter the field's persistent imaginary. Because Asian American studies could not achieve its original objective of fundamentally transforming U.S. capitalist society, it is believed that the university could be an alternative site of continuing revolution. Since realities are expressed through discourse, textual representations of Asian Americans—in the college curriculum, for example—may be considered indicative of the actual social standing of the group.

By seizing on "difference" as an independent variant of (the) "Asian America(n)," one can cut through barriers and connect with other discursive constituencies. The category of gender, for instance, can be linked with feminist or gay and lesbian movements outside the Asian American community in order to form alternative alliances. Similarly, the term "diaspora" can turn the Asian American condition of exile into the global condition of capital and people migration, thus transforming the deprivations of Asian American political and cultural banishment into a celebration of displacement and cosmopolitanism (Said 1990). A view of difference as pure, private, and individual eliminates the historical role of race in the formation of U.S. democracy. The discourse of diaspora, on the other hand, encourages both the kind of "long-distance nationalism" that Benedict Anderson condemns (1994) and the kind of disregard for U.S. politics that the "model minority" thesis insists on.[10] Without discounting the multivalenced formations both "difference" and "diaspora" can helpfully generate, one has to recognize that any movement away from the notion of Asian America as a compelled solidarity not only disregards "race" as a central category of address and analysis, but also virtually dismisses "nation" as a viable ground for critical alliance. When race is erased and the term "racism" is self-censored in the fluid rhetoric of difference, a disregard for Asian American group representation by the privileged class becomes apparent.[11]

The poststructural uses of difference and diaspora have finally come to represent an unsuccessful challenge to the continuing condition of Asian American exclusion and abjection within the United States. If ethnic nationalists of the 1960s try to overcome this condition through a single conception of race and class and its attendant identity politics, the use of difference and diaspora for poststructuralists of the 1990s would seem only (and let me invoke the key deconstructionist concept of "différance") to defer such a condition but not to transcend it. The poststructuralist rewriting of Asian American identity reminds us that the real difference it can make is in helping us consider (the) "Asian America(n)" in historical and material terms, as a collective racial category differentiated within and deferred from the nation. Not until we return to the uneven historical opposition between citizens and aliens, and the contemporary contradiction between the legal assurance of equal rights and the cultural rearticulation of national competence, can we seriously engage the subordination of group differences by the dominant culture as a precondition for formal equality or entertain the possibility of full democratic consent.

Retaining "Asian" as a racial description and "American" as a national signifier is an important step toward such engagement. The notions of difference and diaspora can then meaningfully bring out the important contradictions within both "Asia-Pacific" and "Asian America" that do not diminish the function of the state in either regional or ethnic national formations. They can help expose the inadequacy of an undifferentiated racial collectivity wherein Asian American subjects are supposed to assume identical relations to either the United States or their ancestral lands. And they can also help highlight the essential role of class in post-1965 Asian American demography, wherein the capacity for national transcendence is recognized as class-specific (Espiritu and Ong 1994). As part of a conversation about origin and destination, the concept of the diaspora can be an uneasy but necessary negotiation between capital and labor, the metropolitan and the subaltern, to press the question of whom Asian Americans identify with and where they locate their home. As a group condition, difference challenges the use of universal norms as a means of exclusion and confronts the failure of such "universality" by embracing the "partial" experiences and needs of all kinds of human beings. Only when American citizenship is reconceptualized as a formal commitment to the abstraction of liberty and equality for all can Asian Americans, along with other abjects of the nation, be truly embodied in the constitutive claim "we the people." Contemporary Asian America literature, in this broad sense, is a cultural imagining of the nation; it articulates the perennially deferred yet constantly perfected promise of the "America," to evoke Carlos Bulosan, that "is in the Heart."

Reference Matter

Notes

INTRODUCTION. ALIENATION, ABJECTION, AND ASIAN AMERICAN CITIZENSHIP

1. Kettner fails to address the Asian aspect of the development of American citizenship, an omission that is only partially due to the book's focus on the period from 1608 to 1870.

2. Against the grain of prevailing scholarship, Garry Wills argues that "we have no reason to keep assuming that a Lockean orthodoxy explains the early formation of Jefferson's political thought." There are "more parallels in Montesquieu than in Locke [in the Declaration of Independence] (Wills 1979: 173, 169–75). The term "Atlantic Republicanism" is from J. G. A. Pocock, who contends that instead of Locke it is the combination of Aristotle's thesis of civic human nature and Machiavelli's thesis that "provided a powerful impulse to the American Revolution" (527). For the emergence of American empire as a way of nationalist thinking in the post-Revolution years, see Horsman, esp. 81–97. Also useful is Amy Kaplan and Donald Pease's critical anthology on the cultures of U.S. imperialism.

3. See Cheyfitz 1993 and Maddox 1991 on how the Native American way of life fundamentally troubled the Anglo-American conception of democratic government and citizenship, and P. Wald 1993 on how the cultural premise of possessive individualism disqualified both Indians and blacks from enfranchisement.

A case on the eligibility of Chinese testimony in court, *People v. Hall* (1854) actually established one of the earliest legal precedents in the defense of a racially exclusive American democracy, anticipating the reasoning of *Dred Scott* and the denial of Asian American citizenship. For information on the case, see Takaki 1993: 205–6, and Wu 1972: 41. For a legal history of Asian exclusion and its contestation in courts, see esp. Konvitz 1946, S. Chan 1991, and H. Kim 1994. Unlike the Chinese, who were considered "Indian" and denied political rights in *People v. Hall*, Mexicans were defined through the Treaty of Guadalupe-Hidalgo (1848) as a "white" population and accorded the political-legal status of "free white persons" (Omi and Winant 1986: 75). In theory, "Mexican citizens in the ceded territories would automatically become U. S. citizens unless publicly elected to remain Mexican citizens" (Kettner 1978: 253).

4. Since 1882 the Asian exclusion laws have fanned national anti-immigration sentiment and inadvertently affected southern and eastern European immigration to the United States after World War I (tenBroek et al. 1970: 17). The Immigration Act of 1924, for example, while excluding more Asian groups, also established a national quota system based on the demography of 1890 that favored immigration from northwestern Europe and limited that from southeastern Europe (Hutchinson 1981: 190–94, 484).

5. During exclusion, the Asian was to the European American, object to subject, as Indians and blacks were abject to subject. The removal of Asians from American national space would upset this subject and object opposition and entail a revival of black and white antagonism. I will soon develop Kristeva's category of the "abject" and note the shift toward Asian American abjection in the contemporary United States.

6. While Said treats orientalism mainly as a form of European colonialism, my take on American orientalism tends to focus more on the latter's domestic dimensions, its aspects of "internal colonialism" and its relation to Anglo-American nationalism. See Lisa Lowe on British and French orientalisms (1991a).

7. Fredric Jameson (1988) has argued for a correspondence between the mode of political and economic production and its cultural figuration, thus between "market capitalism" and "realism"; between "monopoly capitalism" and "imperialism,"/"modernism"; and between "late capitalism" and "postmodernism." While my periodization of American orientalism clearly benefits him, a very useful sociological discussion of Asian immigration in monopoly and then transnational capital can be found in Cheng and Bonacich 1984, and in Ong, Bonacich and Cheng 1994, respectively.

While the dominant modes of political economy distinguish the two periods, the dates in the diagram refer specifically to the judicial and legislative assignments of Asian American status. Thus, *People v Hall* (1854) was a legal milestone in the passage of Asian exclusion legislation and the onset of Asian prohibition. The conclusion of exclusion and the acquisition of Asian American formal equality are marked by a dual date because: (1) the 1943 repeal of the Chinese Exclusion Act was replaced with small quotas that practically enforced continued exclusion, and (2) de facto Asian exclusion did not end until the 1965 Immigration Reform Act (Hutchinson 1981: 432–43).

8. Richard Drinnon defines the phrase more broadly as "another name for native-hating—in North America, of 'niggers,' 'Chinks,' 'Japs,' 'greasers,' 'dagoes,' etc.; in the Philippines, of 'goo-goos'; and in Indochina, of 'gooks'" (1980: xvi).

9. Quotation marks appeared around "free white" in the definition of citizenship in the Naturalization Act of 1790 (Kettner 1978: 236). I am not maintaining here that laws and state policies are objective; as Omi and Winant point out, they

continue to support and justify unequal social relations, although in an apparently race neutral manner (1986: 72–78).

10. While Althusser distinguishes between the repressive and ideological apparatuses with the former "function[ing] massively and predominantly *by ideology*," he nevertheless acknowledges a significant convergence of the two, and the "secondary" function of each category in the effect of the other (Althusser 1984: 19).

11. I elaborate on the flexible overlap and structural affinity of "alienation" and "abjection" in the next section.

12. The hyphenated "Asian-American" is the rendering used by the dominant (white) culture; without the hyphen, "Asian American" is the way Asians describe themselves. "Asian-American," in my usage, implies a racial, cultural, and national exclusivity, while "Asian American" does not.

13. The 1965 act responded directly to the movement of transnational capital by absorbing skilled labor abroad, but it also underestimated the racial component of such a professional labor force. As Bill Hing notes, the Kennedy and Johnson administrations thought that the 1965 act would encourage more southern and eastern European immigration; they did not anticipate the Asian influx that "upset the ethnic mix of this country" (Edward Kennedy quoted in Hing 1993: 39–40).

14. For a different application of Kristeva's "abject" in the context of Asian American theater, see Shimakawa 1995.

15. The model minority discourse is conventionally understood to be a national(ist) discourse engaged in by the dominant U.S. culture. Asian American critique of the discourse has generally pointed out its omission of the uneven economic conditions and class disparities among a diverse Asian American population, its neglect of the longer working hours and unaccounted-for-labor that contribute to family income (help from older and younger family members in small family businesses, for example), its concealment of the disparity in education and income between whites and Asians, and that it pits the Asian against other minorities in the classic method of divide and conquer. For a useful review of the subject, see Keith Osajima 1988; Ronald Takaki 1989: 474–84; Sucheng Chan 1991a: 167–81; Gary Okihiro 1994: 139–47; and Ruth Hsu 1996.

Here I also use "model minority" in the international context to suggest how certain Asian "economical miracles" are positioned in the discourse of transnational capital as models of (co)prosperity for the less developed Asian and African countries. My broadening of the "model minority" discourse's neocolonial implications has benefited from the works of Fawcett and Cariño, Arif Dirlik, and Masao Miyoshi. An extensive analysis of the transnational turn in Asian American critical discourse can be found in the book's conclusion.

16. I am alluding to Washington's *Up from Slavery*.

17. See Omi and Winant's (1986) critique of the dominant ethnicity-based paradigm of American historiography and their insightful "racial formations."

18. The dominant cultural practice of putting up a "glass ceiling" significantly qualifies the meritocratic argument of model minority discourse by differentiating between the kinds of qualifications. Resorting to a variation on the old orientalist correspondence between racial innateness and national competency, it justifies the exclusion of Asian Americans from leadership roles by insisting on the immutabil-

ity of Asian cultural passivity and linguistic deficiency. I allude to this practice later when I link Kristeva's concept of the "abject" with Bourdieu's of "distinction."

19. One must note the irony that Reagan's 1984 praise of Asian family and national values (Takaki 1989: 475) contrasts starkly with Senator Blaine's 1879 declaration that the Asiatic "has no regard for family, does not recognize the relationship of husband and wife, does not observe the tie of parent and child, does not have the slightest degree the ennobling and civilizing influences of the hearth stone and the fireside" (Stuart Miller 1969: 3).

20. While we have not seen blatant institutional racism of historical proportions, the legislative proposals in recent years to limit both legal immigration and the rights of legal immigrants are expressive of a die-hard xenophobia. Although "abjection" is used to distinguish the dominant positioning of Asian Americans, the mode of "alienation," I wish to emphasize, is neither quite absent from nor quite defunct in such a positioning. The mass hysteria about Asian economic invasion in the 1980s (concurrent with such symbolic violence as in the movie *Rising Sun* and actual racial violence in the murder of Vincent Chin), and the paranoia about Asian corruption of American politics in the 1990s are prominent examples of how "alienation" always lurks behind "abjection."

21. For another instance of Asian American abjection, see Omi and Takagi's analysis of the affirmative action debate (1996).

22. Again Iris Young has shown us how the abjective process of habitual aversion and avoidance modulates with anxieties over the loss of identity, and how cultural imperialism is enacted through the abjective conditioning of everyday feelings and reactions despite the legal guarantee of equality for all (1990: 141–48). See also Minow 1990, esp. 1–16.

The best illustration of how the law fails to do full symbolic justice to guarantee Asian Americans their equal subject status is perhaps this one liner from *Dragon*, the biographical movie on the martial arts legend, Bruce Lee: "Yes, you are an American citizen," his white mother-in-law addresses Bruce, "but you are not an American."

23. For Gunnar Myrdal, author of *An American Dilemma* (1944), the contradiction of American democracy is not the exclusive juridical interpretation of "the American creed," an abstraction of citizenship rights, but its adulteration by individual values and personal inclinations. For a cogent critique of this definition of the American dilemma, see Ringer 1983: 240–47.

24. Against a prevailing theoretical impatience with structural totality, I have spelled out the terms of oppression particular to Asian Americans in order to reveal the transformative tension between domination and resistance. However, such a formulation of American orientalism may sharpen the theoretical conflict between determinacy and agency and invite criticism from either side. Rather than extensively deal with this hypothetical debate, I wish to alert the reader to works that address these concerns. See Homi Bhabha (1994: 72) on Edward Said (1978); Aijaz Ahmad on Fredric Jameson (Ahmad 1992: 95); Jameson 1988: 354; Ahmad 1992: 120; the implicit rejection by Albert Memmi (1965: 95) of Gilles Deleuze and Félix Guattari 1986; and Henry Louis Gates 1991b: 462.

I use "pre-scriptive" to suggest a prior dominant inscription that prohibits the U.S. inclusion of the Asian, and the "post-scriptive" as a form of Asian American writing back (in)to that national space. The successive legal "pre-scriptions" of Asians, in other words, have inadvertently charted over time a negative space of so-cial affinity among the originally discrete Asian Pacific ethnicities that are capable of becoming a "post-scriptive" "panethnicity" (Espiritu). Though the term "post-scriptive" serves my specific examination of Asian American literature since 1965, I do not mean to imply that Asians did not write and publish in the U.S. before that. There are two points that I wish to emphasize. First, Asian American works had very limited impact beyond the ghetto community and Asian American voices were largely inaudible in public/national culture. Second, the authors were writing with-out the explicit awareness of "Asian America" as a discursive category and concep-tual alternative with which their successors are both blessed and troubled. While these earlier Asian American writers clearly share similar structural positions with their counterparts today, and we may indeed fruitfully situate their work in the American orientalist paradigm that I suggest, I argue against the lumping of these two groups in the establishment of a coherent Asian American tradition. It is not that a comprehensive Asian American literary history cannot be done—indeed it has been admirably accomplished by the pioneer endeavor of Frank Chin and com-pany, and Elaine Kim (1982)—but the question of roots and continuity ought to be pursued with distinctive care. This seems both a justification both of the book's limited period focus and its broad theoretical implications.

25. On different views of the canon's representational functions, see Taylor 1994 and Guillory 1993: vii–xiv, 3–82. Instead of adopting exclusively either a "rep-resentationist" view of cultural artifacts, in which the image is *the* thing, or a "dis-tributionist" view of canonical process, in which the absence of the image is be-lieved to be solely determined by the denial of literacy, in this book I attempt to bring both viewpoints into interactive fruition and then offer my own critical read-ing of representation in Chapter 8 (quoted words are from Guillory).

26. The phrase "professional/managerial class" is taken from Barbara and John Ehrenreich's article of the same title, in which they argued for a new class consist-ing of professionals and managers with a distinctive relationship to the two tradi-tional classes of capitalism, workers and owners. The phrase "Asian American re-naissance" deliberately echoes and expands on Matthiessen's term; he designates the writings of Emerson and others as emblematic of America's "coming to its first ma-turity and affirming its rightful heritage in the whole expanse of art and culture" (Matthiessen 1941: vii).

CHAPTER 1. *AIIIEEEEE!* AND THE PREDICAMENT OF ASIAN AMERICAN ARTICULATION

1. For an examination of the strikes, see the commemorative issue of *Amerasia Journal* (*Salute to the 60s and 70s: Legacy of the San Francisco State Strike*) 15, no. 1 (1989); and chap. 1 of Wei 1993.

2. The fact that the study first appeared in *Amerasia Journal*, an outlet of Asian American expression that originated with the movements and then was anthologized in *Roots*, one of the earliest and now classic texts of Asian American studies, is by itself important.

3. The work of the Sues draws heavily on Gordon W. Allport's analysis of Jewish Americans (Sue 1971: 38, 44), while Tong acknowledges his indebtedness to black nationalists.

4. Since the "traditionalist" is the sole heir of Asian culture, the ideal Asian American, the Sues conclude, is by necessity deprived of its cultural heritage. "The possibility that immigrants can maintain traditional values is highly unlikely since their number is relatively small" the Sues observe, and "concern should be addressed to the functional value of Chinese traits under the present circumstances. If the traits are no longer adaptive for attaining proclaimed goals, then they must be changed" (Sue 1971: 45, 47). While the Sues recognize the historical transformative nature of cultural practice, they seem oblivious to the time of their writing, when the majority of the Asian American population was already becoming immigrant, and a diasporic cultural sensibility was becoming possible through advances in transportation and communication technologies.

5. Both historical and effective at its own moment of articulation, the Cantonese prominence of Chinese Americans that Tong affirms, however, is already changing, and so will the disavowal of Confucian linkage in Asian American culture. For the Neo-Confucian redefinition of transnational capital, see Wei-ming Tu 1991b and 1996, and Dirlik 1995.

6. We examine them first in the context of Chin's theater in the last section of this chapter and treat them more extensively in Chapter 7.

7. I am using "minority discourse" in the general sense defined by Abdul JanMohamed and David Lloyd, as "cultural struggles waged by minorities in the effort to "represent themselves" (1987a: 6). For an elaboration of the nature and context of the concept, see the two issues of *Cultural Critique* (6 and 7) they coedited.

8. See the essays in Tachiki et al. 1971 and Gee et al. 1976; see also Omatsu (1989b) for his association of Asian American movement not with Martin Luther King, Jr., but with Malcolm X (xvi).

9. Chin and Chan cite a speech by David Hilliard, Black Panther Party chief of staff, at a San Francisco Chinatown rally in which he pronounced that Chinese Americans were "the 'Uncle Tom minority' and were contributing to holding the blacks back" (1972: 74). Neither disputes the role Hilliard assigns the Asian American or argues against his misconception that the Asian is part of the institutional infrastructure that subordinates African Americans. More ironic perhaps is the second example Chin and Chan cite, this time from Richard Wright's *Black Boy*. Shorty, the black man who offers the white man a chance to kick his ass for a quarter, is in Chin and Chan's view a Chinese American persona. In accepting Hilliard's allegation, one wonders if the Asian American is being kicked twice, and happily so as well.

10. See John Guillory's important argument (1993: 3–82), Raymond Williams's genealogical study of "Literature" (1985: 185–86), and Kwame Anthony Appiah's elaboration on "Race" (1990a, 274–87).

11. Efforts are being made to translate original Asian language materials about the Asian diaspora into English. Lai et al.'s *Island: Poetry and History of Chinese Immigrants on Angel Island*, Hom's *Songs of Gold Mountain: Cantonese Rhymes from San Francisco Chinatown*, and Kao's *Nativism Overseas: Contemporary Chinese Women Writers* are examples. However, the material limitations on the popularization of these Asian language texts remain strong. The reasons, in my view, are institutional. Asian language material on the diaspora does not fit well into either traditional Asian studies or traditional Asian American studies, both of which are nation-based disciplines. In the former category, indigenous works are favored to the exclusion of immigrant and expatriate works. In the latter category, not only is the discipline largely the terrain of native-born scholars whose Asian language facility is often weak, but the academic reward system itself also dissuades attempt at translation, which is a time-consuming but much undervalued scholarly work. Although global capital restructuring has spurred transnational cultural studies in recent years, it is often the English writing "native" who gets the privilege of speaking for the "local," which is again nation-based—Salman Rushdie can write for India, for example, but not for Indian Britain. The recent transnational turn in Asian American studies will doubtless enhance the importance of Asian languages, but it is unlikely to transcend its status as an attachment to the English Asian American canon.

12. But the kind of dual cultural heritage that informs the ideal Asian American writer in Wand, for example, is the privilege of a well-schooled one, most likely an immigrant with a good Asian and then American education. I do not mean to discount the role of family as the site of education or the possibility that a native Asian American writer could acquire an ideal dual heritage by attending both an American public or private school and an Asian-language school. Many of the problems of ethnic cultural translation that native Asian American writers face have to do with the place and the manner in which Asian culture is received and valued. See Chapter 6 for further elaboration.

In their discussion of ethnic inclusion, Hsu and Palubinskas include three Asian American groups: Chinese, Japanese, and Filipinos. In addition to these ethnicities, Wand includes Korean American and, exceptionally for that period in history, a section on "Polynesian oral literature" that takes into consideration Hawaiians, Samoans, and Tahitians, which the more recent term "Asian-Pacific American" has just began to accommodate (Wand 1974: 9). Despite his inclusiveness, however, Wand seems unaware of a Confucian cultural chauvinism that marks, and in my view mars, his analysis of the Pacific cultures.

13. *No-No Boy* is the title of a novel by John Okada, which owes its posthumous fame to the *Aiiieeeee!* editors' heroic rescue. In it, Ichiro refuses to swear unqualified allegiance to either the Japanese emperor to whom he has no attachment or the American government that violates his constitutional rights; this foreshadows the basic position of Chin et al. with regard to ancestral Asia and white America. The choice of the male noun "boy" is also crucial in understanding the editors' perspective, as will be obvious later.

14. Referring to some immigrant writers, the editors remark that "their being Chinese precludes their ability to communicate the Chinese American sensibility," a logic not only contradictory to the acquired nature of culture that they seem to

embrace but also strangely identical to orientalism, which says that your being racially Asian necessarily precludes your being American (Chin et al. [1974] 1983: xxxviii).

15. The demarcation lines get fuzzy in practical operation, however. For example, Jade Snow Wong's *Fifth Chinese Daughter* (1945) is labeled an Americanized Asian text, while its successor, Monica Sone's *Nisei Daughter*, published eight years later, is hailed as an Asian American book. The structure of cultural conflict so offensive to the *Aiiieeeee!* editors and yet so internal to both autobiographical works is read completely differently. One justification for the difference in their interpretation may be that Wong does not dwell extensively on lives under the shadow of Chinese exclusion, whereas Sone includes the experience of Japanese internment. These choices have a lot to do with the stories' respective time settings, but they reveal nevertheless the ideological positions on which the *Aiiieeeee!* editors seem to have based their judgment.

16. I am thinking of the two prominent aspects of ethnic nationalism: first, the rhetoric of race and repudiation, and second, the integrity of a native ethnic identity. It is worthwhile to note that the transnationalization of Asian American discourse in recent years, like its ethnic nationalization in the 1960s and 1970s, is fundamentally related to the concurrent transformation of African American discourse via Paul Gilroy's *Black Atlantic*.

17. The successful tapping of the mass market for Asian American works remains the achievement of Maxine Hong Kingston's *The Woman Warrior* (1976). The many works excavated and endorsed by the editors of *Aiiieeeee!*, for example, were published by the University of Washington Press until after Kingston's record-breaking debut, as were many other contemporary Asian American works in book form.

18. I am thinking in particular of "Confessions of the Chinatown Cowboy" and *The Chickencoop Chinaman*. For a reading of these two works in the context of Chin's corpus, see Li 1991 and Li 1992b: 319–31. See also earlier analyses of Chin by Elaine Kim (1982) and Cheng Lok Chua (1987).

19. In his pioneering 1933 study of Euro-American literature about Chinese Americans, William Fenn discredits such concocted dialects by pointing out their "obvious distortions as substitution of *I* for *r*, and the indiscriminate addition of *ee*" (1933: 92–100).

20. During his days in Iowa, Frank Chin was often blamed for his failure to explore "the local color of Chinatown." "You know," remarked his instructor, "you're writing about the Chinese in a way that I don't think American people would be interested in," to which Chin retorted, "Because they were just like people, right?" Chin was stunned to learn not only that he "had a point of view" about his people but that his "point of view wasn't white," for he depicted the individuality of the ethnic subject in ways that did not conform to mainstream expectations (Nee and Nee 1972: 379).

CHAPTER 2. CAN MAXINE HONG KINGSTON SPEAK? THE CONTINGENCY OF *THE WOMAN WARRIOR*

1. The focus of this chapter is the interpretive history of *The Woman Warrior*; readers interested in aspects of its textual negotiations should see Li 1988.

2. These exchanges are from Frank Chin, "Letter to Maxine Hong Kingston," July 13, 1976; and Maxine Hong Kingston, "Letter to Frank Chin," August 8, 1976. Permission to quote the correspondence granted by both authors.

3. Kingston's choice of China as the site for her story is especially interesting if one knows that *The Woman Warrior* is not Kingston's first book but her first *published* book. An excerpt from an earlier manuscript was published after *Woman Warrior* as "Duck Boy," which is set in a nonspecific U.S. setting. I believe the shift from the fictional normality of America to exotic China in *The Woman Warrior* was a conscious artistic effort to get her manuscript published.

4. The literary fate of the Eaton sisters, Edith Eaton [Sui Sin Far] and Winnifred Eaton [Onoto Watanna], may crystallize the inevitable relation between an Asian American author's writing and her presumed cultural legitimacy and spatial belonging. See Amy Ling's *Between Worlds*.

5. See *Readers' Guide to Periodical Literature between 1973–1976* for a comprehensive listing of the topics addressed.

6. Elliot's remark is from Chun 1989. As Elaine Kim notes, the editorial marketing of Asian American fiction as autobiography also happens in the case of Carlos Bulosan's *America Is in the Heart* (Kim 1982: 48).

7. Chin, "Letter to Kingston."

8. I am not altogether discrediting poststructural theories of autobiography as self-invention. Rather, I mean to emphasize that autobiography as a generic convention functions for minority writers both as an available channel of expression and as a constrained form of expression. James Olney observes in an analogous situation that "black writers entered the house of literature through the door of autobiography . . . because black history was preserved in autobiographies rather than standard histories" (1980: 15). I might add that in the social construction of literary hierarchy, autobiography has become a peculiarly "ethnic" or "minor" form.

9. It is noteworthy that Chin's reconstruction of *The Woman Warrior*'s reception considerably simplified the camps of opposition as if there were only one community response. The diversity of opinion about the book—some of which we have already sampled—as dictated by gender, class, and professional status is erased in his allegory. See also note 14.

10. The usage is also reflected in English book titles such as Carl Crow's *Foreign Devil in Flowery Kingdom* (Crow 1941).

11. While affirming Kingston's textual negotiation especially of the mainstream audience and the orientalist marketplace, I am not suggesting that the shortchanging of Asian American interests is the only way such interests can be served. Rather, I am pointing to the material dilemma of Asian American writers who are unable to

count on a majority Asian American audience for their creative products. The duality of the audience has in no small measure determined the multiplicity of Asian American form, as I shall demonstrate not only in Kingston's own shift of style when she reconceives her audience, but also in other Asian American works as well.

12. Following Kingston, Morrison won the National Book Critics Circle award in 1977. And after Kingston received the 1980 National Book Award for *China Men*, in 1983 Walker won both the National Book Award and the Pulitzer Prize for *The Color Purple*.

13. The publication of *The Woman Warrior* signaled the beginning professionalization of Asian American writers and of critics as well. In many ways, the categorical viability of "Asian American literature" is currently sustained by the work of both professional Asian American writers and critics. Though the contribution of Asian American academic critics to the legitimation of Kingston is significant, their earlier works were unable to considerably alter the basic critical terms on *The Woman Warrior* set by the predominantly white academic left, who in my view, were principally responsible for the book's initial canonization. For this reason, the remaining analysis of the text's interpretive history concentrates on the work of non–Asian American critics, and address scholarship published by 1991, when the original argument of this chapter was completed.

CHAPTER 3. CANON, COLLABORATION, AND THE CORPOREALITY OF CULTURE

1. A few words of qualification are in order. First, I define canonicity as the status of a text that is reproduced through critical scholarly essays and books, annotations, and anthologies and generally incorporated into academic curricula. Popular critical acclaim is not equivalent to canonical acclaim but may prompt it. Second, although the publication of Asian American authors by commercial and small presses has become more frequent, as determined by the rules of the market, and although Asian American editorial efforts have enabled the preservation of texts in many Asian American anthologies, the Asian American presence in standard American literary anthologies remains locked in the "quota" condition. The exception, again, is the *Heath Anthology of American Literature*, which includes many examples of minority literature and has an Asian American coeditor, Amy Ling. Third, the inclusion of Kingston's "No Name Woman" in mainstream American literary anthologies and the recent publication of the Cliffs Notes guide to Amy Tan's *Joy Luck Club* also signal the geocultural "Asian" prominence of "Asian American" canonical intelligibility.

2. See note 25 in the Introduction for a related discussion of Guillory.

3. For *China Men*'s recharting of American historiography and negotiation of the canon, see Li 1990.

4. Chin's earliest plays, *The Chickencoop Chinaman* and *The Year of the Dragon*, were published in 1981 by the University of Washington Press.

5. Although the sequel to *Aiiieeeee!* is a post–*Tripmaster Monkey* publication, its contents were released in a series of Chin's journalistic essays between *Aiiieeeee!* (1974) and *The Big Aiiieeeee!* (1991) and were thus available to the public.

6. Unless specified otherwise, all quotations from *Tripmaster Monkey* are from the edition cited in the bibliography (Kingston 1989b).

7. Although the Hemingway allusion is clear, Kingston could be drawing from a less obvious source as well. I am thinking of Chin's story "The Only Real Day," first published in 1976, whose protagonist, Yuen, toys with the idea of shooting himself in the mouth (see F. Chin 1988: 77). Kingston's description of Ah Sing's "loud takeover" (3) may be a reference to Chin's favorite mental excursion, which he calls "the movie about me" (F. Chin 1978: 6). The Western composition of his mental reference not only indicates the young artist's sense of the "cool" but also anticipates the difficulty of ethnic recovery.

8. Compare Kingston's recapitulation in Ah Sing with Chin's original statements. "We have no street tongue to flaunt and strut the way the blacks and the Chicanos do" (F. Chin 1976a: 557); "Chinese- and Japanese-Americans have been here for years, strutting and changing language, shaping up a mind, a tongue, a way of making sense people from Asia and white folks in America all find a little strange and have responded with hostility, outrage and maybe a little fear, because we're shouting now. We are shouting to be heard" (F. Chin 1972b: 5); and to Ishmael Reed, "I wanted a legit production in Frisco, in the Year of the Dragon, the Bicentennial year, because the highly-charged 1976 was ripe for the first Chinese American theater downtown and legit. That's what I got. Chinamans who caught the show were pleased to see my work and surprised that the whites didn't cut my bit of Chinatown wisdom, 'Everybody knows Jesus Christ sucked cock at the Last Supper and left his lovers' feet dirty. They don't need the old Charlie Chan. They found Christ'" (F. Chin 1977: 42–43). It is worth noting that Ah Sing does not pose the question "Where's our Beethoven?" How Kingston treats Asian American tradition's emergence in relation to the black "protest novel" and Chin is a point to which I will return.

9. Ah Sing's deliberate act of detachment from his racial identicals is accompanied, not coincidentally, by his unspoken thought, "'Oriental.' Shit," the collective label he wants to dodge.

10. Elsewhere in *Tripmaster Monkey* Kingston asks about Ah Sing: "What had he to do with foreigners? With F.O.B. émigrés? Fifth generation native Californian that he was. Great-Great-Grandfather came on the *Nootka*, as ancestral as the *Mayflower*. . . . His province is America" (41).

11. According to the 1980 census, 62.1 percent of Asian Americans were foreign-born (Fletcher 1992: 14).

12. It is meaningful to see Nanci as Kingston's character-surrogate and Ah Sing her projected Chin both for the romantic possibilities that the narrative aborts and for the theoretical differences that it rehearses.

13. Ah Sing's preoccupation with race and color is accompanied by moments of self-doubt, as in the following:

> Confederates who have an interest in race: the Ku Klux Klan, Lester Maddox, fraternity guys, Governor Faubus, Governor Wallace, Nazis—stupid people on his level.

> The dumb part of himself that eats Fritos and goes to movies was avidly interested in race, a topic unworthy of a great mind. Low-karma shit. (75)

The quote is an example of many such textual maneuvers in which Kingston cautions against the essentialist position on race that she imagines Ah Sing/Chin would take. We shall focus in detail on Kingston's narrative undercutting of race talk after examining her affirmation of its provisional necessity.

14. Using her "accredited" or "canonical" position, Kingston retells well-known Asian texts to an English-speaking audience in order both to legitimate their place in the American setting and to reconstitute the notion of cultural literacy.

15. Chin's story was first published in *Chouteau Review* in 1976.

16. It is interesting to introduce Frank Chin's rare reference to the penis for a contrast. In "The Eat and Run Midnight People," we have this description:

> The beer down my spine killed everything of me but my prick. The prick that grew bigger than New York and nudged the moon in outer space was loose. . . . I was the great rider, Jonah in the whale, a load of shot in my dad's primed harden pumping grease out of Ma's little cunt that night in a backyard chickencoop, in Chinatown, Oakland, California. (F. Chin 1988: 23)

17. Richard Dyer's essay on the male pin-up genre contains a brilliant analysis of the positions of looking and the power relationships involved in its process (1992: 103–19).

18. Again, Wittman Ah Sing: "Martians from outer space and Chinese monks talk alike. Old futs talking fustian. Confucius say this. Confucius say that. Too clean and good for sex. . . . We're all de-balled and other worldly, we don't have the natural fucking urges of the average, that is, the white human being" (320). Kingston is not so much endorsing phallocentrism as she is confirming the reality of Asian American male desexualization in the dominant culture. I will discuss the transformation of this gender focus to a racial one as I continue my reading of the "unzipping" passage.

19. I have substituted "he" for Eliot's original "I" in this quotation from "The Love Song" (Eliot 1973: 451).

20. This is the opening stanza of Whitman's *Song of Myself*, from which Kingston clearly draws many of her key concepts and terms for *Tripmaster Monkey*. Note, for example, not just the name of her protagonist but the chapter titles, such as "Trippers and Askers," "Linguists and Contenders," and "Twisters and Shouters." I have, for the purpose of my argument, changed the positions of the pronouns in Whitman's original lines, which read: "And what I assume you shall assume / For every atom belonging to me as good belongs to you" (25). I again take up the question of race, face, and narrative (ad)dress in Chapter 7.

21. Kingston paraphrases Baldwin when Ah Sing notes "that history is trapped in people means that history is embodied in physical characteristics, such as skin colors" (312). The "willful innocence" phrase seems also indebted to Baldwin, who writes in "Stranger in the Village" that "there is a great deal of will power involved in the white man's naiveté" (1984: 166). This and subsequent references to Baldwin are from his collection of essays, *Notes of a Native Son*.

22. In my view, Kingston's remark to Chin about the genre's black antecedents in the 1950s could not possibly refer to either *Invisible Man* or *Go Tell It on the*

Mountain, two fairly conciliatory works of African American fiction. It is highly probable that in an instance of literary anachronism she actually had in mind Richard Wright's markedly confrontational *Native Son* of an earlier decade, a representative text of the genre that kindles so much of Baldwin's commentary.

23. Richard Fung has commented on a similar feminization in the video representation of gay men's relationships, where more often than not "the Asian man acts the role of the mythologized geisha" (1991: 21). This seems to confirm that racial hierarchy readily crisscrosses sexual stratification regardless of sexual orientation.

24. If white women figure prominently in Carlos Bulosan's autobiographical work as mentors and healers of his American Dream, and signify his acceptance into the nation, they often become in the contemporary ethnic nationalist corpus objects of both desire and compensation for institutionally emasculated Asian American men. See, for example, Shawn Wong's "Good Luck, Happiness and Long Life" (1976) and Frank Chin's "The Eat and Run Midnight People" (in F. Chin 1988).

25. The romantic resolution of the nationalistic *Tripmaster Monkey* does not square off well. The last-minute portrayal of Wittman Ah Sing as a pacifist is redundant because of his earlier characterization as such (137, 190, 235, 242). The sudden dismissal of the ethnic tradition on the base of its innate violence is equally unconvincing not only because it contradicts the novel's prevailing tone of tradition's eulogy, but also because it does not subject the heroic warfare of Western epics to similar critical scrutiny. The narrative end does manage to convey, however, that Wittman Ah Sing's mind is indeed a mixed slate, exemplifying an enabling miscegenation of consciousness. This is evident not only in the protagonist's references to books and movies. Kingston has also revealed how a blend of indigenous and imported theatrical properties and acts pattern Ah Sing's multicultural revue, particularly in the chapters "A Pear Garden in the West" and "Bones and Jones." In an apparent repetition and revision of Chin's *Chickencoop Chinaman*, where Tam claims himself the "result of a pile of pork chop suey thrown up into the chickencoop" (1981: 7), the narrator of *Tripmaster Monkey* declares, "From these chicken scraps and dog scraps, learn what a Chinese American is made up of" (1989b: 277), thus turning the variegated composition of an Asian American into a sign of pride.

26. John Guillory's wording quoted in Gates (1992: 316).

27. Frank Chin's introductory essay in *The Big Aiiieeeee!*, "Come All Ye Asian American Writers of the Real and the Fake," is a deliberate misreading of Kingston's subtitle, "His Fake Book." I am playing on the paradoxical meanings of their usages here to illuminate what Kingston has aptly called her book's anachronism. The preface to *Tripmaster Monkey* reads: "This fiction is set in the 60s, a time when some events appeared to occur months or even years anachronistically."

28. The African American call-and-response theory or deconstructive intertextuality operates much like the ancient Chinese practice of commentaries and exchanges on classic texts. Frank Chin has gone so far as to promote this tradition as a unique Chinese genre. "As a rule of style and literary activity," Chin observes, "it means the fighter writer uses literary forms as weapons of war. . . . The written recital and free association dialog with Sun Tzu became a literary form of their own: commentaries, [which] not only elucidate the nature of the form and forms of

war but [can] be a coded act of war as well" (1985: 112–14). The relationship of *Tripmaster Monkey* to the coded act of war should by now be obvious.

CHAPTER 4. AMERICAN ROMANCES, IMMIGRANT INCARNATIONS

1. All references to and quotations from *Jasmine* in this chapter are to Mukherjee 1989a unless noted otherwise. The novel can be read as a fictional version of Mukherjee's Neo-Platonism and secularized Hinduism. See the interview with her in the *Massachusetts Review* (Carb 1988: 651).

2. Like the other Asian American writers examined in this study, Mukherjee has cashed in on the aesthetic and political meaning of representation. Her adroit rhetorical shifting among "me," "us," and "you" enables the conspicuous yet cleverly concealed authorial "I" to claim for herself the natural outlet for the "lower frequencies," the immigrant blues of contemporary America.

3. Mukherjee dedicated her first story collection, *Darkness* (1985) to Bernard Malamud, whom she also portrays in her "Maximalist" essay as a representative of the Jewish American tradition. Mukherjee's attribution is valid because of the following. Though Abraham Cahan, Mary Antin, and Anna Yezierska preceded Malamud, neither William Dean Howells's promotion of Cahan nor the belated feminist scholarship on Antin and Yezierska has made them "beginnings of the tradition," so to speak. In terms of literary history, Malamud and Isaac Bashevis Singer first constituted the Jewish American canon and by extension the American immigrant tradition. However, Mukherjee's attribution to Malamud also cleverly conceals *Jasmine*'s indebtedness to Mary Antin's autobiography, *The Promised Land* (1912). While I do not focus on this intertextual connection in the following reading of *Jasmine*, I want to point out that Antin's optimistic belief in the distinctively American process of self-transformation and invention is Mukherjee's as well. In both her essay and novel, Mukherjee clearly resonates with the spirit of Antin, whom I quote: "I was born, I have lived, and I have been made over. . . . All the processes of uprooting, transportation, replanting, acclimatization, and development took place in my soul. I felt the pang, the fear, the wonder, and the joy of it. I can never forget, for I bear the scars. But I want to forget—sometimes I long to forget. I think I have done the bidding—I want now to be of today" ([1912] 1997: 1, 3).

4. Mukherjee's essay is interestingly framed by her naturalization ceremony, which is for her less a "bureaucratic exercise" than "a literary experience" (1988a: 1).

5. "It would seem that Americans have a kind of resistance to looking closely at society," Trilling argues. "They appear to believe that to touch accurately on the matter of class, to take full note of snobbery, is somehow to demean themselves" (213–14). It is because of this dismissal of class, the "investigation of the problem of reality beginning in the social field," Trilling feels, that the novel of "its classic intention . . . has never really established itself in America" (1950: 212).

6. "The philosophical doctrine of the romance," Miller contends in *The Raven*

and the Whale, provides the "form in which Young America sought to prove their Americanism" (1965: 339). "American figures, sprung from native soil, big as the mountains, large as the lakes, oratorical as Niagara," he insists, "could not be done in the novel, not by Jane Austen, Bulwer, or Thackery. . . . The great American book had to be big, and it had to be romance" (ibid.: 257). Similarly he asserts in "The Romance and the Novel" that romance is a "providentially given" form that facilitates the most "serious efforts" to express "the meaning of America, of life in America" (1967: 245).

7. Mukherjee's appropriation for her female protagonist of American romance's basic assumption of male mobility in "a world elsewhere," to echo Richard Poirier, is at odds with what Nina Baym has called the "woman's fiction," whose conceptualization of self is deeply embedded in the protagonist's negotiation of social restrictions and possibilities (Baym 1978: 36).

8. In his 1929 story "The Swimmers," Fitzgerald defines America in the following terms: "France was a land, England was a people, but America, having about it that quality of the idea, was hard to utter. . . . It was a willingness of the heart" (quoted by Bruce L. Greenberg in Stern 1986: 237). I thank Norman Bock for alerting me to this source.

9. Jasmine's mating criteria are definite and revealing: "I couldn't marry a man who didn't speak English, or at least who didn't want to speak English. To want English was to want more than you had been given at birth, it was to want the world" (61).

10. In addition to having real relationships, Jasmine is also a "phantom lover" of Du, Bud's, and her adopted Vietnamese son (26), and the "would-be lover" of Darrel (209), whose failure to open a Radio Shack in New Mexico with Jasmine (a version of Vijh & Wife capitalism of Jasmine and Prakash) finally led to his suicide.

11. See the Introduction for a review of the concepts of American citizenship.

12. To become one of the "new breed and generation of North American pioneers," Mukherjee's ideal immigrant will have to fulfill her trajectory from "Unhousement" to "Rehousement," a process of assimilation that entails "breaking away from the culture into which one was born, and in which one's place in society was assured" and "re-rooting oneself in a new culture" (quoted in Hancock 1987: 37, 39).

13. In its embryo form, "Jasmine," the Trinidad Indian nanny of a professor's daughter, succumbs to the man of the house on his "Turkish carpet." The "flower of Trinidad" cannot blossom "in a nothing place" of "the island"; its romantic rapture will have to occur in Ann Arbor (Mukherjee 1988b: 135).

14. Jasmine seems conscious, in a rare moment of authorial irony, of her gender-specific Americanization: "I have had a husband for each of the women I have been. Prakash for Jasmine, Taylor for Jase, Bud for Jane. Half-Face for Kali" (175).

15. Jasmine's abandonment of the Asian male is not exceptional but rather indicative of the absence of intra–Asian American romance. Rainsford may resent his white bride in *Homebase*, but his hinted-at affair with a Chinese American woman is never resumed in the text proper. Rather she is a forever-deferred wish: "She is only the myth of the perfect day until I do get back to her home, she is the summit I must turn to in the end" (Shawn Wong 1979: 79). Shawn Wong's recent *American*

Knees significantly imagines an Asian American love story, but the choice of the novel's protagonist, Raymond, of the Irish Asian American woman over the Vietnamese American one seems also to suggest the novel's limitations.

16. All subsequent references in this chapter to Gish Jen's *Typical American* are from the edition listed in the bibliography.

17. Similar to Mukherjee, Jen also wishes for an Asian American version of the literary renaissance that Saul Bellow and Bernard Malamud once enjoyed (quoted in Brown 1991: 13). This Asian American identification with the white ethnic tradition in general and Jewish tradition in particular (Jen's second novel, *Mona in the Promised Land*, is a more explicit treatment of the Asian and Jewish connection) seems a move similar to that of the Sues' psychoanalytical models in the 1970s. But Mukherjee and Jen are able to center their project in opposition to the "radical left" project of ethnic nationalism in ways that were not possible a decade earlier. Their "centrist" project for Asian immigrants in American culture shares with the ethnic nationalists an affirmation of the United States as the geocultural locale of Asian American imagination, but the analogy stops there. Generally speaking, the centrist is concerned with the power of individual determination in giving consent, while the ethnic nationalist is concerned with the structural effect of excluding consent. If the centrist is relatively inattentive to the effect of race in American culture, the ethnic nationalist may be overburdened by it. These ideological differences are thematically and stylistically mirrored, by and large, by the former's relative indifference to white perception and the latter's preoccupation with ethnic identity in the dominant culture.

18. Jen's concern with Asian American material self-possession is also shared by Steven Lo's *The Incorporation of Eric Chung* (1989) and Glen Cao's *Beijinger in New York* (1993). Published two years before Jen's work by a small press, Lo's novel about a Taiwanese graduate student turned American corporate manager is notable for both its comic vision and its playful tone. Cao's autobiographical novel sold no fewer than 20 million copies in China before it was translated into English. It also was made into a twenty-one-episode television series and aired to an estimated audience of 900 million Chinese; it later became a video blockbuster in Chinese American communities in the United States.

19. See also Francis L. K. Hsu's *Americans and Chinese: Two Ways of Life* and *Rugged Individualism Reconsidered* for a more detailed examination of different individualisms. For Confucianism's impact on European Enlightenment and later on Franklin and Jefferson via the Jesuits and the Physiocrats, see Hunt 1983 (32–35) and Isaacs 1958 (94–96).

20. When asked about the "steel rib" metaphor, Jen explains that it stands "for a strong sense of self, a hefty dose of accomplishment needed by minorities before they can have access to the 'American Dream'" (quoted in Brown 1991: 13). It is worth noting the consistency of Jen's imagery. While money is for Ralph class privilege, a sort of "steel rib" with which to attach himself to "this loose-knit country," it ends up no better than the extra "steel beams" he uses to support his chicken palace, "a building with such a settling problem" that it cannot hold (177–78, 243).

21. A recent report of the U.S. Commission on Civil Rights cites the "glass ceiling" as one of the five prevalent types of employment discrimination against Asian

Americans (Fletcher 1992: 131–36). See also Takaki 1989 for a discussion of job discrimination and Asian American self-employment (13–14). The alien land laws of 1913 and 1921, originally targeted at Japanese Americans but soon extended to cover all Asians, prohibited "aliens ineligible for citizenship" from owning land (Lai and Choy 1971: 99).

22. The house analogy is particularly relevant in view of the fact that Teresa pays part of the mortgage.

23. See Wei-ming Tu's *Confucian Traditions in East Asian Modernity* (1996).

CHAPTER 5. GENES, GENERATION, AND GEOSPIRITUAL (BE)LONGINGS

1. The book's commercial and critical success—275,000 hardcover copies sold, $1.2 million paid for paperback rights, and finalist for both the National Book Award and the National Book Critics Circle award (Holt 1989:2; Simpson 1991:66) —was unprecedented for a first-time author. The book is reported to have sold 4.5 million copies by 1996 (Nguyen 1997: 49).

2. This and all further quotations from *The Joy Luck Club* are taken from the edition listed in the bibliography.

3. Cultural invention or misrepresentation that passes for truth is central to Tan's narrative deployment (Sau-ling Wong 1995).

Since much of *The Joy Luck Club*'s aesthetic appeal lies in "the legendary quality" of "the stories from China" (Seaman 1990: 256), the "*recherches* to old China" that sweep the audience off its feet to be "borne along as if in a dream" (Schell 1989: 28), the relation between its representational mode and its intended audience must be duly noted. Tan's style of narration is akin to the whole genre of explorer accounts whose main motif, according to Marcus and Fischer, is "the romantic discovery by the writer of people and places unknown to the reader" (1986: 129). The concoction of the Chinese idiomatic milieu, the conflation of Chinese festivals, and the calculated use of a vacation topography roughly based on the "scenic wonders of China" all seem to satisfy the voyeuristic inclinations of the armchair reader/traveler. This becomes Tan's trademark, as her later books demonstrate.

4. When the question of her relation to the Asian American community comes up, Tan repeatedly disavows any deliberate connection and emphasizes either the haphazard nature of her character choice ("happening to be Chinese") or their universal significance ("human nature") (see Morris 1994: 219). This universalizing impulse must be appreciated with two facts in mind, however. First, as a former business writer for AT&T, IBM, and other Fortune 500 companies, Tan prides herself on "a real strong batting average on proposals . . . geared to . . . CEOs of major corporations" (Somogyi and Stanton 1991: 27). Second, as Zill and Winglee point out, today's consumers of literature are overwhelmingly white and female.

5. The mother-daughter plot as a model of feminist bonding tends to ignore lesbian desire and identification and accept heterosexual forms of family as the

norm. See Eve Sedgwick's call for "disarticulating . . . the bonds of blood, of law, of habitation, of privacy, of companionship and succor—from the lockstep of their unanimity in the system called 'family'" (1993: 6).

6. The remarks of Tan's characters may reveal the relationship between the author's choice of geography and the configuration of her audience. As Lindo Jong comments in *The Joy Luck Club*, "But now she [Waverly] wants to be Chinese, it is so fashionable" (253), Helen of *The Kitchen God's Wife*, Tan's second novel, will point out, "Hard life in China, that's very popular now" (Tan 1991: 80). Given these self-referential statements, it is not difficult to see Tan's dual accommodation of orientalism, first in her affirmation of China as the natural homeland of Chinese Americans, and second in her inflation of the China stock on the orientalist marketplace.

7. Although Chin began exploring the potential of Asian American folk texts as early as the 1970s, it was not fully developed in his own work until *Donald Duk*, published at the same time as *The Big Aiiieeeee!* It was Kingston who first gave the Asian material its American significance.

8. The "real" refutes three "fake" assumptions that "the first yellows . . . were sojourners; Asian culture is anti-individualistic, mystic, passive, collective, and morally and ethically opposite to Western culture; [and] Chinese and Japanese culture are so misogynistic they don't deserve to survive" (Chin et al. 1991: 9).

9. Kingston's prefiguring of *The Big Aiiieeeee!* in *Tripmaster Monkey* and Chin's refiguring of *The Woman Warrior* in *Donald Duk* (1991) sufficiently demonstrate their textual collaboration on the subject of Asian cultural tradition in the United States. Despite this imaginative convergence, or perhaps because of it, Asia also becomes a field of ideological difference as well as commercial rivalry. Part of the reason that *The Big Aiiieeeee!* finally came out after what seems an endless struggle with editors and presses, I suspect, is due to its declared war against the big publishing houses and Kingston and Tan. This opposition, with its self-proclaimed authenticity and community base, appeals to presses that hope to profit from its publication. As a textbook, the anthology competes with the works of Kingston and Tan for the considerable college market, in which multicultural studies are being integrated into the traditional curriculum.

10. In *The Big Aiiieeeee!*, however, Chin misattributes the notion of the collective unconscious to Freud.

11. In his 1985 essay, which contains the rudimentary ideas that will develop into *The Big Aiiieeeee!*, Chin has this to say: "Chinese civilization is founded on history. Specifically the five classics, selected by Confucius the historian, are the basis of Chinese civilization. . . . Religion as the foundation of civilization is a sissy notion in Chinese thought. . . . The epic tradition of Homer and the Bible. . . . The perpetual power, the submissive individual, the civilization founded on religion" (Chin 1985: 115).

12. I use "character" in two senses of the word, to mean distinctive personal qualities and a symbol of Chinese writing. Recall also Kingston's liberal elaboration of Chin's reading of the Chinese first-person pronoun in *Tripmaster Monkey* (Kingston 1989b: 319).

13. Although it is well known that Confucianism exerted tremendous influence

via the French Jesuits upon the evolution of European Enlightenment, which is often hailed as the philosophical origin of the American Revolution, no one has gone as far as Chin does, to my knowledge, in directly attributing the source of American democracy to an Asian philosophy of antiquity (see Raymond Dawson in general; and Fairbank 1983: 155–58).

14. It is to Chin's credit that he never comes to the point of spelling out the Western opposite of Asian learning. We know, however, that the devaluation of rote memory in Western theories of pedagogy is accompanied not only by the elevation of "critical thinking" as the desirable alternative but the racialization of epistemological practices as well. In this instance, the catechistic method of old is eliminated from the Western historical tradition and imbued with a specific Eastern slant. What Chin responds to is a new paradigm that emerges from this transformation, which dictates learning by repetition and imitation as exclusively Asian and learning by creative thinking and problem solving as appropriately Western.

15. See both Diana Fuss's *Essentially Speaking* and bell hooks's review of the book (hooks 1991). For efforts at examining "whiteness," see *American Quarterly* 47, no. 2 (September 1995).

16. I am thinking in particular of the history of exclusion, which targeted discrete Asian groups and led to the negative construction of Asian American collectivity. See section I, note 24 (on the "pre-scriptive") of the Introduction for a brief review of the history and its influence on Asian American definition.

17. Chin's description of the Asian subconscious bears some resemblance to that of the Indian subaltern group whose "*strategic* use of positivistic essentialism in a scrupulously visible political interest" Gayatri Spivak affirms (Guha and Spivak 1988: 13). See also Mudimbe's chapter "The Panacea of Otherness" (in Mudimbe 1988) and Appiah's "The Uncompleted Argument: Du Bois and the Illusion of Race" (Appiah 1986) for analyses of Sartre's point on the negritudinal stage.

18. As long as Asian American subjects are kept safely away from the center of power, myth only remains as a permissible and containable (though nevertheless enabling) generic instrument for Asian American literary legitimation. We may note the similarity between the use of Asian myth and the employment of conjuring in the dialect and stories of Charles Chestnutt or the element of the primitive and the folk in the Harlem Renaissance era (Andrews 1980: 39–73; Huggins 1971: 90–136; and Carby 1988: 125–43). In all these cases, the realization of an ethnic subjectivity involves the necessary self-engineering of difference in order to mediate the mainstream market.

19. I discuss these in greater detail in the next chapter and in the Conclusion.

20. In Chin's case, the Asian universal also betrays a thinly disguised Sinocentricism of old that disregards Asian regional cultural differences and rivalries. I am thinking mainly of the two World Wars, the Korean and Vietnam Wars, and the Cold War, though the civil wars in China, other regional wars, and the wars between communist and capitalist modes of production had a similar formative impact on Asian culture.

21. The pan-Asian mythology that Chin claims are "the staples of childhoods from Korea to Japan, to China, Vietnam, Laos, Thailand, and Cambodia" (40) does not expressly cover, however, "the American born generations and the colonial mid-

dle-class immigrants," who in his view, are "likewise indoctrinated in white supremacy, in Singapore, Hong Kong, and Christian Taiwan" (Chin et al. 1991: 8–9).

CHAPTER 6. ECCENTRIC HOMES: TOPOGRAPHY, PEDAGOGY, AND MEMORY

1. A "cultural arbitrary," according to Bourdieu and Passeron (1977), is the culture into which a child is born and over which he or she has no choice or control.

2. Intriguingly, both Johnny and Maxine begin backtalking after they start attending public school. Theirs is the first generation of schoolchildren after de jure segregation was pronounced dead in California on June 14, 1947 (Low 1982: 135). With the disappearance of visible barriers and the illusion of inclusion, Chinese-language schools and Chinese families began playing a smaller role in the education of their children.

3. This and all subsequent quotations from *Donald Duk* are from the edition listed in the bibliography.

4. The Chinese classic *Shui Fu* (*Water Margins*) provides Chin with both the heroes of his textual allusions and, it seems, his conceptual parameters of Chinatown as an island. The imagery at the end of the block quotation as well as analogies of Lian Shan, the marshy headquarters of peasant rebels in *Water Margins*, to that of Okefenokee in Georgia and the Everglades in Florida reinforce the sense of isolation and freedom with which Chin imbues his Chinatown.

5. This brings to mind Chalsa M. Loo's sociological study of a rather different nature, *Chinatown: Most Time, Hard Time* (Loo 1991).

6. Chin's surreal collage of myth and reality shares with Kingston's and Yep's fables an inattention to representational accuracy. Keeping in mind that he charged Kingston with violating the original texts, we note that Chin's own conflation in the episode of the track-laying competition is equally serious (114–17). The rebel soldiers of the Water Margin could never have galloped side by side with the heroic warrior Kwan Kung in "real" historical time, for between Kwan Kung's Three Kingdoms and the outlaws' Song Dynasty is a gap of eight to eleven centuries. But like Kingston's use of Mu Lan, Chin's poetic license seems equally empowering for Donald's recognition and registering of racial pride.

7. Chin's ethnocentric agenda of racial uplifting is responsible for his lack of interest in distinguishing the social status of knowledge. His refusal to recognize the superiority of late capitalist technological and managerial knowledge over pre-industrial modes of craftsmanship and culinary art and the humanistic knowledge of the arts and literature is not purely cultural in motivation. It is also coupled with his deep mistrust of the Asian American professional managerial class, whose knowledge constitutes a challenge both to his racialist formation of Asian American consciousness and his desire for class transcendence.

8. Along with resignation to racism as a fact of life and an effusive optimism that defies social conditions is a striking mellowing of Chin's earlier confrontational

stance toward the dominant white culture. Readers familiar with his repudiative oeuvre may be astounded to hear Daisy Duk's remark, apparently with authorial approval: "What's wrong with racists, anyway? We have been living with them for over a hundred years now, and we get along with them fine" (150).

9. This and all subsequent quotations from *Bone* are from Ng 1993 as listed in the bibliography.

10. Leon's recapitulation of his life rhythm echoes that of Bak Goong in Kingston's *China Men*: "Work. Work. Work. Eat. Eat. Eat. Shit and piss. Sleep. Work. Work" (100).

11. Ng's use of Ona is similar to Wayne Wang's use of Chan in his San Francisco Chinatown movie *Chan Is Missing* (1981). If Wang's intention is to showcase the Chinatown diaspora and unfix a unitary identity, Ng's is to link individual destiny to the conditions of her historical inheritance.

12. Although Ng shows little explicit interest in the school curriculum, Leila, the schoolteacher, implies that public education is ineffective in radically changing the lot of the Chinatown folk. In addition to Bourdieu on French education, see also the important work of Apple (1982, 1989), Giroux (1988), and Aronowitz and Giroux (1985) on the American school system.

13. The one moment when the entire Leon family feels happy is when everyone is "drunk with forgetfulness" (102).

14. Ng's narrative solution resembles that of both *The Woman Warrior* and Sandra Cisneros's *House on Mango Street* (see Yarbro-Bejarano 1991 on the latter). It is also important to note that the end of the novel is not its chronological end. Leila's departure from Chinatown has already been succeeded by her frequent return to it, though not as a permanent resident.

15. All subsequent quotations from *Turning Japanese* are taken from Mura 1991.

16. "The confusion and general discomfort I felt with her [Gisela] seemed to come from a sense of danger or uncertainty, an inability to decipher her words and actions. . . . The way she both held herself back and smiled at me frustrated, kept me from moving the conversation into a looser tone, something more friendly, jocular, less sexually vague" (147).

17. Mura's responses to Gisela and Yuri also coincide with the U.S. commercial readings of Witt, a German national, and Yamaguchi, an American citizen of Japanese descent. That Witt has a great number of commercial endorsements on American television and Yamaguchi has had few demonstrates that the United States is still constructed and identified as exclusively white. It is perhaps unironic that Yamaguchi is a prominent spokeswoman for the contact lens industry, appearing in ads for lenses that can turn her brown eyes blue or green, enabling the "alien" to become both a "native" daughter and an American "national." This equation of whiteness with Americanness was reinforced in the news coverage of the 1998 Winter Olympics. After Tara Lipinski took the gold medal for figure-skating over her teammate Michelle Kwan, MSNBC ran the headline, "American Beats Out Kwan" (February 20, 1998). In this sense, the judgment about race and nation behind the Supreme Court decisions on *Hirabayashi* and *Baumgartner* during World War II— in which the native-born Japanese American was considered an enemy alien but the naturalized German American a true citizen—is still powerful in our times. The

difference is such national distinctions are no longer made by the state but by the dominant capital. (On the legal differentiation of German and Japanese Americans, see Konvitz 1946: 139–40, 246–47. For a review of the different modes of American orientalism and European American nationalism, see the discussion of alienation and abjection in the Introduction.)

CHAPTER 7. THE LOOK, THE ACT, THE TRANSVESTIC, AND THE TRANSPIRATIONAL ASIAN

1. Unless otherwise noted, the quotations of Hwang are from the Plume edition of *M. Butterfly*, listed in the bibliography as Hwang 1989.

2. Though Hwang's intertext is apparently Puccini's opera, he does not use its exact title, *Madama Butterfly*. In conflating the title, he evokes John Luther Long's original short story of the same title, which was the basis for playwright/director David Belasco's relatively obscure 1900 stage production as well as the now famous Puccini operatic production in 1904. I follow Hwang's usage in the text, and the Puccini work is the understood subtext.

3. In addition to the prestigious Tony, the awards heaped on *M. Butterfly* include Drama Desk awards, the Outer Critics Circle award for best Broadway play, and the John Gassneer award for the best new American play (Street 1989: 42–43). For a useful analysis of the play's reception, see Angela Pao.

4. I would like to suggest that the original theater-going audience was unlikely to have eluded the bombardment of media, which made the Bouriscot/Shi sex scandal the talk of the town and marketed the play as an adaptation of the real event. The reader of the script, however, learns from the playwright's notes that Song is a man.

5. At the 1989 Association for Asian American Studies convention, which David Henry Hwang attended, I witnessed probably the most direct and fervid charge against the play so far. One female Asian student from U.C. Berkeley tearfully asked Hwang how he could "do this [pander] to us," leaving the genuinely troubled playwright frantic to clear away "misreadings." A law professor from the University of Hawaii agreed with other negative readings when he accused the play of promoting invisible-turned-devious Asian American maleness. Aware of the inherent irony of his proposal, he nevertheless chanted, "Give me Bruce Lee or Give me Death." "If it comes down to Bruce Lee or Song Liling, I'll take Bruce any day [because] at least Bruce was up front with his enemies—it was not his style to masquerade" (Chang 1989).

6. The interpretation of *M. Butterfly* in the traditions of Beijing Opera or Japanese Kabuki, though appealing, presumes Hwang's intuitive command of Asian cultural heritages. I remain deeply suspicious both of the orientalist slant in this mode of reading and a similar Western homoerotic interpretation of Asian theatrical practices.

7. For a reading of Hwang's Asian American trilogy, *FOB*, *The Dance and the Railroad*, and *Family Devotions*, see Li 1992a: 187–94.

8. The challenges to the traditional white feminist construction of woman's identity by Afro-American feminists, postcolonial feminists, and gay and lesbian critics are well-known, but other complications of gender identity are not. See Stanley Aronowitz's astute commentary on the representational power reversal of working-class men and upper-class women, which brings class to bear on gender construction (1992: 193–209). My reading of *M. Butterfly*, however, focuses on the gendering of race.

9. As Ted Polhemus and Lynn Proctor have noted, "clothes are major signifiers of power on the international political scene. When the West is in the ascendant, other nations dress in Western clothes; but when the relations of power shift, the leaders of non-Western nations can wear their national clothes" (quoted in Dyer 1986: 91).

10. Both the positive responses of the academic left and the negative responses of Asian American male critics are, in my estimation, "minority" responses. Brustein's and Neely's responses are in the mainstream and quite representative of the broader audience response. As Marjorie Garber's survey of the initial Western coverage of the real event shows, the American magazine *People*, unlike the European print media, directed its contempt not at Boursicot but at Shi, the treacherous Chinese diva, who misled "the occidental tourist" with a tube of a K-Y jelly (1992: 236). If the British and the French instinctively detach themselves by branding one of their own queer and stupid, the American media further extricate themselves by blaming the Other, a tendency repeatedly reinforced by the theater reviews. Since *People*'s readers shall by no accident become the majority audience of *M. Butterfly*, we may reasonably ask in what ways the playwright has endeavored to unsettle his audience, whose perceptions are both determined by and determining of the orientalist paradigm.

11. This quotation from the *New York Times* is taken from Hwang's "Playwright's Notes," which precede the text of *M. Butterfly*.

12. It ought to be noted that *M. Butterfly*'s stage production blurred the distinction between Japanese and Chinese expressive forms, evoking a conflated and romanticized Orient that few Broadway audiences are able to perceive.

13. In an interview in *Drama Review*, Hwang explained that the avoidance of Song's frontal nudity was a result of an aesthetic debate between director John Dexter and himself. Dexter thought a candid revelation of Song's penis would be "distracting," capable of riveting audience attention when it should be devoted to Gallimard. "So we decided to stage the scene the way we did," Hwang says, "with Song Liling *downstage* and Gallimard *upstage* where we were basically seeing his reaction" DiGaetani 1988: 150; italics mine). Though feeling perfectly attuned to the idea of a deconstructivist *M. Butterfly*, Hwang too concedes that he "knew it would not hurt in commercial or career terms to be able to create a great part for a white male." The result is his struggle "to find a structure that would keep his audience at a comfortable distance from the sexually threatening story line" (Henry 1989), a struggle whose success in suturing white (male) subjectivity we have already witnessed.

14. I am paraphrasing Du Bois's "double consciousness" to illustrate the Asian American dilemma. The dilemma has been reenacted in the much publicized controversy over *Miss Saigon* (1990), in which Hwang argued for Asian American employment equity in the theater and then retreated from his position (see Hulbert 1991). For opposite arguments on *Miss Saigon*, see Rich 1988 and Iyer 1990, and Holly 1990 and Sun 1990.

The controversy is later dramatized in Hwang's "Face Values" (1993), which calls for peeling back the skin to reveal the common core of humanity in all of us. See Kelly 1993a and 1993b for the media coverage of the production. I here thank the playwright for generously sharing the script of his play with me.

15. After receiving favorable journalistic reviews across the nation, *Pangs of Love* won the Art Seidenbaum award (the *Los Angeles Times* Book award for first fiction) and *Ploughshares'* first-book award in 1991.

16. Critics may disagree with my conclusion because "Love on the Rocks" characterizes Buddy Lam as Chinese. In the same way that I refuse to consider *M. Butterfly* a play primarily about Asian Americans unless read oppositionally, I reason that the story is not about Asians. Among the six sections of "Love on the Rocks," four first-person narrations and two omniscient ones, the supposed protagonist Buddy never gets a chance to speak. He is multiply framed by his white contacts—his wife, his lover, her friend, and his mother-in-law, but forever unable to represent himself. Lam's racial identification is shrouded with layers of whiteness that ultimately peripheralize him as a passive object of representation. Like its immediate predecessor, "Disturbing the Universe," a revisionist fable of baseball's Chinese origins with rather subversive effects, "Love on the Rocks" is Louie's experimentation with "transpirational" coding, to which I turn next.

17. Unless otherwise noted, all quotations from Louie's short stories are from *Pangs of Love* (Louie 1991).

18. Not coincidentally, Louie decides to make his writerly tension explicit when he racially identifies the protagonist in "Birthday." Calling the radio psychologist after he was jilted, Wallace Wong, the story's first-person narrator, was advised by the producer of the show that "if [he] wanted the listeners' sympathy [he] should consider dropping the 'Chinese stuff'" (9). Wong refused, and as a result he did not get on the air. In view of Louie's statements about his initial trouble getting published, the producer represents the editor whose advice to omit identifying ethnic markers as a condition of publication and public understanding the author has taken to heart.

19. The intimation of reproduction is very much at the heart of *Pangs of Love*, which shares with such works as Kingston's *China Men* in relating the theme of procreation with the dilemmas of Asian American national belonging.

20. To illustrate how race acts on the ideological unconscious of knowledge acquisition, I asked a class of thirty to identify the image of the protagonist in "The Movers" as they visualized him while reading the story. In a class of roughly half Asians and half non-Asians (including whites, Jews, Latinos, and blacks), all but one, an Asian student, thought he was white. Since there is little direct textual evidence of his Asian physicality, this multiracial class argued, it never occurred to them that they could or should read him otherwise. The single dissenting voice in

the class reasoned, however, that since the dust jacket features a picture of Louie, she always had his image in mind while processing the story. I told her to imagine being given a library copy without the dust jacket or a paperback edition without the author's picture and asked whether those circumstances would alter her image of the protagonist. Slightly flustered, she insists that it would not have made any difference because the author's last name would remain unmistakably Asian. I have to applaud her effort in willing Asian Americans into being.

Worth noting is the fact that the last name is not a certain indicator of a person's racial identity even when it is not an alias. Acquisition of Asian names by marriage or the loss of such names in biracial children are examples that come to mind. What the class encounter demonstrates, however, is the importance of authorship both for ethnic literary scholarship and in the larger politics of cultural representation, to which I turn in the next chapter.

CHAPTER 8. ETHNIC AGENCY AND THE CHALLENGE OF REPRESENTATION

1. See Taylor 1994 and John Guillory 1993 for the opposing views on the canon.

2. For a delineation of Vietnamese American emergence through collaboration, see Truong's "Vietnamese American Literature: 1975–1990" (1993). The quotations in the text are from her talk at the April 1994 UCLA conference, "Strategizing Asian American Cultures." I thank the author for providing me with a copy of her manuscript.

3. Henry Louis Gates has written persuasively on white impersonation of the ethnic and the question of authenticity (see Gates 1991a). Though he gives consideration to the importance of both authorial identity and textual mediation, he is more concerned about sounding a warning against variations of the essentialist thesis and affirming writing as an imaginative exercise. For a contrast to Gates, see Houston Baker's illuminating understanding of race as "gross features" (1986: 186).

4. Albert Memmi's lament about "the colonized's depersonalization [by] the mark of the plural" can be read as an implicit rejection of Deleuze and Guattari, and considered applicable to the American national context (Memmi 1965: 85).

CONCLUSION. ASIAN AMERICAN IDENTITY IN DIFFERENCE AND DIASPORA

NOTE: *This chapter draws heavily from "Meaningful Interruptions: Insurgency and Institutionalization of Asian American Literary Studies," a paper I presented at the 1994 Modern Language Association convention in San Diego.*

1. Portions of this chapter were originally published in *Race, Gender and Class* 4, no. 3 (1997): 40–53. The following list of recent Asian American anthologies is a sample rather than an exhaustive list: Asian Women United of California's *Making Waves* (1989); Lim and Tsutakawa's *The Forbidden Stitch* (1989); Watanabe and Bruchac's *Home to Stay* (1990); *Engendering Visions* (*Asian Pacific American Journal*, Spring/Summer 1993); *Witness Aloud* (*Asian Pacific American Journal*, Fall/Winter 1993); Hagedorn's *Charlie Chan Is Dead* (1993); Hong's *Growing Up Asian American* (1993); Ratti's *A Lotus of Another Color* (1993); Yep's *American Dragons* (1993); *Amerasia Journal*'s special literary issues, *Burning Cane* (Hong et al. 1991) and *Dimensions of Desire* (Leong 1994); Lim-Hing's *The Very Inside* (1994); Hongo's *The Open Boat* (1993) and *Under Western Eyes* (1995); Kudaka's *On a Bed of Rice* (1995); and Shawn Wong's *Asian American Literature* (1995b).

2. Besides specific studies on Asian American literature, James Moy's work on theater (1993), Gina Marchetti and Darrell Hamamoto's work on movie and television (1993, 1994), David Palumbo-Liu's *Ethnic Canon* (1995), and E. San Juan's book on the "dialectics of Philippines-U.S. literary relations" (1996) all help expand and enrich the Asian American cultural discourse. See also Lim and Ling 1992, Cheung 1997, and two special journal issues on Asian America, Ng and Wan 1997 and Kim and Lowe 1997.

3. In addition to Louie's "transpirational" strategies in fiction writing, quite a number of Asian American filmmakers have assumed similar tactics of representational racial evasion as apparent concessions to the mainstream. Wayne Wang's *Smoke* (1995) and *Blue in the Face* (1995), George Huang's *Swimming with Sharks* (1994), and Desmond Nakano's *White Men's Burden* (1994) are examples that come to mind.

4. See esp. Clifford's "On Collecting Art and Culture" in Clifford 1988: 215–52.

5. See the 1989 Association of Asian American Studies Conference Proceedings (Hune, Kim, Fugita, and Ling 1991) from which the following discussion is drawn. It is regrettable that the argument in this chapter was formulated before the publication of the special issue of *Amerasia Journal*, "Thinking Theory in Asian American Studies" (vol. 21, nos. 1/2, [1995]) in which leading scholars debate similar issues.

6. Though not explicitly engaging the relation between Asian and Asian American studies, a special issue of *Daedalus* (Tu 1991) and Rey Chow's *Writing Diaspora* (1993) address significant aspects of the Asian diaspora.

7. See the introduction in Pease 1994 and Appadurai 1993. Both speak to the transnational theoretical challenges that increasingly influence the field of Asian American studies.

8. His use of the hyphen between "Asian" and "American" and his discussion of the "sides" of the term seem to suggest some conflict between the sides, whether cultural, racial, or national.

9. The charge that the term "Asian American" is indifferent to people of Pacific origin or does not accommodate ethnic diversity ignores the semantic evolution of the term over the years.

10. See R. Radhakrishnan's related criticism of Foucault's poststructuralism (1990: 76), and Dirlik's warning against postcolonialism (1994).

11. By calling attention to the specter of class in the theoretical resort to difference and diaspora, we are not only recalling the original missions of Asian American studies in social transformation but also recognizing its limitation as an academic discipline. For Asian American identity politics to be truly effective, it seems, we must not confuse politics and political practice. While Asian American electoral politics, academic politics, movement/grass roots/community politics, and cultural politics are all interwoven, distinctions need to be made among them so that there will be no substitution of one kind of politics for the other or of one group's interests by another group.

Works Cited

Ahmad, Aijaz. 1992. *In Theory: Classes, Nations, Literatures.* London: Verso.

Althusser, Louis. 1984. *Essays on Ideology.* London: Verso.

Anderson, Benedict. 1983. *Imagined Communities: Reflections on the Origin and Spread of Nationalism.* London: Verso.

———. 1994. "Exodus." *Critical Inquiry* 20, no. 2 (Winter): 314–27.

Andrews, William. 1980. *The Literary Career of Charles Chesnutt.* Baton Rouge: Louisiana State University Press.

Antin, Mary. [1912] 1997. *The Promised Land.* Ed. Werner Sollors, with introduction and notes. New York: Penguin.

Appadurai, Arjun. 1993. "Patriotism and Its Futures." *Public Culture* 5: 411–29.

Appiah, Kwame Anthony. 1986. "The Uncompleted Argument: Du Bois and the Illusion of Race." In *"Race," Writing, and Difference,* ed. Henry Louis Gates, Jr., 21–37. Chicago: University of Chicago Press.

———. 1990a. "Race." *Critical Terms for Literary Study,* ed. Frank Lentricchia and Thomas McLaughlin, 274–87. Chicago: University of Chicago Press.

———. 1990b. "Racisms." In *Anatomy of Racism,* ed. David Theo Goldberg, 3–17. Minneapolis: University of Minnesota Press.

Apple, Michael W. 1982. *Cultural and Economic Reproduction in Education: Essays on Class, Ideology and the State.* London: Routledge and Kegan Paul.

———. 1989. *Teachers and Texts: A Political Economy of Class and Gender Relations in Education.* New York: Routledge.

Aronowitz, Stanley. 1992. *The Politics of Identity: Class, Culture, Social Movements.* New York: Routledge.

Aronowitz, Stanley, and Henry Giroux. 1985. *Education Under Siege: The Conservative, Liberal and Radical Debate over Schooling.* Granby, Mass.: Bergin and Garvey.

Asian Women United of California, ed. 1989. *Making Waves: An Anthology of Writings by and About Asian American Women.* Boston: Beacon.

Baker, Houston A., Jr. 1981. "Generational Shifts and the Recent Criticism of Afro-American Literature." *Black American Literature* 15 (Spring): 3–21.

———. 1984. "To Move Without Moving: Creativity and Commerce in Ralph Ellison's Trueblood Episode." In *Black Literature and Literary Theory*, ed. Henry Louis Gates, Jr., 221–48. New York: Methuen.

———. 1986. "Caliban's Triple Play" (Critical Response to *"Race," Writing, and Difference*). *Critical Inquiry* 13, no. 1 (Autumn): 182–96.

Baker, Martin. 1981. *The New Racism: Conservatives and the Ideology of the Tribe*. London: Junction.

Bakhtin, M. M. 1981. *The Dialogical Imagination*. Ed. Michael Holquist. Austin: University of Texas Press.

Baldwin, James. [1955] 1984. *Notes of a Native Son*. Boston: Beacon.

Balibar, Etienne, and Immanuel Wallerstein. 1991. *Race, Nation, Class: Ambiguous Identities*. London: Verso.

Bammer, Angelika. 1994. "Mother Tongues and Other Strangers: Writing 'Family' Across Cultural Divides." In *Displacements: Cultural Identities in Question*, ed. Angelika Bammer, 90–109. Bloomington: Indiana University Press.

Barnes, Clive. 1972. "Stage: Identity Problem, 'Chickencoop Chinaman' at American Place." *New York Times*, June 13.

Baym, Nina. 1978. *Woman's Fiction: A Guide to Novels by and About Women in America, 1820–1870*. Ithaca, N.Y.: Cornell University Press.

Bellah, Robert N., William M. Sullivan, Ann Swidler, and Steven M. Tipton, eds. [1985] 1986. *Habits of the Heart: Individualism and Commitment in American Life*. New York: Harper and Row.

Bhabha, Homi K. 1994. *The Location of Culture*. New York: Routledge.

Blackburn, Sara. 1977. "Notes of a Chinese Daughter." *Ms*, Jan.: 39–40.

Bourdieu, Pierre. 1977. *An Outline of a Theory of Practice*. Trans. Richard Nice. New York: Cambridge University Press.

———. 1984. *Distinction: A Social Critique of the Judgment of Taste*. Trans. Richard Nice. Cambridge, Mass.: Harvard University Press.

———. 1985. "The Social Space and the Genesis of Groups." *Theory and Society* 14, no. 6: 723–44.

Bourdieu, Pierre, and Jean-Claude Passeron. 1977. *Reproduction in Education, Society and Culture*. London: Sage.

Brooks Peter. 1993. *Body Work: Objects of Desire in Modern Narrative*. Cambridge, Mass.: Harvard University Press.

Brown, Elizabeth A. 1991. "New Novelist Tries to Break the 'Ethnic Box.'" *Christian Science Monitor*, Mar. 25.

Brustein, Robert. 1988. "Transcultural Blends." *New Republic*, Apr. 25: 28–29.

Bulosan, Carlos. [1943] 1990. *America Is in the Heart*. Seattle: University of Washington Press.

Burning Cane. 1991. *Amerasia Journal* 17, no. 2 (Special issue): 1–121.

Butler, Judith. 1990. *Gender Trouble: Feminism and the Subversion of Identity*. New York: Routledge.

———. 1991. "Imitation and Gender Insubordination." In *Inside/Out: Lesbian Theories, Gay Theories*, ed. Diana Fuss, 13–31. New York: Routledge.

———. 1993. *Bodies That Matter: On the Discursive Limits of "Sex."* New York: Routledge.

Cao, Glen. 1993. *Beijinger in New York*. Trans. Ted Wang. San Francisco: Cypress.

Carb, Alison B. 1988. "An Interview with Bharati Mukherjee." *Massachusetts Review* 29, no. 4: 645–54.

Carby, Hazel V. 1988. "Ideologies of the Black Folk: The Historical Novel of Slavery." In *Slavery and the Literary Imagination*, ed. Deborah E. McDowell and
Arnold Rampersad, 125–43. Baltimore: Johns Hopkins University Press.

Cawelti, John G. 1976. *Adventure, Mystery, and Romance: Formula Stories as Art and
Popular Culture*. Chicago: University of Chicago Press.

Chan, Jeffery Paul. 1977. "The Mysterious West." *New York Review of Books*, Apr.
28: 41.

Chan, Sucheng. 1978. "Contextual Frameworks for Reading *Counterpoint*." *Amerasia Journal* 5, no. 1: 115–29.

———. 1991a. *Asian Americans: An Interpretive History*. Boston: Twayne.

———. 1991b. "The Exclusion of Chinese Women, 1870–1943." In *Entry Denied:
Exclusion and the Chinese Community in America, 1882–1943*, ed. Sucheng
Chan, 94–146. Philadelphia: Temple University Press.

———, ed. 1991. *Entry Denied: Exclusion and the Chinese Community in America,
1882–1943*. Philadelphia: Temple University Press.

Chang, Williamson. 1989. "*M. Butterfly*: Passivity, Deviousness and the Invisibility
of the Asian-American Male." Sixth National Conference of the Association
for Asian American Studies. New York, June 3.

Chase, Richard. 1957. *The American Novel and Its Tradition*. New York, Doubleday.

Cheng, Lucie, and Edna Bonacich. 1984. *Labor Immigration Under Capitalism: Asian
Workers in the United States Before World War II*. Berkeley: University of California Press.

Cheung, King-Kok. 1990. "The Woman Warrior Versus the Chinaman Pacific:
Must a Chinese American Critic Choose Between Feminism and Heroism?"
In *Conflicts in Feminism*, ed. Marianne Hirsch and Evelyn Fox Keller, 234–51.
New York: Routledge.

———. 1993. *Articulate Silences: Hisaye Yamamoto, Maxine Hong Kingston, Joy
Kogawa*. Ithaca, N.Y.: Cornell University Press: 1993.

———, ed. 1997. *An Interethnic Companion to Asian American Literature*. New York:
Cambridge University Press.

Cheyfitz, Eric. 1993. "Savage Law: The Plot Against American Indians in *Johnson
and Graham's Lessee v. M'Intosh* and *The Pioneer*." In *Cultures of United States
Imperialism*, ed. Amy Kaplan and Donald E. Pease, 109–28. Durham, N.C.:
Duke University Press.

Chin, Frank. 1972a. "Confessions of the Chinatown Cowboy." *Bulletin of Concerned
Asian Scholars* 4, no. 3: 58–70.

———. 1972b. "Don't Pen Us Up in Chinatown." *New York Times*, Oct. 8.

———. 1976a. "Backtalk." In *Counterpoint: Perspectives on Asian America*, ed.
Emma Gee et al., 556–57. Los Angeles: Asian American Studies Center,
UCLA.

———. [1972] 1976b. "Food for All His Dead." In *Asian American Authors*, ed.
Kai-yu Hsu and Helen Palubinskas, 48–61. Boston: Houghton.

———. 1976c. "Where I'm Coming From." *Bridge* 4, no. 3: 28–29.

———. 1977. "Letter to Y'Bird." *Y'Bird Magazine* 1, no. 1: 42–45.

———. 1978. "The Sixties: Hail and Farewell." *The Weekly: Seattle's Newsmagazine*,
Aug. 9: 6–8.

———. 1981. *The Chickencoop Chinaman and the Year of the Dragon*. Seattle: University of Washington Press.

———. 1985. "This Is Not an Autobiography." *Genre* 8 (Summer): 109–30.

———. 1988. *The Chinaman Pacific & Frisco R.R. Co.* Minneapolis: Coffee House.

———. 1991. *Donald Duk*. Minneapolis: Coffee House.

Chin, Frank, and Jeffery Paul Chan. 1972. "Racist Love." In *Seeing Through Shuck*, ed. Richard Kostelanetz, 65–79. New York: Ballantine.

Chin, Frank, Jeffery Paul Chan, Lawson Fusao Inada, and Shawn Wong, eds. [1974] 1983. *AIIIEEEEE! An Anthology of Asian-American Writers*. Washington, D.C.: Howard University Press.

———. 1991. *The Big Aiiieeeee! An Anthology of Chinese and Japanese American Literature*. New York: Meridian.

Chin, Marilyn. 1989. "Writing the Other: A Conversation with Maxine Hong Kingston." *Poetry Flash: The Bay Area's Poetry Review* (Sept.): 1.

Ching, Frank, and Frank Chin. 1972. "Who's Afraid of Frank Chin, or Is it Ching?" *Bridge* 2, no. 2: 29–34.

Cho, Fiona. 1993. "Daddy, I Don't Know What You're Talking." *Critical Mass: A Journal of Asian American Cultural Criticism* 1, no. 1 (Fall): 57–62.

Chow, Rey. 1991. *Woman and Chinese Modernity: The Politics of Reading Between West and East*. Minneapolis: University of Minnesota Press.

———. 1993. *Writing Diaspora: Tactics of Intervention in Contemporary Cultural Studies*. Bloomington: Indiana University Press.

Chu, Louis. [1961] 1979. *Eat a Bowl of Tea*. Seattle: University of Washington Press.

Chua, Cheng Lok. 1987. "Frank Chin." In *Critical Survey of Drama: Supplement*, ed. Frank N. Magill, 45–51. Eaglewood Cliffs, N.J.: Salem.

Chun, Gloria H. 1989. "Metaphysician of Orientalism: Maxine Hong Kingston." Sixth National Conference of the Association for Asian American Studies. New York, June 3.

Clifford, James. 1988. *The Predicament of Culture: Twentieth-Century Ethnography, Literature, and Art*. Cambridge, Mass.: Harvard University Press.

———. 1992. "Traveling Cultures." In *Cultural Studies*, ed. Lawrence Grossberg, Cary Nelson, and Paula Treichler, 96–111. New York: Routledge,

Crow, Carl. 1941. *Foreign Devil in Flowery Kingdom*. London: Hamish Hamilton.

Cumings, Bruce. 1993. "Rimspeak; or the Discourse of the 'Pacific Rim.'" In *What Is in a Rim? Critical Perspectives on the Pacific Region Idea*, ed. Arif Dirlik, 29–47. Boulder, Colo.: Westview.

Currier, Susan. 1980. "Maxine Hong Kingston." In *Dictionary of Literary Biography Yearbook: 1980*, ed. Karen Rord et al., 235–41. Detroit: Gale Research.

Dawson, Raymond, ed. 1964. *The Legacy of China*. Oxford: Clarendon.

Deleuze, Gilles, and Félix Guattari. 1986. *Kafka: Toward a Minor Literature*. Trans. Dana Polan. Minneapolis: University of Minnesota Press.

Demetrakipoulos, Stephanie A. 1980. "The Metaphysics of Matrilinearism in Women's Autobiography: Studies of Mead's *Blackberry Winter*, Hellman's *Pentimento*, Angelou's *I Know Why the Caged Bird Sings*, and Kingston's *The Woman Warrior*." In *Women's Autobiography: Essays in Criticism*, ed. Estelle C. Jelinek, 180–220. Bloomington: Indiana University Press.

DiGaetani, John Louis. 1988. "*M. Butterfly*: An Interview with David Henry Hwang." *TDR: The Drama Review* 33, no. 3 (Fall): 141–53.

Dirlik, Arif. 1992. "The Asia-Pacific Idea: Reality and Representation in the Invention of Regional Structure." *Journal of World History* 3, no. 1: 55–79.

———. 1993a. "The Asian Pacific Idea in Asian-American Perspective." In *What Is in a Rim? Critical Perspectives on the Pacific Region Idea*, ed. Arif Dirlik, 305–29. Boulder, Colo.: Westview.

———. 1993b. "Introducing the Pacific." In *What Is in a Rim? Critical Perspectives on the Pacific Region Idea*, ed. Arif Dirlik, 1–11. Boulder, Colo.: Westview.

———. 1994. "The Postcolonial Aura: Third World Criticism in the Age of Global Capitalism." *Critical Inquiry* 20, no. 2 (Winter): 328–56.

———. 1995. "Confucius in the Borderlands: Global Capitalism and the Reinvention of Confucianism." *Boundary 2* 22, no. 3 (Fall): 229–73.

———, ed. 1993. *What Is in a Rim? Critical Perspectives on the Pacific Region Idea.* Boulder, Colo.: Westview.

Doane, Mary Ann. 1982. "Film and the Masquerade: Theorising the Female Spectator." *Screen* 23, no. 3/4: 74–87.

Drinnon, Richard. 1980. *Facing West: The Metaphysics of Indian-Hating and Empire Building.* Minneapolis: University of Minnesota Press.

Du Bois, W. E. B. [1903] 1979. *The Souls of Black Folk.* New York: Dodd, Mead.

Dyer, Richard. 1986. *Heavenly Bodies: Film Stars and Society.* New York: St. Martin's.

———. 1992. *Only Entertainment.* New York: Routledge.

———. 1993. *The Matter of Images: Essays on Representations.* New York: Routledge.

Eagleton, Terry. 1994. "Discourse and Discos: Theory in the Space Between Culture and Capitalism." *Times Literary Supplement,* July 15: 3–4.

Eakin, John Paul. 1985. *Fictions in Autobiography: Studies in the Art of Self-Invention.* Princeton, N.J.: Princeton University Press.

Eaton, Edith [Sui Sin Far]. 1982. Excerpts from *Leaves from the Mental Portfolio of a Eurasian.* In *Turning Shadow into Light: Art and Culture of the Northwest's Early Asian/Pacific Community,* ed. Mayumi Tsutakawa and Alan Chong Lau, 88–90. Seattle: Young Pine.

Eder, Richard. 1991. "Meeting the Twain" [Review of *Pangs of Love*]. *Los Angeles Times Book Review,* June 16: 3.

Ehrenreich, Barbara and John. 1979. "The Professional Managerial Class." In *Between Labor and Capital,* ed. Pat Walker, 5–48. Boston: South End Press.

Eliot, T. S. 1973. "The Love Song of J. Alfred Prufrock." In *The Norton Anthology of Modern Poetry,* ed. Richard Ellmann and Robert O'Clair, 449–52. New York: W. W. Norton.

Ellison, Ralph. 1966. *Shadow and Act.* New York: Signet.

Endo, Russell, and William Wei. 1988. "On the Development of Asian American Studies Programs." In *Reflections on Shattered Windows: Promises and Prospects for Asian American Studies,* ed. Gary Y. Okihiro et al., 5–15. Pullman: Washington State University Press.

Engendering Visions: Roles, Reversals and Revolutions. 1993. *Asian Pacific American Journal* 2, no. 2 (Special issue, Spring/Summer): 1–146.

Espiritu, Yen Le. 1992. *Asian American Panethnicity: Bridging Institutions and Identities.* Philadelphia: Temple University Press.

Espiritu, Yen Le, and Paul Ong. 1994. "Class Constraints on Racial Solidarity Among Asian Americans." In *The New Asian Immigration in Los Angeles and Global Restructuring,* ed. Paul Ong, Edna Bonacich, and Lucy Cheng, 295–322. Philadelphia: Temple University Press.

Fabian, Johannes. 1983. *Time and the Other: How Anthropology Makes Its Object.* New York: Columbia University Press.

Fairbank, John King. 1983. *The United States and China.* 4th ed. Cambridge, Mass.: Harvard University Press.

Fanon, Frantz. 1967. *Black Skin, White Masks.* Trans. Charles Lam Markmann. New York: Grove.

Fawcett, James T., and Benjamin V. Cariño, eds. 1987. *Pacific Bridges: The New Im-*

migration from Asia and the Pacific Islands. New York and Honolulu: Center for Migration Studies and the East-West Center.

Fenn, William Purviance. 1933. *Ah Sin and His Brethren in American Literature*. Peipin, China: College of Chinese Studies.

Fiedler, Leslie. 1991. *Fiedler on the Roof: Essays on Literature and Jewish Identity*. Boston: David R. Godine.

Fish, Stanley. 1980. *Is There a Text in This Class?* Cambridge, Mass.: Harvard University Press.

———. 1997. "Boutique Multiculturalism, or Why Liberals Are Incapable of Thinking About Hate Speech." *Critical Inquiry* 23 (Winter): 378–95.

Fitzgerald, F. Scott. [1925] 1986. *The Great Gatsby*. New York: Collier/Macmillan.

Fletcher, Arthur A. 1992. *Civil Rights Issues Facing Asian Americans in the 1990s: A Report of the United States Commission on Civil Rights*. Washington, D.C.: United States Commission on Civil Rights.

Fong, Katheryn M. 1977. "An Open Letter/Review." *Bulletin of Concerned Asian Scholars* 9, no. 4 (Oct.–Dec.): 67–69.

Franklin, Benjamin. 1958. *Autobiography and Other Writings*. Ed. Russel B. Nye. Boston: Houghton Mifflin / Riverside.

Fung, Richard. 1991. "Looking for My Penis: The Eroticized Asian in Gay Video Porn." In *How Do I Look: Queer Film and Video*, ed. Bad Object-Choices, 145–68. Seattle: Bay.

Fuss, Diana. 1989. Essentially Speaking: Feminism, Nature, and Difference. New York: Routledge.

Gallop, Jane. 1988. *Thinking Through the Body*. New York: Columbia University Press.

Garber, Marjorie. 1992. *Vested Interests: Cross Dressing and Cultural Anxiety*. New York: Routledge.

Gates, Henry Louis, Jr. 1987. *Figures in Black: Words, Signs, and the "Racial" Self*. New York: Oxford University Press.

———. 1991a. "'Authenticity,' or the Lesson of Little Tree." *New York Times Book Review*, Nov. 24: 1.

———. 1991b. "Crticial Fanonism." *Critical Inquiry* 17 (Spring): 457–470.

———. 1992a. *Loose Canons: Notes on Culture Wars*. New York: Oxford University Press.

———. 1992b. "African American Criticism." In *Redrawing the Boundaries: The Transformation of English and American Literary Studies*, ed. Stephen Greenblatt and Giles Gunn, 303–19. New York: Modern Language Association of America.

Gee, Emma, et al., eds. 1976. *Counterpoint: Perspectives on Asian America*. Los Angeles: Asian American Studies Center, UCLA.

Gerard, Jeremy. 1988. "David Hwang: Riding on the Hyphen." *New York Times Magazine*, Mar. 13: 44, 88–89.

Gilbert, Sandra, and Susan Gubar, eds. 1985. *The Norton Anthology of Literature by Women: The Tradition in English*. New York: Norton.

Gilroy, Paul. 1993. *The Black Atlantic: Modernity and Double Consciousness*. Cambridge, Mass.: Harvard University Press.

Giroux, Henry A. 1988. *Teachers and Intellectuals: Toward a Critical Pedagogy of Learning*. Granby, Mass.: Bergin & Garvey.

Graff, Gerald. 1992. *Beyond the Cultural Wars: How Teaching Conflicts Can Revitalize American Education*. New York: Norton.

Gramsci, Antonio. 1971. *Selections from the Prison Notebooks*. Ed. and trans. Quinton Hoare and Geoffrey Nowell Smith. New York: International.

Grewal, Gurleen. 1993. "Born Again American: The Immigrant Consciousness in *Jasmine*." In *Bharati Mukherjee: Critical Perspectives*, ed. Emmanuel S. Nelson, 181–96. New York: Garland.

Guha, Ranajit, and Gayatri Chakravorty Spivak, eds. 1988. *Selected Subaltern Studies*. New York: Oxford University Press.

Guillory, John. 1993. *Cultural Capital: The Problems of Literary Canon Formation*. Chicago: University of Chicago Press.

Haedicke, Janet. 1992. "David Henry Hwang's *M. Butterfly*: The Eyes on the Wing." *Journal of Dramatic Theory and Criticism* 7, no. 1: 27–44.

Hagedorn, Jessica, ed. 1993. *Charlie Chan Is Dead: An Anthology of Contemporary Asian American Fiction*. New York: Penguin.

Hamamoto, Darrell Y. 1994. *Monitored Peril: Asian Americans and the Politics of TV Representation*. Minneapolis: University of Minnesota Press.

Hancock, Geoff. 1987. "An Interview with Bharati Mukherjee." *Canadian Fiction Magazine* 59: 30–44.

Harvey, David. 1989. *The Condition of Postmodernity*. Cambridge: Basil Blackwell.

Heath, Stephen. 1986. "Joan Riviere and the Masquerade." In *Formations of Fantasy*, ed. Victor Burgin, James Donald, and Cora Kaplan, 45–61. New York: Methuen.

Helms, Mary W. 1988. *Ulysses' Sail: An Ethnographic Odyssey of Power, Knowledge, and Geographic Distance*. Princeton, N.J.: Princeton University Press.

Henry, William A., III. 1989. "When East and West Collide—Profile." *Time*, Aug. 14: 62–64.

Hetternan, William A., and Mark Johnston, eds. 1991. *The Harvest Reader*. 2d ed. San Diego: Harcourt Brace Jovanovich.

Hing, Bill Ong. 1993. *Making and Remaking Asian America Through Immigration Policy: 1850–1990*. Stanford, Calif.: Stanford University Press.

Hirsch, Marianne. 1989. *The Mother/Daughter Plot: Narrative, Psychoanalysis and Feminism*. Bloomington: Indiana University Press.

Hite, Molly. 1991. "Postmodern Fiction." In *The Columbia History of the American Novel*, ed. Emory Elliott et al., 697–725. New York: Columbia University Press.

Hobsbawm, Eric, and Terence Ranger. 1992. *The Invention of Tradition*. New York: Cambridge University Press.

Holly, Ellen. 1990. "Why the Furor over '*Miss Saigon*' Won't Fade." *New York Times*, Aug. 26.

Holt, Patricia. 1989. "The Shuffle over 'Joy Luck.'" *San Francisco Chronicle Book Review*, July 26: 2.

Hom, Marlon K. 1987. *Songs of Gold Mountain: Cantonese Rhymes from San Francisco Chinatown*. Berkeley: University of California Press.

Homsher, Deborah. 1979. "*The Woman Warrior*, by Maxine Hong Kingston: A Bridging of Autobiography and Fiction." *Iowa Review* 10, no. 4 (Fall): 93–98.

Hong, Maria, ed. 1993. *Growing Up Asian American: An Anthology*. New York: William Morrow.

Hongo, Garrett, ed. 1993. *The Open Boat: Poems from Asian America*. New York: Anchor.

———, ed. 1995. *Under Western Eyes: Personal Essays from Asian America*. New York: Anchor.

hooks, bell. 1991. "Essentialism and Experience." *American Literary History* 3, no. 1 (Spring): 172–83.

———. 1992. *Black Looks: Race and Representation*. Boston: South End Press.

Horn, Miriam. 1988. "The Mesmerizing Power of Racial Myths." *U.S. News and World Report*, Mar. 28,: 52–53.

Horsman, Reginald. 1981. *Race and Manifest Destiny: The Origins of American Racial Anglo-Saxonism*. Cambridge, Mass.: Harvard University Press.

Horton, Karen. 1979. "Honolulu Interview: Maxine Hong Kingston." *Honolulu Today*, Dec.: 49–56.

Hsu, Francis L. K. 1953. *Americans and Chinese: Two Ways of Life*. New York: Henry Schuman.

———. 1971. *The Challenge of the American Dream: The Chinese in the United States*. Belmont, Calif.: Wadsworth.

———. 1983. *Rugged Individualism Reconsidered: Essays in Psychological Anthropology*. Knoxville: University of Tennessee Press.

Hsu, Kai-yu, and Helen Palubinskas, eds. 1976. *Asian American Authors*. 1972. Boston: Houghton.

Hsu, Ruth Y. 1996. "'Will the Model Minority Please Identify Itself?' American Ethnic Identity and Its Discontents." *Diaspora* 5, no. 1 (Spring): 37–63.

Hu-DeHart, Evelyn. 1991. "From Area Studies to Ethnic Studies: The Study of the Chinese Diaspora in Latin America." In *Asian Americans: Comparative and Global Perspectives*, ed. Shirley Hune, Hyung-chan Kim, Stephen Fugita, and Amy Ling, 5–16. Pullman: Washington State University Press.

Huggins, Nathan Irvin. 1971. *Harlem Renaissance*. New York: Oxford University Press.

Hulbert, Dan. 1991. "'Butterfly Creator': Saigon Battle Has Been Fought." *Atlanta Journal-Constitution*, Apr. 28.

Hune, Shirley. 1977. *Pacific Migration to the United States*. Washington, D.C.: Smithsonian Institution.

Hune, Shirley, Hyung-chan Kim, Stephen Fugita, and Amy Ling, eds. 1991. *Asian Americans: Comparative and Global Perspectives*. Pullman: Washington State University Press.

Hunt, Michael H. 1983. *The Making of a Special Relationship: The United States and China to 1914*. New York: Columbia University Press.

Hurston, Zora Neale. 1990. *Their Eyes Were Watching God*. New York: Harper and Row.

Hutchinson, E. P. 1981. *Legislative History of American Immigration Policy: 1798–1965*. Philadelphia: University of Pennsylvania Press.

Hwang, David Henry. 1989. *M. Butterfly: With an Afterword by the Playwright*. New York: Plume.

Ignatiev, Noel. 1995. *How the Irish Became White*. New York: Routledge.

Isaacs, Harold R. 1958. *Scratches on Our Minds: American Images of China and India*. New York: John Day.

Iwasaki, Bruce. 1971. "Response and Change for the Asian in America: A Survey of Asian American Literature." In *Roots: An Asian American Reader*, ed. Amy Tachiki et al., 89–100. Los Angeles: Asian American Studies Center, UCLA.

———. 1976. "Introduction to Literature." In *Counterpoint: Perspectives on Asian America*, ed. Emma Gee et al., 452–63. Los Angeles: Asian American Studies Center, UCLA, 1976.

Iyer, Pico. 1990. "The Masks of Minority Terrorism." *Time*, Sept. 3: 86.

Jameson, Fredric. 1981. *The Political Unconscious: Narrative as a Socially Symbolic Act*. Ithaca, N.Y.: Cornell University Press.

———. 1988. "Cognitive Mapping." In *Marxism and the Interpretation of Culture*, ed. Cary Nelson and Lawrence Grossberg, 347–57. Chicago: University of Illinois Press.

JanMohamed, Abdul R., and David Lloyd. 1987a. "Introduction: Toward a Theory of Minority Discourse." *Cultural Critique* 6 (Spring): 5–12.

———. 1987b. "Introduction: Minority Discourse—What Is to Be Done?" *Cultural Critique* 7 (Fall): 5–17.

Jehlen, Myra. 1986. *American Incarnation: The Individual, the Nation and the Continent*. Cambridge, Mass.: Harvard University Press.

———. 1987. "The Novel and the Middle Class in America." In *Ideology and Classic American Literature*, ed. Sacvan Bercovitch and Myra Jehlen, 125–44. New York: Cambridge University Press.

Jen, Gish. 1991. *Typical American*. Boston: Houghton Mifflin.

———. 1996. *Mona in the Promised Land*. New York: Knopf.

Johnson, Diane. 1977. "Ghosts." *New York Review of Books*, Feb. 3: 19–21.

Jones, Leroi, and Larry Neal, eds. 1968. *Black Fire: An Anthology of Afro-American Writing*. New York: William Morrow.

Juhasz, Suzanne. 1980. "Towards a Theory of Form in Feminist Autobiography: Kate Millet's *Flying* and *Sita*; Maxine Hong Kingston's *The Woman Warrior*." In *Women's Autobiography: Essays in Criticism*, ed. Estelle C. Jelinek, 211–37. Bloomington: Indiana University Press.

———. 1985. "Narrative Technique and Female Identity." In *Contemporary American Women Writers: Narrative Strategies*, ed. Catherine Rainwater and William J. Sheick, 174–89. Lexington: University Press of Kentucky.

Kao, Hsin-sheng C. 1993. *Nativism Overseas: Contemporary Chinese Women Writers*. Albany: State University of New York Press.

Kaplan, Amy. 1993a. "Black and Blue on San Juan Hill." In *Cultures of United States Imperialism*, ed. Amy Kaplan and Donald E. Pease, 219–36. Durham, N.C.: Duke University Press.

———. 1993b. "'Left Alone with America': The Absence of Empire in the Study of American Culture." In *Cultures of United States Imperialism*, ed. Amy Kaplan and Donald E. Pease, 3–21. Durham, N.C.: Duke University Press.

Kelly, Kevin. 1993a. "Hwang's 'Face Value' Flops on Its Farce." *Boston Globe*, Feb. 15.

———. 1993b. "Hwang Looks Beyond 'Face Value.'" *Boston Globe*, Feb. 17.

Kemnitz, Charles. 1983. "The Hand of Forging Personal Narrative." *Genre* 16 (Summer): 175–89.

Kennedy, X. J. and Dorothy M. 1985. *The Bedford Reader*. New York: Macmillan.

Kettner, James H. 1978. *The Development of American Citizenship, 1608–1870*. Chapel Hill: University of North Carolina Press.

Kim, Elaine H. 1982. *Asian American Literature: An Introduction to the Writings and Their Social Contexts*. Philadelphia: Temple University Press.

———. 1990. "'Such Opposite Creatures': Men and Women in Asian American Literature." *Michigan Quarterly Review* 29, no. 1: 68–93.

———. 1993. "Preface." In *Charlie Chan Is Dead: An Anthology of Contemporary Asian American Fiction*, ed. Jessica Hagedorn, vii–xiv. New York: Penguin Books.

Kim, Elaine H., and Lisa Lowe, eds. 1997. *New Formations, New Questions: Asian American Studies*. Positions: East Asia Cultures Critique 5, no. 2 (Special issue, Fall).

Kim, Hyung-chan. 1994. *A Legal History of Asian Americans, 1790–1990*. Westport, Conn.: Greenwood.

Kim, Royong. 1986. *Clay Walls*. Sag Harbor, N.Y.: Permanent Press.

Kingston, Maxine Hong. 1976. *The Woman Warrior: Memoirs of a Girlhood Among Ghosts*. New York: Vintage Books.

———. 1977. "Duck Boy." *New York Times Magazine*, June 12: 54.

———. 1980. *China Men*. New York: Ballantine.

———. 1982. "Cultural Mis-readings by American Reviewers." In *Asian and American Writers in Dialogue: New Cultural Identities*, ed. Guy Amirthanayagam, 55–65. London: Macmillan.

———. 1989a. "The Novel's Next Step." *Mother Jones*, Dec.: 37–41.

———. 1989b. *Tripmaster Monkey: His Fake Book*. New York: Alfred A. Knopf.

———. 1991. "Personal Statement." In *Approaches to Teaching Kingston's* The Woman Warrior, ed. Shirley Geok-lin Lim. New York: Modern Language Association of America.

Klein, Dianne. 1989. "Monkeying with Myths." *Los Angeles Times*, May 11.

Knepler, Henry and Myrna, eds. 1983. *Crossing Cultures: Readings for Composition*. New York: Macmillan.

Knippling, Alpana Sharma. 1993. "Toward an Investigation of the Subaltern in Bharati Mukherjee's *The Middleman and Other Stories* and *Jasmine*." In *Bharati Mukherjee: Critical Perspectives*, ed. Emmanuel S. Nelson, 143–59. New York: Garland.

Kondo, Dorinne K. 1990. "*M. Butterfly*: Orientalism, Gender, and a Critique of Essentialist Identity." *Cultural Critique* 16 (Fall): 5–29.

Konvitz, Milton R. 1946. *The Alien and the Asiatic in American Law*. Ithaca, N.Y.: Cornell University Press.

Krist, Gary. 1991. "The Ratchety Process of Change" [Review of *Pangs of Love*]. *New York Times Book Review*, July 14: 13–14.

Kristeva, Julia. 1982. *The Powers of Horror: An Essay on Abjection*. Trans. Leon S. Roudiez. New York: Columbia University Press.

Kroll, Jack. 1972. "Primary Color." *Newsweek*, June 19: 53.

———. 1988. "The Diplomat and the Diva: A Bizarre Affair in China" [Review of *M. Butterfly*]. *Newsweek*, Apr. 4: 75.

Kudaka, Geraldine. 1995. *On a Bed of Rice: An Asian American Erotic Feast*. New York: Anchor.

Laclau, Ernesto. 1992. "Universalism, Particularism, and the Question of Identity." *October* 61 (Summer): 83–90.

Laclau, Ernesto, and Chantal Mouffe. 1985. *Hegemony and Socialist Strategy: Towards a Radical Democratic Politics*. London: Verso.

Lai, H. M., and P. P. Choy, eds. 1971. *Outlines: History of the Chinese in America*. San Francisco: Chinese American Studies Planning Group.

Lai, H. M., P. P. Choy, Genny Lim, and Judy Yung, eds. 1980. *Island: Poetry and History of Chinese Immigrants on Angel Island: 1910–1940*. San Francisco: Chinese Culture Foundation.

Lauter, Paul, et al., eds. 1990. *The Heath Anthology of American Literature*. Lexington, Mass.: D. C. Heath.

Lentricchia, Frank. 1983. *Criticism and Social Change*. Chicago: University of Chicago Press.

Leonard, John. 1976. "In Defiance of Two Worlds." *New York Times*, Sept. 17.

———. 1989. "Of Thee Ah Sing." *The Nation*, June 5: 768–72.

Leong, Russell, ed. 1994. *Dimensions of Desire: Other Asian and Pacific American Sexualities. Amerasia Journal* 20, no. 1: v–viii, 1–210.

Lew, Julie. 1989. "How Stories Written for Mother Became Amy Tan's Best Seller." *New York Times*, July 4.

Li, David Leiwei. 1988. "The Naming of a Chinese American 'I': Cross-Cultural Sign/ifications in *The Woman Warrior*." *Criticism* 30, no. 4: 497–515.

———. 1990. "*China Men*: Maxine Hong Kingston and the American Canon." *American Literary History* 2, no. 3 (Fall): 482–502.

———. 1991. "The Formation of Frank Chin and Formations of Chinese American Literature." In *Asian American Studies: Comparative and Global Perspectives*, ed. Shirley Hune et al., 211–22. Pullman: Washington State University Press.

———. 1992a. "Filiative and Affiliative Textualization in Contemporary Chinese American Literature." In *Understanding Others: Cultural and Cross-Cultural Studies and The Teaching of Literature*, ed. Joseph Trimmer and Tilly Warnock, 177–200. Urbana, Il.: National Council of Teachers of English.

———. 1992b. "The Production of Chinese American Tradition: Displacing American Orientalist Discourse." In *Reading the Literatures of Asian America*, ed. Shirley Lim and Amy Ling, 319–31. Philadelphia: Temple University Press.

———. 1994. "Meaningful Interruptions: Insurgency and Institutionalization of Asian American Literary Studies." Paper given at the Annual Meeting of the Modern Language Association, San Diego, Dec. 28.

———. 1997. "Race, Gender, Class and Asian American Literary Theory." *Race, Gender and Class: An Interdisciplinary and Multicultural Journal* 4, no. 3: 40–53.

Lim-Hing, Sharon, ed. 1994. *The Very Inside: An Anthology of Writing by Asian and Pacific Islander Lesbian and Bisexual Women*. Toronto: Sister Vision Press.

Lim, Shirley, and Amy Ling eds. 1992. *Reading the Literatures of Asian America*. Philadelphia: Temple University Press.

Lim, Shirley, and Mayumi Tsutakawa, eds. 1989. *The Forbidden Stitch: An Asian American Women's Anthology*. Corvallis, Ore.: Calyx.

Ling, Amy. 1990. *Between Worlds: Women Writers of Chinese Ancestry*. New York: Pergamon.

Lo, Steven C. 1989. *The Incorporation of Eric Chung*. New York: Workman.

Loo, Chalsa M. 1991. *Chinatown: Most Time, Hard Time*. New York: Praeger.

Louie, David Wong. 1989. "Contributor's Note." In *The Best of American Short Stories (1989)*, ed. Margaret Atwood, 320–21. Boston: Houghton Mifflin.

———. 1991. *Pangs of Love*. New York: Knopf.

Low, Victor. 1982. *The Unimpressible Race: A Century of Educational Struggle by the Chinese in San Francisco*. San Francisco: East/West Publishing.

Lowe, Lisa. 1991a. *Critical Terrains: French and British Orientalisms*. Ithaca, N.Y.: Cornell University Press.

———. 1991b. "Heterogeneity, Hybridity, Multiplicity: Marking Asian American Differences." *Diaspora* 1, no. 1 (Spring): 24–44.

———. 1996. *Immigrant Acts: On Asian American Cultural Politics*. Durham, N.C.: Duke University Press.

Lyotard, Jean-François. 1989. *The Postmodern Condition*. Trans. G. Bennington and B. Massumi. Minneapolis: University of Minnesota Press.

Lukács, Georg. 1971. *The Theory of the Novel: A Historical-Philosophical Essay on the Forms of Great Epic Literature*. Trans. Anna Bostock. Cambridge, Mass.: MIT Press.

McCarthy, Terry. 1998. "In Defense of 'Asian Values.'" *Time*, Mar. 16: 40.

McDowell, Deborah E. 1989. "Boundaries: Or Distant Relations and Close Kin."

In *Afro-American Literary Study in the 1990s*, ed. Houston A. Baker, Jr., and Patricia Redmond, 51–70. Chicago: University of Chicago Press.

McNeil, Jean. 1993. "Vietnamese Voices: *A Good Scent from a Strange Mountain* by Robert Olen Butler." *Times Literary Supplement*, Dec. 10: 19.

McQuade, Donald, et al., eds. 1987. *The Harper American Literature*. New York: Harper and Row.

Macpherson, C. B. 1962. *The Political Theory of Possessive Individualism: Hobbes to Locke*. Oxford: Oxford University Press.

Maddox, Lucy. 1991. *Removals: Nineteenth-Century American Literature and the Politics of Indian Affairs*. New York: Oxford University Press.

Mar, Laureen. 1983. "The Immigration Act of 1924." In *Breaking Silence: An Anthology of Contemporary Asian American Poets*, ed. Joseph Bruchac, 181. Greenfield Center, N.Y.: Greenfield Review.

Marchetti, Gina. 1993. *Romance and the "Yellow Peril": Race, Sex, and the Discursive Strategies in Hollywood Fiction*. Berkeley: University of California Press.

Marcus, George E., and Michael E. Fischer. 1986. *Anthropology as Cultural Critique: An Experimental Moment in the Human Sciences*. Chicago: University of Chicago Press.

Matthiessen, F. O. 1941. *American Renaissance: Art and Expression in the Age of Emerson and Whitman*. New York: Oxford University Press.

Mazumdar, Sucheta. 1991. "Asian American Studies and Asian Studies: Rethinking Roots." *Asian Americans: Comparative and Global Perspectives*, ed. Shirley Hune, Hyung-chan Kim, Stephen Fugita, and Amy Ling, 29–44. Pullman: Washington State University Press.

Memmi, Albert. 1965. *The Colonizer and the Colonized*. Trans. Howard Greenfield. New York: Orion.

Michie, Helena. 1991. "Not One of the Family: The Repression of the Other Woman in Feminist Theory." In *Feminisms: An Anthology of Literary Theory and Criticism*, ed. Robyn R. Warhol and Diane Price Herndl, 58–68. New Brunswick, N.J.: Rutgers University Press.

Miller, Perry. 1956. *Errand into the Wilderness*. New York: Harper and Row.

———. 1965. *The Raven and the Whale: The War of Words and Wits in the Era of Poe and Melville*. New York: Harcourt, Brace.

———. 1967. *Nature's Nation*. Cambridge, Mass.: Harvard University Press.

Miller, Stuart Creighton. 1969. *The Unwelcome Immigrant: The American Image of the Chinese: 1785–1882*. Berkeley: University of California Press.

Minh-ha, Trihn T. 1989. *Woman, Native, Other: Writing Postcoloniality and Feminism*. Bloomington: Indiana University Press.

Minow, Martha. 1990. *Making All the Difference: Inclusion, Exclusion and American Law*. Ithaca, N.Y.: Cornell University Press.

Miyoshi, Masao. 1993. "A Borderless World? From Colonialism to Transnationalism and the Decline of the Nation-State." *Critical Inquiry* 19, no. 4 (Summer): 726–51.

Morante, Linda. 1987. "From Silence to Song: The Triumph of Maxine Hong Kingston." *Frontiers* 9, no. 2: 78–82.

Mori, Toshio. [1949] 1985. *Yokohama, California*. Seattle: University of Washington Press.

Morris, Gregory L. 1994. *Talking Up a Storm: Voices of the New West*. Lincoln: University of Nebraska Press.

Morrison, Toni. 1992. *Playing in the Dark: Whiteness and the Literary Imagination*. Cambridge: Harvard University Press.

Mouffe, Chantal. 1992. "Citizenship and Political Identity." *October* 61 (Summer): 28–32.

Moy, James. 1990. "David Henry Hwang's *M. Butterfly* and Philip Kan Gotanda's *Yankee Dawg You Die*: Repositioning Chinese American Marginality on the American Stage." *Theatre Journal* 42, no. 1: 48–56.

———. 1993. *Marginal Sights: Staging the Chinese in America*. Iowa City: University of Iowa Press.

Mudimbe, V. Y. 1988. *The Invention of Africa: Gnosis, Philosophy, and the Order of Knowledge*. Bloomington: Indiana University Press.

Mukherjee, Bharati. 1985. *Darkness*. New York: Penguin.

———. 1988a. "Immigrant Writing: Give Us Your Maximalists!" *New York Times Book Review*, Aug. 28: 1.

———. 1988b. *The Middleman and Other Stories*. New York: Fawcett Crest.

———. 1989a. *Jasmine*. New York, Fawcett Crest.

———. 1989b. "Wittman at the Golden Gate." *Washington Post Book World*, Apr. 16: 1.

Mura, David. 1991. *Turning Japanese: Memoirs of a Sansei*. New York: Anchor.

Myers, Victoria. 1986. "The Significant Fictivity of Maxine Hong Kingston's *The Woman Warrior*." *Biography* 9, no. 2: 112–25.

Nee, Victor G., and Brett de Bary Nee. 1972. *Longtime Californ': A Documentary Study of an American Chinatown*. New York: Pantheon. Reissued, with index, by Stanford University Press, Stanford, Calif., 1986.

Neely, Kent. 1991. "Intimacy or Cruel Love: Displacing the Other by Self Assertion." *Journal of Dramatic Theory and Criticism* 5, no. 2: 167–73.

Ng, Fae Myenne. 1993. *Bone*. New York: Hyperion.

Ng, Wendy, and Qum Wan, eds. 1997. *Race, Gender and Class: Asian American Voices*. *Race, Gender and Class: An Interdisciplinary and Multicultural Journal* 4, no. 3 (Special issue, Fall): 5–179.

Ngugi, wa Thiong'o. 1986. *Decolonizing the Mind: The Politics of Language in African Literature*. London: James Currey.

Nguyen, Lan N. 1997. "The Next Amy Tan." *A. Magazine*, Feb./Mar.: 46–51, 55.

Nonini, Donald M. 1993. "On the Outs on the Rim: An Ethnographic Grounding of the 'Asia-Pacific' Imaginary." In *What Is in a Rim? Critical Perspectives on the Pacific Region Idea*, ed. Arif Dirlik, 161–82. Boulder: Westview.

Okada, John. [1957] 1990. *No-No Boy*. Seattle: University of Washington Press.

Okihiro, Gary Y. 1991a. "African Studies and Asian American Studies: A Comparative Analysis and Commentary." In *Asian Americans: Comparative and Global Perspectives*, ed. Shirley Hune et al., 17–28. Pullman: Washington State University Press.

———. 1991b. *Margins and Mainstreams: Asians in American History and Culture*. Seattle: University of Washington Press.

Oliver, Edith. 1972. "Off Broadway" [Review of *The Chickencoop Chinaman*]. *New Yorker*, June 24: 46.

———. 1988. "Poor Butterfly" [Review of *M. Butterfly*]. *New Yorker*, Apr. 4: 72.

Olney, James, ed. 1980. *Autobiography: Essays Theoretical and Critical*. Princeton, N.J.: Princeton University Press.

Omatsu, Glenn. 1989a. "The 'Four Prisons' and the Movements of Liberation." *Amerasia Journal* 15, no. 1 (Special isue): xv–xxx.

———, ed. 1989b. *Salute to the 60s and 70s: Legacy of the San Francisco State Strike*. *Amerasia Journal* 15, no. 1 (Special issue): xi–xxx, 3–320.

Omi, Michael, and Howard Winant. 1986. *Racial Formation in the United States: From the 1960s to the 1980s*. New York: Routledge and Kegan Paul.

Omi, Michael, and Dana Takagi, eds. 1995. *Thinking Theory in Asian American Studies. Amerasia Journal* 21, nos. 1 & 2 (Special issue): v–xv, 1–169.

———. 1996. "Situating Asian Americans in the Political Discourse on Affirmative Action." *Representations* 55 (Special issue): 155–62.

Ong, Caroline. 1989. "Demons and Warriors." *Times Literary Supplement*, Sept. 15–21: 998.

Ong, Paul, Edna Bonacich, and Lucy Cheng, eds. 1994. *The New Asian Immigration in Los Angeles and Global Restructuring.* Philadelphia: Temple University Press.

Osajima, Keith. 1988. "Asian Americans as the Model Minority: An Analysis of the Popular Press Image in the 1960s and 1980s." In *Reflections on Shattered Windows: Promises and Prospects for Asian American Studies*, ed. Gary Y. Okihiro et al., 165–74. Pullman: Washington State University Press.

Palumbo-Liu, David, ed. 1995. *The Ethnic Canon: Histories, Institutions and Interventions.* Minneapolis: University of Minnesota Press.

Pao, Angela. 1992. "The Critic and the Butterfly: Socio-cultural Contexts and the Reception of David Henry Hwang's *M. Butterfly.*" *Amerasia Journal* 18, no. 3: 1–16.

Parker, Andrew, Mary Russo, Doris Sommer, and Patricia Yeager, eds. 1992. *Nationalisms and Sexualities.* New York: Routledge.

Pease, Donald E., ed. 1994. *National Identities and Post-Americanist Narratives.* Durham, N.C.: Duke University Press.

Pfaff, Timothy. 1980. "Talk with Mrs. Kingston." *New York Times Book Review*, June 15: 1.

Pitkin, Hanna Fenichel. 1967. *The Concept of Representation.* Berkeley: University of California Press.

Pocock, J. G. A. 1975. *The Machiavellian Moment: Florentine Political Thought and the Atlantic Republican Tradition.* Princeton, N.J.: Princeton University Press.

Poirier, Richard. 1966. *A World Elsewhere: The Place of Style in American Literature.* New York: Oxford University Press.

Publishers Weekly. 1989. "Tripmaster Monkey." Feb. 3.

Radhakrishnan, R. (Rajagopalan). 1990. "Toward an Effective Intellectual: Foucault and Gramsci?" In *Intellectuals: Aesthetics, Politics, Academics*, ed. Bruce Robins, 57–99. Minneapolis: University of Minnesota Press.

Radway, Janice A. 1985. *Reading the Romance: Women, Patriarchy, and Popular Literature.* Chapel Hill: University of North Carolina Press.

Ratti, Rakesh. 1993. *A Lotus of Another Color: An Unfolding of the South Asian Gay and Lesbian Experience.* Boston: Alyson.

Rea, Kenneth W., ed. 1977. *Early Sino-American Relations, 1841–1912: The Collected Articles of Earl Swisher.* Boulder, Colo.: Westview.

Reising, Russell. 1986. *The Unusable Past: Theory and the Study of American Literature.* New York: Methuen.

Rich, Frank. 1988. "'*M. Butterfly*,' a Story of a Strange Love, Conflict and Betrayal." *New York Times*, Mar. 21.

———. 1990. "Johnathan Pryce, '*Miss Saigon*' and Equity's Decision." *New York Times*, Aug. 10.

Ringer, Benjamin. 1983. *"We the People" and Others: Duality and America's Treatment of Its Racial Minorities.* New York: Tavistock Publications.

Riviere, Joan. 1986. "Womanliness as a Masquerade." In *Formations of Fantasy*, ed. Victor Burgin, James Donald, and Cora Kaplan, 35–44. New York: Methuen.

Roy, Anindyo. 1993. "The Aesthetics of an (Un)willing Immigrant: Bharati Mukherjee's *Days and Nights in Calcutta* and *Jasmine*." In *Bharati Mukherjee: Critical Perspectives*, ed. Emmanuel S. Nelson, 127–41. New York: Garland.

Russo, Mary. 1986. "Female Grotesques: Carnival and Theory." In *Feminist Studies / Critical Studies*, ed. Teresa de Lauretis, 213–29. Bloomington: Indiana University Press.

Said, Edward W. 1978. *Orientalism*. New York: Vintage.

———. 1983. *The World, the Text, and the Critic*. Cambridge, Mass.: Harvard University Press.

———. 1990. "Reflections on Exile." In *Out There: Marginalization and Contemporary Cultures*, ed. Russell Ferguson, Martha Gever, Trinh T. Minh-ha, and Cornel West, 357–66. New York: New Museum of Contemporary Art.

San Juan, E. 1996. *The Philippine Temptation: Dialectics of Philippines-U.S. Literary Relations*. Philadelphia: Temple University Press.

Santos, Bienvenido N. [1955] 1992. *Scent of Apples: A Collection of Short Stories*. Seattle: University of Washington Press.

Sauvage, Leo. 1988. "Spring Salad" [Review of *M. Butterfly*]. *New Leader*, Apr. 18: 22–23.

Saxton, Alexander. 1971. *The Indispensable Enemy: Labor and the Anti-Chinese Movement in California*. Berkeley: University of California Press.

Schell, Orville. 1989. "Your Mother Is in Your Bones." *New York Times Book Review*, Mar. 19: 3.

Schreiber, Le Anne. 1989. "The Big, Big Show of Wittman Ah Sing." *New York Times Book Review*, Apr. 23: 9.

Schuck, Peter H., and Rogers M. Smith. 1985. *Citizenship Without Consent: Illegal Aliens in the American Polity*. New Haven, Conn.: Yale University Press.

Seaman, Donna. 1990. "The Booklist Interview: Amy Tan." *Booklist*, Oct. 1: 256–57.

Sedgwick, Eve Kosofsky. 1993. *Tendencies*. Durham, N.C.: Duke University Press.

Shapiro, Michael J. 1988. *The Politics of Representation: Writing Practices in Biography, Photography, and Policy Analysis*. Madison: University of Wisconsin Press.

Shimakawa, Karen. 1995. "Swallowing the Tempest: Asian American Women on Stage." *Theatre Journal* 47: 367–80.

Shrodes, Caroline, et al., eds. 1985. *The Conscious Reader*. New York: Macmillan.

Silverman, Kaja. 1992. "The Lacanian Phallus." *differences: A Journal of Feminist Cultural Studies* 4, no. 1 (Spring): 84–115.

Simpson, Janice C. 1991. "Fresh Voices Above the Noisy Din." *Time*, June 3: 66–67.

Solberg, S. E. 1989. "Between the Lines." *Seattle Weekly*, Apr. 10: 47.

Sollors, Werner. 1986. *Beyond Ethnicity: Consent and Descent in American Culture*. New York: Oxford University Press.

Sommer, Doris. 1990. "Irresistible Romance: The Foundational Fictions of Latin America." In *Nation and Narration*, ed. Homi K. Bhabha, 71–98. New York: Routledge.

Somogyi, Barbara, and David Stanton. 1991. "Amy Tan: An Interview." *Poets and Writers* 19, no. 5: 24–32.

Sone, Monica. [1953] 1979. *Nisei Daughter*. Seattle: University of Washington Press.

Spivak, Gayatri Chakravorty. 1981–83. "French Feminism in an International Frame." *Yale French Studies* 62–63: 154–84.

———. 1987. *In Other Worlds: Essays in Cultural Politics*. New York: Methuen.

————. 1988a. "Can the Subaltern Speak?" In *Marxism and the Interpretation of Culture*, ed. Cary Nelson and Lawrence Grossberg, 271–313. Chicago: University of Illinois Press.

————. 1988b. "Subaltern Studies: Deconstructing Historiography." In *Selected Subaltern Studies*, ed. Ranajit Guha and Gayatri Chakravorty Spivak, 3–32. New York: Oxford University Press.

————. 1993. *Outside in the Teaching Machine*. New York: Routledge.

Stacey, Judith. 1994. "Scents, Scholars, and Stigma: The Revisionist Campaign for Family Values." *Social Text* 40 (Fall): 51–75.

Steinberg, Sybil. 1989. "Bharati Mukherjee: PW Interviews." *Publishers Weekly*, Aug. 25: 46–47.

Stern, Milton R. 1986. *Critical Essays on F. Scott Fitzgerald's "Tender Is the Night."* New York: G. K. Hall.

Street, Douglas. 1989. *David Henry Hwang*. Boise, Idaho: Boise State University.

Sue, Stanley and Derald. 1971. "Chinese-American Personality and Mental Health." *Amerasia Journal* 1, no. 2: 36–49.

Sui Sin Far. See Edith Eaton.

Sumida, Stephen H. 1991. *And the View from the Shore: Literary Traditions of Hawai'i.* Seattle: University of Washington Press.

Sun, Shirley. 1990. "For Asians Denied Asian Roles, 'Artistic Freedom' Is No Comfort." *New York Times*, Aug. 26.

Tachiki, Amy, et al., eds. 1971. *Roots: An Asian American Reader*. Los Angeles: Asian American Studies Center, UCLA.

Takaki, Ronald T. 1989. *Strangers from a Different Shore: A History of Asian Americans*. Boston: Little, Brown.

————. 1993. *A Different Mirror: A History of Multicultural America*. Boston: Little Brown.

Talbot, Stephen. 1990. "Talking Story: Maxine Hong Kingston Rewrites the American Dream." *Image* (*San Francisco Examiner* Magazine), June 22: 6–17.

Tan, Amy. 1989. *The Joy Luck Club*. New York: G. P. Putnam's.

————. 1991. *The Kitchen God's Wife*. New York: G. P. Putnam's.

Taylor, Charles. 1994. "The Politics of Recognition." In *Multiculturalism: A Critical Reader*, ed. David Theo Goldberg, 75–106. Cambridge: Basil Blackwell.

tenBroek, Jacobus, Edward N. Barnhart, and Floyd W. Matson. 1970. *Prejudice, War and the Constitution*. Berkeley: University of California Press.

Tong, Ben. 1971. "The Ghetto of the Mind: Notes on the Historical Psychology of Chinese-America." *Amerasia Journal* 1, no. 3: 1–31.

————. 1977. "Critic of Admirer Sees Dumb Racist." *San Francisco Journal*, May 11: 6.

Trilling, Lionel. 1950. *The Liberal Imagination: Essays on Literature and Society*. New York: Viking.

Truong, Monique T. D. 1993. "Vietnamese American Literature: 1975–1990." *Amerasia Journal* 19, no. 3: 27–50.

————. 1994. "On *A Good Scent from a Strange Mountain*: A Talk." UCLA Conference on "Strategizing Asian American Cultures." Los Angeles, April.

Tu, Wei-ming. 1991a. "Cultural China: The Periphery as the Center." *Dædalus* 120, no. 2: 1–32.

————. 1991b. *The Living Tree: The Changing Meaning of Being Chinese Today*. *Dædalus* 120, no. 2 (Special issue): 1–226. Reissued in slightly revised form by Stanford University Press, Stanford, Calif., 1991.

————, ed. 1996. *Confucian Traditions in East Asian Modernity: Moral Education and*

Economic Culture in Japan and the Four Mini-Dragons. Cambridge, Mass.: Harvard University Press.

Tyler, Anne. 1989. "Manic Monologue." *New Republic,* Apr. 17: 44–45.

Tyler, Carole-Anne. 1991. "Boys Will Be Girls: The Politics of Gay Drag." In *Inside/Out: Lesbian Theories, Gay Theories,* ed. Diana Fuss, 32–70. New York: Routledge.

Uyematsu, Amy. 1971. "The Emergence of Yellow Power in America." In *Roots: An Asian American Reader,* ed. Amy Tachiki et al., 9–13. Los Angeles: Asian American Studies Center, UCLA.

Wald, Alan. 1987. "Theorizing Cultural Difference: A Critique of the 'Ethnicity School.'" *Melus* 14, no. 2 (Summer): 21–33.

Wald, Priscilla. 1993. "Terms of Assimilation: Legislating Subjectivity in the Emerging Nation." In *Cultures of United States Imperialism,* ed. Amy Kaplan and Donald E. Pease, 59–84. Durham, N.C.: Duke University Press.

Walker, Pat, ed. 1979. *Between Labor and Capital.* Boston: South End.

Wallace, Michele. 1978. *Black Macho and the Myth of Superwoman.* New York: Dial.

Walsh, Joan. 1990. "Asian Women, Caucasian Men: The New Demographics of Love." *Image* (*San Francisco Examiner* Magazine), Dec. 2: 11–16.

Wand, David Hsin-Fu, ed. 1974. *Asian American Heritage: An Anthology of Prose and Poetry.* New York: Washington Square.

Wang, Wayne. 1984. *Chan Is Missing.* Honolulu: Bamboo Ridge.

Watanabe, Sylvia, and Carol Bruchac, ed. 1990. *Home to Stay: Asian American Women's Fiction.* Greenfield Center, N.Y.: Greenfield Review.

Wei, William. 1993. *The Asian American Movement.* Philadelphia: Temple University Press.

West, Cornel. 1993. "The New Cultural Politics of Difference." In *The Cultural Studies Reader,* ed. Simon During, 203–17. New York: Routledge.

Williams, Raymond. 1985. *Keywords: A Vocabulary of Culture and Society.* Rev. ed. New York: Oxford University Press.

Wills, Garry. 1979. *Inventing America: Jefferson's Declaration of Independence.* New York: Doubleday.

Willis, Susan. 1991. *A Primer for Daily Life.* New York: Routledge.

Witness Aloud: Lesbian, Gay and Bisexual Asian/Pacific American Writings. 1993. *Asian Pacific American Journal* 2, no. 1 (Special issue, Fall/Winter): 1–131.

Wolfe, Tom. 1971. "Bok Gooi, Hok Gooi and T'ang Jen: or Why There Is No National Association for the Advancement of Chinese Americans." *New York,* Sept. 27: 35–41.

Wong, Jade Snow. [1945] 1989. *Fifth Chinese Daughter.* Seattle: University of Washington Press.

Wong, Nellie. 1978–79. "*The Woman Warrior.*" [A Review] *Bridge* 6, no. 4: 46–48.

Wong, Sau-ling C. 1993. *Reading Asian American Literature: From Necessity to Extravagance.* Princeton, N.J.: Princeton University Press.

———. 1995. "'Sugar Sisterhood': Situating the Amy Tan Phenomenon." In *The Ethnic Canon: Histories, Institutions and Interventions,* ed. David Palumbo-Liu, 174–210. Minneapolis: University of Minnesota Press.

Wong, Shawn Hsu. 1976. "Good Luck, Happiness and Long Life." In *Counterpoint: Perspectives on Asian America,* ed. Emma Gee et al., 464–70. Los Angeles: Asian American Studies Center, UCLA.

———. 1979. *Homebase.* New York: I. Reed.

———. 1995a. *American Knees.* New York: Simon and Schuster.

———. 1995b. *Asian American Literature: A Brief Introduction and Anthology.* New York: Harper Collins College.

Woodside, Alexander. 1993. "The Asia-Pacific Idea as a Mobilizing Myth." In *What Is in a Rim? Critical Perspectives on the Pacific Region Idea*, ed. Arif Dirlik, 13–27. Boulder, Colo.: Westview.

Wu, Chen-Tsu, ed. 1972. *"Chink!"* New York: Meridian / Times Mirror.

Yamamoto, Hisaye. 1988. *Seventeen Syllables and Other Stories.* Latham, N.Y.: Kitchen Table.

Yarbro-Bejarano, Yvonne. 1991. "Chicana Literature from a Chicana Feminist Perspective." In *Feminisms: An Anthology of Literary Theory and Criticism*, ed. Robyn R. Warhol and Diane Price Herndl, 732–37. New Brunswick, N.J.: Rutgers University Press.

Yep, Laurence. 1975. *Dragonwings.* New York, Harper and Row.

———. 1993. *American Dragons: Twenty-Five Asian American Voices.* New York: Harper Collins.

You, Guoen, et al., eds. 1964. *A History of Chinese Literature.* Beijing: People's Literature.

Young, Iris Marion. 1990. *Justice and the Politics of Difference.* Princeton, N.J.: Princeton University Press.

Yung, Judy. 1986. *Chinese Women of America: A Pictorial History.* Seattle: University of Washington Press.

Zill, Nicholas, and Marianne Winglee. 1990. *Who Reads Literature? The Future of the United States as a Nation of Readers.* Washington, D.C.: National Endowment for the Humanities.

Index

In this index an "f" after a number indicates a separate reference on the next page, and an "ff" indicates separate references on the next two pages. A continuous discussion over two or more pages is indicated by a span of page numbers, e.g., "57–59." *Passim* is used for a cluster of references in close but not consecutive sequence.

Library of Congress Cataloging-in-Publication Data

Li, David Leiwei
   Imagining the nation : Asian American literature and cultural consent /
David Leiwei Li.
      p.   cm. — (Asian America)
   Includes bibliographical references and index.
   ISBN 0-8047-3400-3 (alk. paper)
      1. American literature—Asian American authors—History and criticism.
2. Literature and society—United States—History.   3. Asian Americans—
Intellectual life.   4. Asian Americans in literature.   I. Title.   II. Series.
PS153.A84L5   1999
810.9'895—dc21   98-24578

  ⊗ This book is printed on acid-free, recycled paper.

Original printing 1998
Last figure below indicates year of this printing:
07 06 05 04 03 02 01 00 99 98